Lecture Notes in Business Information Processing 423

More information about this series at http://www.springer.com/series/7911

Artem Polyvyanyy · Stefanie Rinderle-Ma (Eds.)

Advanced Information Systems Engineering Workshops

CAiSE 2021 International Workshops
Melbourne, VIC, Australia, June 28 – July 2, 2021
Proceedings

Springer

Editors
Artem Polyvyanyy (iD)
The University of Melbourne
Carlton, VIC, Australia

Stefanie Rinderle-Ma (iD)
Technical University of Munich
Garching, Germany

ISSN 1865-1348   ISSN 1865-1356 (electronic)
Lecture Notes in Business Information Processing
ISBN 978-3-030-79021-9   ISBN 978-3-030-79022-6 (eBook)
https://doi.org/10.1007/978-3-030-79022-6

This Springer imprint is published by the registered company Springer Nature Switzerland AG
The registered company address is: Gewerbestrasse 11, 6330 Cham, Switzerland

Preface

The International Conference on Advanced Information Systems Engineering (CAiSE) has a longstanding tradition as a premier venue for Information Systems Engineering research on highly innovative and relevant topics with rigorous methods. In 2021, CAiSE featured the special conference theme of uncertainty, which reflects upon the ongoing situation with the COVID-19 pandemic and the challenges that have to be addressed through Intelligent Information Systems. The uncertainty aspect and the global situation also hit the CAiSE conference organization. Originally, CAiSE 2021 was planned as a live event to be held during June 28 – July 2, 2021, in Melbourne, Australia, but due to the ongoing pandemic it was held online.

Traditionally, the CAiSE main track is flanked by the two working conferences BPMDS and EMMSAD, as well as a number of high-quality workshops that address inspiring and future topics of Information Systems Engineering. In 2021, a total of eight workshops were selected based on criteria such as quality, innovativeness, and potential to spark discussions at the workshop.

This volume contains the papers presented at the CAiSE workshops during 29–30 June, 2021, 33 papers were submitted, out of which 14 full papers and 1 short paper were accepted for the following workshops:

- *BC4IS*: 1st International Workshop on Blockchain for Information Systems
- *EMoBI*: 3rd International Workshop on Ethics and Morality in Business Informatics
- *KET4DF*: 3rd International Workshop on Key Enabling Technology for Digital Factories
- *MOBA*: 1st International Workshop on Model-driven Organizational and Business Agility
- *NeGIS*: 2nd International Workshop on Next Generation Information Systems

These workshops reflect a broad range of exciting topics and trends ranging from blockchain technologies via digital factories, ethics, and business agility to the next generation of Information Systems.

We would like to thank the chairs of the workshops for their excellent job in difficult times. Also, we thank the reviewers for their timely and constructive work. We thank Springer for the swift communication and support of the proceedings production process. Finally, we thank Marcello La Rosa as General Chair and Laura Juliff as Organization Chair of CAiSE for supporting us with the workshop website and the Easychair conference management system.

May 2021

Artem Polyvyanyy
Stefanie Rinderle-Ma

Contents

MOBA

MOBA 2021 Preface

The International Workshop on Model-driven Organizational and Business Agility (MOBA) builds on the identity of the successful, and long-running, International Workshop on Enterprise and Organizational Modeling and Simulation (EOMAS), and its cooperation with CAiSE, maintaining the modeling aspect but reshaping the focus and scientific research on organizational and business agility.

A generic notion of agility as a capability to rapidly response to changes and to reduce uncertainty in an increment-based way has become critically important for all stages of the life cycle of modern IT systems. Methodological principles and practical tools of agility have been adopted in practice by multiple organizations to improve their services and incremental design of better products. So, the growing challenges need scientific inquiry, research, and rigorous solutions.

Addressing such challenges, the MOBA workshop aims at growing a multi-disciplinary community of researchers and practitioners, which will help consolidate efforts in detecting, modeling, improving, and disseminating best agility practices and theories. One of the main objectives of the workshop is to study different agility phenomena from a systemic viewpoint, distinguishing between the endogenous agility inside an organization and the exogenous agility of business connections with external parties. Common principles of model-driven research and engineering of organizational or technical artefacts will guarantee consistency and interoperability of the results obtained.

In order to model and study organizational and business agility in a system context, we inevitably join together most of research themes developed in the scope of EOMAS, like enterprise architecture, semantic interoperability, model-driven design of information systems, models validation, and business value co-creation.

This year, as part of MOBA 2021, we continued the Master and Doctoral Consortium, which attracted young talent to present and discuss their work, and thus allow them to obtain feedback and encouragement. We would like to express our sincere thanks to the existing EOMAS and emerging MOBA communities: the authors, the Program Committee, the CAiSE organizers, and the chairs for their enthusiasm and devotion. We are grateful to all of the participants for their contributions and we are looking forward to meeting again at the second edition of MOBA in 2022!

June 2021

Eduard Babkin
Joseph Barjis
Russell Lock
Pavel Malyzhenkov
Vojtech Merunka
Robert Pergl

MOBA 2021 Organization

Executive Committee

General Chair

Eduard Babkin   National Research University Higher School of Economics, Nizhny Novgorod, Russia

Program Chairs

Joseph Barjis	San Jose State University, USA
Russell Lock	Loughborough University, UK
Pavel Malyzhenkov	National Research University Higher School of Economics, Nizhny Novgorod, Russia
Vojtech Merunka	Czech Technical University in Prague, Czech Republic
Robert Pergl	Czech Technical University in Prague, Czech Republic

Program Committee

Eduard Babkin	National Research University Higher School of Economics, Nizhni Novgorod, Russia
Joseph Barjis	San Jose State University, USA
Anna Bobkowska	Gdansk University of Technology, Poland
Alexander Bock	University of Duisburg-Essen, Germany
Luiz Olavo Bonino	University of Twente, the Netherlands
Mahmoud Boufaida	Mentouri University of Constantine, Algeria
Peter de Bruyn	University of Antwerp, Belgium
Simona Colucci	Politecnico di Bari, Italy
Francesco M. Donini	Università degli Studi della Tuscia, Italy
Samuel Fosso Wamba	Toulouse Business School, France
Sergio Guerreiro	Instituto Superior Tecnico, University of Lisbon, Portugal
Giancarlo Guizzardi	Free University of Bozen-Bolzano, Italy
Georg Grossmann	UniSA STEM, Australia
Kristina Hettne	Leiden University, the Netherlands
Frantisek Hunka	University of Ostrava, Czech Republic

Rossi Kamal	Kyung Hee University, Korea
Dmitry Kudryavtsev	St. Petersburg University, Russia
Alexei Lapouchnian	University of Toronto, Canada
Yann Le Franc	E-Science Data Factory, France
Russell Lock	Loughborough University, UK
Pavel Malyzhenkov	National Research University Higher School of Economics, Nizhni Novgorod, Russia
Peter McQuilton	University of Oxford, UK
Vojtech Merunka	Czech Technical University in Prague and Czech University of Life Sciences, Czech Republic
Martin Molhanec	Czech Technical University in Prague, Czech Republic
Peter Mutschke	GESIS - Leibniz Institute for the Social Sciences, Germany
Maria Ntaliani	Agricultural University of Athens, Greece
Gautham Pallapa	VMware, USA
Josef Pavlicek	Czech University of Life Sciences, Czech Republic
Petra Pavlíčkovà	Czech Technical University in Prague, Czech Republic
Robert Pergl	Czech Technical University in Prague, Czech Republic
Patrizia Ribino	ICAR-CNR, Italy
Ben Roelens	Open University of the Netherlands, the Netherlands, and Ghent University, Belgium
Victor Romanov	Russian Plekhanov University, Russia
Gustavo Rossi	Universidad Nacional de La Plata, Argentina
Adrian Rutle	Western Norway University of Applied Sciences, Norway
Erik Schultes	GO FAIR International Support and Coordination Office, the Netherlands
Janis Stirna	Stockholm University, Sweden
Michal Valenta	Czech Technical University in Prague, Czech Republic
Steven van Kervel	Formetis BV, Belgium
Michael Verdonck	Ghent University, the Netherlands
Jan Verelst	University of Antwerp, Belgium

Agility Driven Learning for Educational Organizations

Sergey Avdoshin⬛, Elena Pesotskaya$^{(\boxtimes)}$ ⬛, Divani Kuruppuge⬛,
and Angelina Strashnova

HSE University, 20 Myasnitskaya ulitsa, 101000 Moscow, Russian Federation
{savdoshin,epesotskaya,dkuruppuge_1,aastrashnova_1}@hse.ru

Abstract. Agility as a capability to rapidly respond to changes and to reduce uncertainty in an increment-based way is also critically important in Educational Organizations, such as Colleges, Universities, online learning platforms, and educational service providers. Nowadays, people can easily get access to educational courses, and the ability to provide a personalized educational track and change it depending on an agile business context is critically important. The user needs to identify the target specialization or job and get the shortest path with the list of recommended courses and alternatives. This paper summarizes the key ideas relating to methodological principles and practical tools of agility that can be applicable to educational organizations and suggests the model that builds a unique educational path, based on users behavior, data on existing courses, and personal information. The suggested model uses gamification techniques to boost short-term motivation and allows customizing and rebuilding the educational track, also considering churn rate and the educational progress of the user.

Keywords: Agility · Education · Personalization · Gamification · Learning

1 Introduction

New technologies are reshaping the future of work. Employers will seek out candidates that can continuously learn new skills. It means that specific knowledge will need to be continuously updated, and employees will need to adapt to be part of the world's future workforce.

The educational and learning system must adapt to the automation and digitalization challenges that influence business and jobs demanding new skills and competencies. Especially since the COVID-19 pandemic situation negatively influenced the unemployed and stressed the need to become skilled in other jobs to find alternative work.

The majority of professionals are not fully confident that they have all the skills needed to manage their career development [1]. The idea is to empower individuals to drive their own learning journey and suggest pathways towards actual jobs. Lifelong learning programs must be flexible to help people develop their own career and skills

© Springer Nature Switzerland AG 2021
A. Polyvyanyy and S. Rinderle-Ma (Eds.): CAiSE 2021 Workshops, LNBIP 423, pp. 5–16, 2021.
https://doi.org/10.1007/978-3-030-79022-6_1

plans. Not all modern educational organizations are able to provide an individual trajectory of education. Students need flexibility to choose their own learning paths based on their skills. That is why agility in education will help students to adapt to change and seek out better career opportunities.

The goal of this research is to study agility in educational processes and organizations, understand how agility can be introduced to educational organizations and, based on the findings, propose a high-level approach on how to use an individual educational track to assist a person's growth in their changing career. To reach the goal, the authors investigate the principles of building an Agile driven educational organization and propose a *Model-driven Educational Agility Framework* that supports personalized and flexible learning to maximize the effect and, in the shortest time, achieve personal and career goals.

A proposed Framework aims to optimize the formation of educational courses by customizing the educational product for the goals and behavior of a potential user. In this paper, after the introduction, the second section investigates the Agility phenomena in the education process and shows the key trends in this area. The third section analyzes the consumer interests, their needs and requirements, and suggests the Model-driven Educational Agility Framework based on identified user requirements and individual user behavior. The fourth section of the paper is dedicated to discussion, considering the limitations that apply to this study. The final section presents conclusions drawn from the research and avenues for further research.

2   Related Work on the Agile Phenomena in the Educational Process

The Agile concept is derived from the organizational psychology discipline [2]. The definition of agility is the ability to respond to business challenges and to deal with rapidly changing global markets to provide high-quality and high-performing products or services, including providing customer-configured products and services [3].

These Agile phenomena first was introduced to the software engineering course curricula to make student teams practice in real software projects [4]. Many conferences, seminars, webinars and training courses, and Agile user groups on agile development, are taking place in different parts of the world [5]. Later, it was proved that Agile methodology can be used in teaching other subjects such as mathematics and others [6]. Agile education is consistent with student oriented characteristics. The main responsibilities are handed to students for self-learning, adaptive thinking, regular student-teacher feedback cycles, testing of student's extra skills and knowledge gain, continuously evolving learning through self-direction and mentored learning.

Many authors have reworked Agile manifesto's four values as alternative learning models. Such an interpretation, that particularly focuses on active and collaborative learning, was offered by Stewart et al. [7]. A similar rework that narrowly focused on an 'Agile e-learning' method was suggested by Tesar and Sieber [8]. Agile competencies are not only limited to technical skills but also reinforce social skills [9]. Agile values and principles are much wider than technical skills, even though they are important.

2.1 University and Students Perspective

Currently, the Agile Teaching/Learning Methodology is based on the best practice and ideas from the field of software engineering and taken from Agile software methodologies for higher education [10]. In order to systematize the results, a university can customize the training and implementation of individual tracks compliance with the outlined standards. Universities should devote more time to practical tasks, solving business cases, and involving companies in the learning process.

While choosing an education provider students consider the time scale of obtaining relevant knowledge, its quality and relevance in the employment market. They also take into account the specific characteristics of the provider, the possibility of the individual trajectory and ability to drive the process [11].

2.2 Postgraduates and Employee's Perspective

Being no longer a modern trend, but a reality, the concept of Agile has penetrated the business and corporate life, demanding the same from employees. Employees then acquire additional knowledge on the job, sometimes using third-party resources and educational services. Sometimes, people have to change their field of expertise or activity, and then we are talking about a total retraining and upskilling of the knowledge base.

A survey by Ahmed et al. [13] determined the main soft necessary for IT specialists: analytical and problem solving, organizational skills, fast learning, interpersonal skills, team playing, open and adaptable to change, and ability to work innovatively. A study on job requirements by analyzing online job advertisements in Netherlands' three most popular IT-job portals [14] identified skill related qualifications that are demanded by employers which are soft skills, language proficiency, communication, and analytical skills.

This is a rather difficult step for a person who seeks to change their career path, since a person does not always know how this can be achieved. Studying at the university may seem too long, choosing courses on your own might be difficult and erroneous. This undermines self-confidence and motivation to achieve goals.

2.3 Companies/Employers Perspective

Changes in technologies and markets are happening very quickly, so it is worth talking not only about choosing a profession, but also about choosing a field of activity and competencies crucial for a successful career. It is very difficult to predict the demand and success of professions, therefore, constant training and mastering of new competencies will allow specialists to remain in demand.

It became more convenient for employers to reskill the current employees instead of hiring new ones. Employees are supporting this as they want to stay employed and can upskill their skills using the convenience of online courses. According to a recent McKinsey Global Survey, 87% of executives said they are experiencing a skill shortage or expecting it for several years, which is why there is a trend towards online education and retraining [12].

A person who possesses Agile skills will always be in demand in the labor market, and will also be able to negotiate on what conditions to cooperate with companies. The capability of an organization to develop distinctive business practices and services or products which are hard to be copied by their competitors is referred to by business competencies [15].

3 Model-Driven Educational Agility Framework

3.1 The Analysis of Key Stakeholders and Their Needs

In order to determine a framework of a Model-driven Educational Agility, the authors identified what the audience needs and what it lacks now, namely, the interests of consumers and service providers (Table 1). The customers and end users interests should be considered as the highest priority, while potential employers and social structures are secondary categories.

Table 1. The analysis of the key Stakeholders needs

Stakeholder	Needs	Impact
1. End users (or Students) - learners who will use the product in the process of gaining knowledge	Getting relevant skills in the most efficient way	High. Fully determine the relevance and development of the product
2. Customers - EdTech companies and educational organizations, for which the product will be a business asset	Identifying and producing an educational product to be demanded by the end users	Medium-High. Design the product and provide it in the market
3. Employers - potential student recruiters	An influx of quality workforce whose skills satisfy the employer's needs	Medium-Low. Has a direct impact on the needs of the end users
4. Social structures and institutions (Ministry of Education, schools, etc.)	Improving the quality of education in society	Medium-Low. Controls the system and the quality of education

To shape the framework of a Model-driven Educational Agility a survey-based study was conducted among respondents aged 14 to 70 years from Russia's regions (73%) and megalopolises (27%). The primary aim of the study was to draw up a more accurate portrait and understand the ultimate goals and needs of the end users. The secondary – to assess the motivational keys of the educational services users.

A survey concluded that the prevailing goals differ as well as motivation keys.

1. *Adulthood*. Education is a hobby, a desire to try and understand oneself, a skill "forced by parents". *The motivational key*: "Parents say it's right".
2. *From 18 to 22*. Getting tertiary education, and obtaining the second degree only in the case when there is a potential shortage of knowledge acquired at the university/college during the first round. *The motivational key:* "I could learn harder if I understand the value or can manage my education".

3. *From 22 to 28.* Already understood what knowledge and skills they did not get at the university and what they lack/dislike at work. They purposefully follow a certain skill in order to realize themselves. Development of soft skill prevails. *The motivational key:* "I want to improve my skills, I am searching for self-development".
4. *From 28 to 34.* Want to improve their qualifications and digital skills or dream of changing their profession, improving the current state of affairs. *The motivational key:* "I want to improve the quality of living, both social and material".
5. *From 34 to 45+.* The desire to get a potential second optional training to occupy their leisure time prevails, no longer considering a sharp change in the activity/career. *The motivational key:* I want stability, but ready to perfect my skills, follow the trends.
6. After 45. A certain hobby or obtaining new unique knowledge, which are difficult to acquire on their own due to a decrease in mental faculties. *The motivational key:* "Easier to adapt to the rapidly changing environment, speak the same language with the technologies".

According to the research, 3 main reasons for dropping out were identified. The first one is "financial circumstances" (47%). Often, the educational service users did not experience financial difficulties, but believed that the investment in education was not justified. The second is "the loss of motivation" to learn (25%). The reasons varied: from a lack of sufficient time to a change in activity and family circumstances. The last one is "lack of relevance of content" (19%), the course either offered the knowledge that the user already had, or the user expected more.

Considering the results of the survey-based study, we can conclude that the main tasks of the educational agility purposes should include identifying patterns in changing user behavior and adaptation of the educational path to the needs of the student (end user). Furthermore, it is pivotal that the student has the necessary and most suitable content. Regulation and retention of student motivation is also very important. We assume the results of this research should be a *Model-driven Educational Agility Framework* for the development of the educational products which will allow for adapting the existing educational tracks to each student's needs, thereby increasing the effectiveness of online learning.

3.2 Design Methodology

To develop the Model-driven Educational Agility Framework for the shaping of necessary skills in the chosen profession and ensuring the effectiveness of obtaining these skills, a combination of the following methods should be considered:

- *Expert judgement* and professional expertise from educational providers for the validation of the educational content.
- *Methodical processing* for the educational materials design and integration into the learning process.
- *Graph theory* for the knowledge obtaining process analysis in order to build the most effective learning paths and track the "gaps" in knowledge.
- *Data analysis* for the classification and prediction of students' behavior and predicting decision-making to maintain motivation and increase retention.

- *Gamification* and game mechanics in training within the player's social type for the student's motivation.

We suggest to use a framework that consists of five stages.

Stage 1. Preparing an educational track. The purpose is to validate educational materials for compliance with the target skills and ensure the logic of the top training track using a competence map [16] (Table 2). A map reflects what new skills the student needs to develop and the existing skills to be acquired during education. Such an assessment of skills will allow us to determine the connections in the educational product components, allowing the product to anticipate what the student lacks.

Table 2. Competency map structure

Priority	Competence (What task to be solved?)	Skill (existed)	Skill (acquired)	How to test?
N	Competence N	Skill N	Skill #N.1	Test #1.1
		Skill #N. n	Skill #1.2	Test #1.2

The next stage provides the methodological processing of the competence map [17] to determine an educational product that uniquely covers all the target skills of the student demanded by the future career path. It is based on the injection of skills from the competence map into the components/modules of the course. The training program designed to preserve the logic of the interrelationships of skills will be an example of the traditional educational path (Fig. 1), and is a sequence of connected vertices.

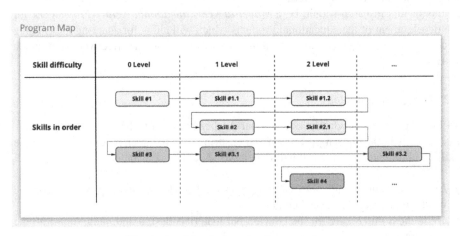

Fig. 1. Traditional educational program map

For these purposes, we construct a graph [18] with the vertices corresponding to the skills from the competence map (Fig. 2).

Stage 2. Analysis of critical indicators. As an input data, we should use the existing users behavior within the educational track (module execution speed, outflow time, etc.). The broadest and most complete dataset should be evaluated since the classification or clustering will reveal the most correlated characteristics.

In the framework of the stage, we need to estimate the weights of the vertices and set the following average values to be compared in the future. Thus, we will need to fix the following values: the average execution time of each module or the weight of the vertex of the educational graph, the outflow time, or the average time of absence of the student in the system (Table 3). In this case, the sample must be cleared of outliers, and the standard deviation level can be set independently.

Table 3. Key metrics for the student behavior analysis

№	Metric	Formula
1	**Outflow time** (the average time of the user's absence on the educational platform/course)	$E(T_{out}) = \frac{\sum_{i=0}^{k} n_i (E(T_{ex}) - t_{on}(i))}{N}$
2	**Execution speed** (the average module execution time and presence on the platform/course from the beginning to completion)	$E(T_{ex}) = \frac{\sum_{i=0}^{k} t_i n_i}{N}$ where t_i - average time to acquire a skill n_i - number of skills, with an average time t_i N - total skills in the competency map $t_{on}(i)$ - time spent on a platform during the period of module execution

The next step is to build a classification model, identifying the most significant or correlating features, and train the model. The model will allow us to track the correlation between the available data/features and the resulting indicator. This way, we can classify user behavior within each module. The logic of calculating logistic regression [19] is constructing an exponential entity (plane or curve) based on the indicators of the features, marking the training data, and determining the target indicator depending on the location relative to the entity.

As a result of applying the model, we obtain a classifier of students to the behavior on each educational track module and the most correlated features with the behavior [20]. Getting the average module execution time ensures that there are vertex weights in the graph, which are necessary for calculating the path. Moreover, the constructed classification model will allow us to predict the student's behavior.

Stage 3. Student testing. At the entrance to the educational track, the student is tested for the existing skills to predict the subsequent behavior. Processing of this data is important to analyze the student's primary educational needs, target skills, and existing ones. The next step is to determine the player's type by Bartle classification [21, 22] and identify the motivational keys for the success of the student's stimulation by a particular game mechanic. It will allow us to identify students belonging to a particular class of behavior within each module and answer the question "do we have a motivational increase or decrease".

Stage 4. Building a primary path and customization. Building a primary path based on graphs to build the most effective way to acquire skills, taking into account existing skills and user needs. Our task is to identify the most effective learning method from the graph, i.e., the shortest path (Fig. 2).

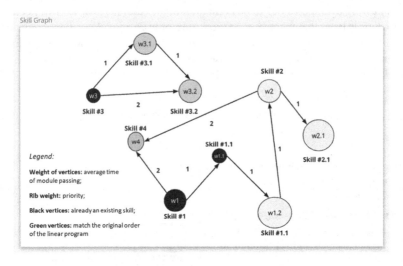

Fig. 2. Skill-driven educational graph

The basis for solving this problem can be the Dijkstra algorithm [23]. The following rules should be taken into account. Existing skills should be marked as passed vertices of the graph.

1. The travel time of the path must be calculated relative to the sum of all the weights of all the vertices not traversed;
2. The passage's priorities from the more negligible skill to the important one determine the length of the edge connecting the two skills. Simultaneously, the closer the skill is in the order of competencies, the shorter the edge length is;
3. When visiting a point, it is marked as passed, we should not return to it;
4. If a vertex has no uncovered neighbors, the algorithm moves to the following minimum unvisited vertex;
5. The algorithm terminates when all vertices have been visited.

This task's result is the most efficient sequence of graph traversals in terms of time and the inherent logic of skill relationships. For the student, it is a sequence of modules. Later, the student can independently change the order of the educational track components, taking into account their interests and priorities. Customization of the educational path for skills/educational modules prioritization, marking the skills as "motivated" or "undesirable". The system should allow for such customization if the logic and rules applied when building a crawl path in the graph are followed.

Stage 5. Training and adaptation. The main stage of implementing flexibility is the student's learning process with further analysis of the key indicators of "success". Student learning and adaptation supposes a constant scanning of students' motivation metrics [24] and applying measures to improve *outflow time* and *execution time*. In case of a significant change in the indicator, one of 4 scenarios can be applied (Fig. 3):

1. If the indicators are kept within the norm, changes are not possible, or only possible if desired. However, when a student reaches the "unmotivated module", it is necessary to either reduce the level of significance or apply motivational mechanics, preventing the decline in advance indicators.
2. In the case of increasing the module completion time but maintaining the outflow time within the norm, the conclusion is made about the complexity of the material or the lack of skills on the student's part. A preventive measure, in this case, is either an offer to the student to master the previous skill (if it exists), or a rearrangement of the graph, with the transition modules, which provides an increase in the learning's interest.
3. In the case of an increase in the outflow time, we conclude that the user exhibits reduced motivation. The most effective solution is to use game mechanics that directly affect the student's primary main motivational key [21]. Hence, gamification is a way of motivating learners through game design principles in the learning environment. To sustain the students' motivation has been a difficult task in education, thus the attention gained by gamification in educational context is significant [25].
4. In the case of an increase in both the outflow time and the module's execution time, it is necessary to provide for the option of losing motivation based on the complexity of the received content. It should involve changing or reducing the complexity of the module in the graph, and then using the gamification mechanics to increase motivation.

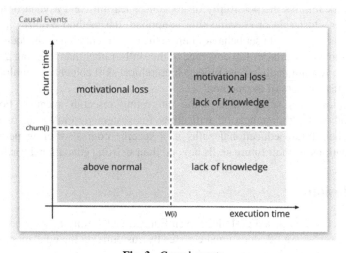

Fig. 3. Causal events

Accordingly, the process of early development and subsequent application of game mechanics supposes determining the player's type [26], his motivational keys [27]; setting a goal or target hypothesis that will be further tested on the student; determining the plan and matching the goal and type of the game mechanics and evaluating the mechanics' effectiveness, and then deciding whether to rework the gamification goals or the chosen mechanics. A timely impact on the motivation and adaptation of the educational path is carried out based on the demonstrated resulting indicators.

4 Discussion

This research has provided shows some interesting results. However, to draw conclusions on whether the proposed framework can actually improve the quality of education (speed and result), it is necessary to conduct a long-term test on a sufficient sample of students:

1. Initial A/B testing [28] on one existing product with an assessment of the retention metric and the effectiveness of the course. This test aims to evaluate the effectiveness of the application of the learning logic's application.
2. Testing on several various educational products. The leading measurable indicator will be student satisfaction and optimization of developing and adapting the educational track. This test aims to check the effectiveness of the methodology in the development and implementation of an educational product.
3. Testing mechanics in various fields or paradigms of online education [29]. The purpose of this testing is primarily to test the scalability of this hypothesis.

Based on the test results, the hypotheses must be accepted or refuted. If the hypotheses are accepted, the model should be considered at a higher level of abstraction and evaluation of the system's effectiveness within the framework of business processes and possible growth points.

As always, there are certain limitations that should be taken into consideration. First, the framework implies the possibility of non-linear learning and asynchronous input. Second, when clustering or classification is applied, the method requires a «product history», an assessment of user behavior before the implementation of the methodology. Third, the framework implies full coverage of the skills, rather than teaching a skill, and the more the program includes and reflects hierarchical skill content and multilevel, the higher the effectiveness of the method.

Nevertheless, this study opens some interesting research avenues. For example, the methodology's application will allow for systematic clustering of students, predicting their future educational paths in a specific course, offering personalized recommendations on their future skills beyond their existing educational track.

5 Conclusion

In our research we proposed a Model-driven Educational Agility Framework aimed to optimize the formation of educational courses by customizing the educational product for the goals and behavior of a potential user.

The model builds the path of a person's professional success in education and, makes it transparent and achievable for the user. It will help to determine the main patterns of student performance and behavior within the educational course throughout the entire learning path. The next step would be to optimize the process of adaptation of the student's educational track, taking into account his needs, existing characteristics and classifying behavior. And finally, to control the level of student motivation and increase the effectiveness of student learning by providing the tailored education materials.

The proposed model allows to solve the main problem of a potential student: it forms a high-quality personal educational track, and supports motivation for learning.

References

1. Accenture: It's learning. Just not as we know it: how to accelerate skills acquisition in the age of intelligent technologies. Accenture (2018). https://www.accenture.com/_acnmedia/Thought-Leadership-Assets/PDF/Accenture-Education-and-Technology-Skills-Research.pdf. Accessed 17 Feb 2021
2. Goldman, S.L., Nagel, R.N., Preiss, K.: Management, technology and agility: the emergence of a new era in manufacturing. Int. J. Technol. Mang. **8**(1–2), 18–38 (1993)
3. Bernardes, E.S., Hanna, M.D.: A theoretical review of flexibility, agility and responsiveness in the operations management literature: toward a conceptual definition of customer responsiveness. Int. J. Oper. Prod. Manag. **29**(1), 30–52 (2009). https://doi.org/10.1108/01443570910925352
4. Alfonso, M.I., Botia, A.: An iterative and agile process model for teaching software engineering. In: IEEE International Conference on Software Engineering Education and Training (CSEE&T), pp. 9–16 (2005). https://doi.org/10.1109/CSEET.2005.5
5. Morien, R.: Pedagogical agility and agile methodologies in computer system development education. Int. J. Adv. Intell. Paradig., 1–7 (2018). https://doi.org/10.1504/IJAIP.2018.092943
6. Duvall, S., Hutchings, D., Kleckner, M.: Changing perceptions of discrete mathematics through Scrum-based course management practices. J. Comput. Sci. Coll. **33**(2), 182–189 (2017)
7. Stewart, J.C., DeCusatis, C.S., Kidder, K., Massi, J.R., Anne, K.M.: Evaluating agile principles in active and cooperative learning. In: Proceedings of Student-Faculty Research Day, CSIS, Pace University, B3 (2009)
8. Tesar, M., Sieber, S.: Managing blended learning scenarios by using agile e-learning development. In: 2010 Proceedings of the IADIS International Conference E-Learning, vol. 2, pp. 125–129 (2010)
9. Parsons, D., MacCallum, K.: Agile and Lean Concepts for Teaching and Learning; Bringing Methodologies from industry to the Classroom. Springer, Singapore (2019)
10. Chun, A.H.W.: The agile teaching/learning methodology and its e-learning platform. In: Liu, W., Shi, Y., Li, Q. (eds.) ICWL 2004. LNCS, vol. 3143, pp. 11–18. Springer, Heidelberg (2004). https://doi.org/10.1007/978-3-540-27859-7_2
11. Kanij, T., Grundy, J.: Adapting teaching of a software engineering service course due to COVID-19. In: 2020 IEEE 32nd Conference on Software Engineering Education and Training (CSEE&T), Munich, Germany, pp. 1–6 (2020). https://doi.org/10.1109/CSEET49119.2020.9206204
12. Agrawal, S., Smet, A.D., Poplawski, P., Reich, A.: Beyond hiring: How companies are reskilling to address talent gaps: survey. McKinsey & Company, 20 February 2020. https://www.mckinsey.com/business-functions/organization/our-insights/beyond-hiring-how-companies-are-reskilling-to-address-talent-gaps. Accessed 10 Dec 2020

13. Ahmed, F., Capretz, L.F., Campbell, P.: Evaluating the demand for soft skills in software development. IT Prof. **14**(1), 44–49 (2012)
14. Daneva, M., Wang, C., Hoener, P.: What the job market wants from requirements engineers? An empirical analysis of online job ads from the Netherlands. In: 2017 ACM/IEEE International Symposium on Empirical Software Engineering and Measurement (ESEM), Toronto, ON, Canada, pp. 448-453 (2017).https://doi.org/10.1109/ESEM.2017.60
15. Yusuf, Y.Y., Sarhadi, M., Gunasekaran, A.: Agile manufacturing: the drivers, concepts and attributes. Int. J. Prod. Econ. **62**(1), 33–43 (1999). https://doi.org/10.1080/00207543.2018.1530478
16. Sánchez Carracedo, F., et al.: Competency maps: an effective model to integrate professional competencies across a STEM curriculum. J. Sci. Educ. Technol. **27**(5), 448–468 (2018). https://doi.org/10.1007/s10956-018-9735-3
17. Perera, S., Babatunde, S., Zhou, L., Pearson, J., Ekundayo, D.: Competency mapping framework for regulating professionally oriented degree programmes in higher education. Stud. High. Educ. **42**(12) (2016). https://doi.org/10.1080/03075079.2016.1143926
18. Gugnany, A., Ponnalagy, K., Kuma, V.: Generating unified candidate skill graph for career path recommendation. In: 2018 IEEE International Conference on Data Mining Workshops (ICDMW) (2018). https://doi.org/10.1109/ICDMW.2018.00054
19. Zhilina, E.V.: Using binary logistic regression to assess the quality of an adaptive test. Journal Vestnik TSU № 334, Russia, Tomsk (2010)
20. Pyke, S.W., Sheridan, P.: Logistic regression analysis of graduate student retention. Can. J. High. Educ. **23**, 44–64 (1993)
21. Jia, Y., Xu, B., Karanam, Y., Voida, S.: Personality-targeted gamification: a survey study on personality traits and motivational affordances. In: Proceedings of the 2016 CHI Conference on Human Factors in Computing Systems - CHI 2016. ACM (2016). https://doi.org/10.1145/2858036.2858515
22. Hakulinen, L., Auvinen, T.: The effect of gamification on students with different achievement goal orientations. In: 2014 International Conference on Teaching and Learning in Computing and Engineering (LaTiCE), pp. 9–16. IEEE (2014) https://doi.org/10.1109/latice.2014.10
23. Thomas, H.C., Charles, I.L., Ronald, L.R., Clifford, S.: Algorithms: Construction and Analysis = Introduction to Algorithms, 2nd edn. Williams, Moscow (2006). S. 1296, ISBN 0-07-013151-1
24. Kim, K., Frick, T.: Changes in student motivation during online learning. J. Educ. Comput. Res. **44**(1), 1–23 (2011). https://doi.org/10.2190/EC.44.1.a
25. Dichev, C., Dicheva, D.: Gamifying education: what is known, what is believed and what remains uncertain: a critical review. Int. J. Educ. Technol. High. Educ. **14**(1), 1–36 (2017). https://doi.org/10.1186/s41239-017-0042-5
26. Hamary, J., Tuunanen, J.: Player types: a meta-synthesis. Trans. Digit. Games Res. Assoc. **1**(2), 29–53 (2014). https://doi.org/10.26503/todigra.v1i2.13
27. Kumar, J.: Gamification at work: designing engaging business software. In: Marcus, A. (ed.) DUXU 2013. LNCS, vol. 8013, pp. 528–537. Springer, Heidelberg (2013). https://doi.org/10.1007/978-3-642-39241-2_58
28. Kohavi, R., Longbotham, R.: Online controlled experiments and A/B testing. In: Sammut, C., Webb, G.I. (eds.) Encyclopedia of Machine Learning and Data Mining, pp. 922–929. Springer, Boston (2017). https://doi.org/10.1007/978-1-4899-7687-1_891
29. Sharma, V., Dogra, J.: Study of new paradigm shift towards online learning and analysis of E-management education. Int. J. Mark. Manag. Res. (IJMMR) **3**(1) (2012). ISSN 2229-6883

Agile Game in Online Environment

Ondřej Havazík[1]([✉]), Petra Pavlíčková[2], and Josef Pavlíček[1]

[1] Faculty of Economics, CULS, Kamýcká 129, Prague – Suchdol, 165 00 Prague,
Czech Republic
{havazik,pavlicek}@pef.czu.cz
[2] Faculty of Information Technology, CTU, Thákurova 9, Prague 6, 160 00 Prague,
Czech Republic
petra.pavlickova@fit.cvut.cz

Abstract. The outbreak of the global coronavirus pandemic worsened the conditions for teaching, and it was necessary to teach students to use technologies and tools of remote communication, such as Skype, Google meets or today's most popular software from Microsoft - MS Teams. Since we primarily teach agile project management using practical methods, specifically games, it was necessary to invent and design a game that can be played through remote communication channels, not only in classes with students' physical presence. The game was designed in ADLM software, which stands for Application Life-cycle Management, called JunoOne. Through this tool, the course of the entire project (agile game) will be recorded in the game, and students will be able to try not only the style of agile project management in the Scrum framework but also in the real tool used in practice. This paper's main goal is to present the created agile game in a real tool and the concept of how to play the game remotely. Unfortunately, the game as such has not yet been played due to the bad pandemic situation.

Keywords: Agile game · JunoOne · Project · Students · Task

1 Introduction

Agile approaches have recently been gradually applied in many companies, including large corporations such as banks. Thanks to today's fast-paced times, companies are forced to come up with new or improved products in a much shorter time than before, and they are helped to do so by agile methodologies.

1.1 Scrum Framework

Scrum is framework that helps people, teams and organizations generate value through adaptive solutions and helps to manage their projects. Scrum is built upon by the collective intelligence of the people using it. Rather than provide people with detailed instructions, the rules of Scrum guide their team cooperation, communication and interactions.

© Springer Nature Switzerland AG 2021
A. Polyvyanyy and S. Rinderle-Ma (Eds.): CAiSE 2021 Workshops, LNBIP 423, pp. 17–25, 2021.
https://doi.org/10.1007/978-3-030-79022-6_2

Scrum is an iterative, incremental approach to optimize predictability and to control and manage risk. It combines four formal events for inspection and adaptation within an iterative event, the Sprint. Basic Scrum artifacts are transparency, inspection, and adaptation [1].

- **Transparency** - Significant aspects of the process must be visible to those responsible for the output. Transparency requires that these aspects be defined clearly through a common standard.
- **Inspection** - Scrum participants often check for Scrum artifacts. They move towards the goal of the sprint to reveal unwanted deviations. Inspection should never interfere with work as such.
- **Adaptation** - Adaptation speaks of continuous improvement, of the ability to adapt based on the results of control. Successful use of Scrum depends on people becoming more proficient in living five values which are commitment, focus, openness, respect, and courage

The Scrum Team commits to achieving its goals and to supporting each other. Their primary focus is on the work of the Sprint to make the best possible progress toward these goals. The Scrum Team and its stakeholders are open to cooperate and communicate inside the team. Scrum Team members respect each other, they are independent people, and are respected in the team. The Scrum Team members have the courage to do the right thing, to work on tough problems [1].

1.2 Agile Game

According to Anslow and Maurer [2] teaching agile software development at universities is difficult. When teaching agile software development, it is important to see the following factors such as student collaboration in teams, customer communication, and well-defined scope. Kropp and Meier [3] found that using agile methodologies in teaching had a positive impact on student learning outcomes, based on experiments with these methods.

It can, therefore, be said that when teaching agile management, it is appropriate to use a practical way of teaching [4].

Based on the above we introduced the Agile game in our paper [4] where we described our concept of Agile Game and also we presented the results of playing this Agile game with the master students during the winter semester in the academic year 2019/2020.

The design of the agile game is very important part of the team's research. This agile game helps students to understand the agile approach of the project in a Scrum.

Our research was carried out on students of the 2nd year of the follow-up master's degree in study program informatics on Faculty of Economics and Management, Czech University of Life Sciences in Prague. The total number of players participating in the game was 63 students. The 63 students were divided into 12 teams, each team consisting of 5 players (some teams consisted of 6 players). Every team has one person who represented the customer in the game (usually a teacher). The game was played with students on two different days; each day, about 30 students came; one customer was assigned to each group [4]. Our research team also designed our Agile game in JIRA tool, detailed concept was presented in paper [5].

This paper's main goal is to design our Agile game in such an environment to play it remotely, ideally online. The concept of designing this Agile game remotely in an online environment is described in the second part of this paper, Materials, and Methods. For this reason, we have chosen JunoOne tool as the right tool for our purposes.

1.3 JunoOne

JunoOne is ADLM solution for software development companies, software delivery companies, and software integrators, worldwide invented by Czech company Denevy s.r.o. It comes with a solution designed to simplify and streamline the software development process. It's possible to create all kinds of projects, oversee the proper management of development and testing processes, control, organize and be effective. JunoOne offers a comprehensive and clear way of working and it's fully compatible with Jira, GitLab, and Slack [6]. This tool consists of all the basic necessary sections for project management, including dashboard, task management, schedule, test execution, issue management, design, timesheet, remote work, etc. JunoOne contains a lot of useful functions and benefits that allow you to manage different types of projects effectively, and these are [6] (Table 1):

Table 1. Functions and benefits.

Functions	Benefits
Set of functions from analysis through planning, development to test	Effective implementation of Test processes
Variably configurable reporting	Easy integration with JIRA, GitLab and Slack
Complete task and bug management process	Effective reporting and exports
Configurable notification templates	Clear dashboards
Advanced request management	Configurable widgets
Effective role and feature management	Requirements mapping and detailed overview about their status
Active directory	Using proven and reliable technology
Custom fields	

2   Materials and Methods

This part describes the most important part of the whole paper, and that is the concept of converting an agile game into a computer tool for project management JunoOne so that the game can be played with students remotely (online via MS Teams for example, this tool is used as an elected tool for distance study at CULS). The agile game will not be analyzed and described in-depth. This is what our previous article deals with, where the concept of the game in board form is described in detail [4]. The tool is created primarily in English, but the game has content in the Czech language for a straightforward reason. Although it would be better to have the game in English, it is quite possible (very likely) that students who do not have English at the appropriate level would not clearly understand the tasks. Therefore, it would distort the agile game results based on some students' language barrier and not based on game errors.

2.1 What Students Need to Play the Game Remotely?

To successfully play an agile game remotely, students only need a few necessary things, which can arrange quite easily.

Requirements:

- Notebook or PC.
- Stable internet connection.
- Software for remote communication – MS Teams.
- Internet browser such a Google Chrome, Mozilla Firefox, Safari etc.
- Access to the software tool JunoOne.

As you can see from the points above, several things are needed to be able to play remotely. The basic and most important thing is definitely to have a laptop or desktop computer (tablet or mobile phone is not enough). To be able to play the game remotely and smoothly, it is necessary to have a stable internet connection (ideally via wifi). For the game, it is very important to have an internet browser installed for playing the game, through which the JunoOne tool in which the game was created will open, as well as access to the draw.io page, in which graphic designs will be implemented (internet browser of any type). For individual teams to be able to communicate with each other and at the same time be able to add teachers to the team freely, all participants in the game must have the MS Teams program installed. This communication software was also chosen because integration into JunoOne and MS Teams is planned for the future via some form of a plugin. For a better evaluation of the results of the game, individual 90-min calls will be recorded. Lastly, students must have access to the JunoOne application, which runs on the domain https://czu.juno.one. It is the teacher's responsibility (game facilitator) to ensure that all students have access to the application and the project called "agile game".

2.2 Preparing Students for the Game

Students cannot start playing an agile game without teachers explaining the rules, content and describing the principle of agile management of the Scrum project on which the game is based. One lesson must be organized, explaining everything in detail to the students, and materials will be given to prepare them for the game. Without this, it is not possible to play the game properly with students without negatively affecting the game's outcome.

2.3   Implementing of Individual Tasks

As already mentioned in chapter 3.1., It is necessary to have a web browser installed to use the draw.io page actively. This simple, although potent software is used primarily to create graphs, flow, or, for example, simple wireframes of pages. If students prefer, they can use an alternative in classic painting, which can be found on every computer with a pre-installed MS Windows operating system. The software in the form of draw.io was chosen because it is enough to have an Internet browser installed on it. It is not necessary to install any application locally, which is also cross-platform. In the future, it is still possible that a software change will be made based on a survey of the tools used in practice.

2.4   Concept of the Game in Tool JunoOne

The agile game was created in the tool as a separate project. This project's basic concept will always be cloned according to the number of individual teams that play the game. The project will be named after the number of the relevant team and accessible only to students of the team and instructors who lead the game.

After students open their project, they will be primarily interested in what epics and user stories they have in the design section, which can be seen in the picture below (Fig. 1).

Fig. 1. List of US and Epics

The whole backlog of tasks that are to be handled for the projects' duration consists of 5 Epics, which are further broken down into 17 User stories, and these are consist of one or two particular tasks. These 17 User Stories are associated with 20 unique tasks, most of which have only one specific task, some exceptionally two. Among the important attributes of each task (of any type) are the priority of the task, which can be low, medium, high or critical.

And the second important attribute is the status of the task. All tasks are placed in the backlog by default, from where the Product Owner prioritizes them together with his team to individual Sprints to handle them as efficiently as possible. The JunoOne tool has six states in which we can find tasks, and they will be used only four of them for demonstration in our game because they are the most important for our purposes and these are:

- Backlog - waiting to be included in the future Sprint.
- To do - they must be completed by the end of the actual Sprint.
- In progress – someone from the team is currently working on the task.
- Done – the task is completed and accepted by the customer (teacher).

One of the most important parts of the whole game will be the Scrum board for students, after which they will move the tasks during the project and plan for the upcoming as well as accept the completed tasks after the Sprint. Before the start of each Sprint, it will be necessary to move tasks from the backlog to the "To do" column, which will be tasks that this Sprint must complete, and tasks that were not completed in the last Sprint should also be performed (Fig. 2).

Fig. 2. Scrum board

As can be seen in the picture above, the progress of a specific sprint is recorded here. In the column "In progress" there are two specific tasks on which selected students from the team are working right now (graphic roles in the team). In the column "Done" it is possible to see the tasks that the students completed and were accepted by the customer (teacher/game coordinator).

2.5 Process the Handover and Acceptance of a Specific Task

Suppose someone from the team (a specific student) completes one of the tasks assigned to him/her for the solution (creates a specific graphic design). It is necessary to upload it correctly to the specific task and give it to the customer to accept the solution design.

The following steps are required for the task to be submitted correctly to the customer for approval. First, the student must open the task's detail and add a draft with the text "Request for acceptance" to the comment (see Fig. 3). The student must not forget the critical thing after uploading the completed task and comments with the request for acceptance is to assign the task to the customer using the "Assignee" button on the right in the corner. Assuming the customer is not satisfied, he adds a comment with what needs to be fixed and assigns the task back to the solver. Assuming that the customer is satisfied and accepts the solution, he writes a comment stating that the solution is accepted and assigned a task to the product owner, whose responsibility is to move it to the "Done" status.

Fig. 3. Acceptance request on the customer

2.6 Game over

An agile game can end in several ways. The most common end is the expiration of all 6 sprints in which the game is played (90 min). After the time limit expires, all key parts of the project can be accepted, and the project as such is accepted and declared fulfilled. On the other hand, the project may also end with the non-completion of some parts, and at that time, in practice, it would be necessary to move deadlines, and the project would cost more money (at best, at worst it could be rejected, and the company could withdraw from the contract or demand penalties). The best ending is if students manage to move all the specific tasks into the "Done" section. It means that all tasks were created and accepted before the time end of the last sprint. The game ends prematurely by fulfilling everything required.

2.7 Game Evaluation

The results described in our first paper [4] concern evaluating the game as such (pros and cons) and finding out how many students had some practical experience with an agile approach and framework Scrum. The aim was also to determine whether the game came to students more interesting and beneficial for understanding the issue. The second part, which deals with the analysis of team roles, will be described in the future in a separate paper. We want to verify several hypotheses on this online version of the agile game, which should be evaluated using both a questionnaire survey, observation, and the appropriate test, which will verify students' knowledge.

3 Discussion

New Scrum Guide [1] is mainly about agile mindset and new artifacts are transparency, inspection, and adaptation as were described in section Introduction. These most important ideas, also confirms Zuzuna Šochova on her blog [7].

Nowadays in pandemic situation COVID-19 is very important to think about how to play our game in online environment. The same reason to create an Agile game had the team Doug Husovsky et all in their paper [8]. We designed our Agile game in JIRA and now we created in JunoOne tool. And we believe that will help a lot to understand the Scrum and students will like it as they liked our previous version. And we hope that our Agile game played remotely will help to reduce the lack of information during the pandemic situation. About the recent lack of information discuss paper Joseph Crawford [9] and we hope that in our research we are helping to solve the situation. Also the authors Tadesse and Muluye came to the same conclusion [10].

4 Conclusion

Due to the coronavirus pandemic, it was not possible to play the game in an alpha version, which must first be tested in people's presence to catch the biggest shortcomings of the game. Then it will be possible to play it remotely in a beta version. After successfully playing the beta version of the game, it will be possible to start playing the game with students the following semester.

Nowadays, distance learning due to the unfavorable pandemic situation around the world has become a big topic. Because so far, we have had a game created only in the board form and the JIRA form, which was not ready for remote play, we were not able to play the game with the students in 2020/21 at all. In the course evaluation, it often appeared that the students were disappointed that they did not enjoy the game this year. Based on all the above reasons, we decided to design the game to be played remotely with students, which would save a lot of work and time, even if normal contact teaching. A clear plan for the future is to play the game remotely with the students and evaluate whether it is as successful and beneficial as the agile game's board version and whether the game is playable in an online environment at all in our form. We would also like to confirm that playing the game will provide students a piece of practical knowledge and experience. We would evaluate their subsequent acquired knowledge using a test that students would receive after theoretical teaching of agile project management and Scrum framework compared to the test results after playing an online agile game. It should also be much easier to play with a wider range of students, thanks to the ability to play the game from the comfort of their homes.

Acknowledgements. The results and knowledge included herein have been obtained owing to support from the following institutional grants. Internal grant agency of the Faculty of Economics and Management, Czech University of Life Sciences in Prague, grant no. 2019A0008, "Analýza týmových rolí v IT projektech pomocí speciální hry AGILNĚ".

References

1. Schwaber, K., Sutherland, J.: Scrum Guide V7. https://scrumguides.org/docs/scrumguide/v2020/2020-Scrum-Guide-US.pdf#zoom=100
2. Anslow, C., Maurer, F.: An experience report at teaching a group based agile software development project course. In: SIGCSE 2015 - Proceedings of the 46th ACM Technical Symposium on Computer Science Education, pp. 500–505 (2015). https://doi.org/10.1145/2676723.2677284
3. Kropp, M., Meier, A.: Teaching agile software development at university level: values, management, and craftsmanship. In: 2013 26th International Conference on Software Engineering Education and Training, pp. 179–188 (2013). https://doi.org/10.1109/CSEET.2013.6595249
4. Havazik, O., Pavlickova, P.: Using a simulation game in the education. In: Fejrar Jiří, F.M. (ed.) Proceedings of the 17th International Conference Efficiency and Responsibility in Education 2020 (ERIE 2020), pp. 76–82 (2020)
5. Havazik, O., Pavlickova, P.: How to design agile game for education purposes in JIRA, pp. 331–334 (2020). https://doi.org/10.1109/codit49905.2020.9263937
6. Denevy: JunoPro. https://juno.one/
7. Šochová, Z.: Nový Scrum guide. https://soch.cz/blog/category/management/agile/scrum-management/
8. Husovsky, D., Schlaver, J., Stewart, R.: Virtual Agile Games to Strengthen Distributed Teams. https://www.agileconnection.com/article/virtual-agile-games-strengthen-distributed-teams
9. Crawford, J., et al.: COVID-19: 20 countries' higher education intra-period digital pedagogy responses. J. Appl. Learn. Teach. 3(1), 1–20 (2020). https://doi.org/10.37074/jalt.2020.3.1.7
10. Tadesse, S., Muluye, W.: The impact of COVID-19 pandemic on education system in developing countries: a review. Open J. Soc. Sci. **08**, 159–170 (2020). https://doi.org/10.4236/jss.2020.810011

Filling the Gap Between Business and Application Development Using Agile BORM

Himesha Wijekoon[1,2]([✉]), Boris Schegolev[1], and Vojtěch Merunka[1,3]

[1] Department of Information Engineering, Faculty of Economics and Management,
Czech University of Life Sciences Prague, Prague, Czech Republic
{wijekoon,schegolev,merunka}@pef.czu.cz
[2] Department of Industrial Management, Faculty of Science,
University of Kelaniya, Kelaniya, Sri Lanka
himesha@kln.ac.lk
[3] Department of Software Engineering, Faculty of Nuclear Sciences and Engineering,
Czech Technical University in Prague, Prague, Czech Republic
vojtech.merunka@fjfi.cvut.cz

Abstract. Agile software development is the most popular methodology used in today's software engineering. Agility in software development does not mean the resignation to the accuracy and quality of meeting user requirements. However, it is apparent that the tasks of requirements engineering are taken lightly or often overlooked in agile projects due to project cost. One of the main reasons for this is the lack of efficient and easy to use modelling tools which can be used for the purposes of business modelling and initial software design. Therefore, there is a need for good modelling tools which can be easily used by both non-technical users and software developers which can fill the gap between business needs and identified software requirements. This paper presents BORM as a feasible solution for this in an agile software development environment.

Keywords: Requirements Engineering · Business modelling · BORM · Agile software development · Business process reengineering

1 Introduction

A software engineering process should begin with Requirements Engineering. However, elicitation, verification and validation of the requirements are sometimes considered to be outside the scope of software engineers' work. In this regard, software engineers rely on customers, business analysts or domain specialists to finalize the requirements specification. Furthermore, agile methods which have become widely used these days do not even assume that the requirements are accurately identified at the beginning of the software development lifecycle [12]. However, with our experience we believe the requirements engineering process must involve software engineers. In this regard, software engineering intersects with business engineering and management consulting.

A. Polyvyanyy and S. Rinderle-Ma (Eds.): CAiSE 2021 Workshops, LNBIP 423, pp. 26–38, 2021.
https://doi.org/10.1007/978-3-030-79022-6_3

The business organizations decide to develop software to streamline their business processes. Therefore, business software is intertwined with the business processes. The situation will not improve in cases where business processes are not reviewed and optimized before implementing software to support them. Hence Organization Modeling (OM) or Business Process Reengineering (BPR) is a crucial part of such software development. However, there is a major problem which arises in the first stages of the software development life cycle [2, 10]. In the initial stages requirements for the system should be specified. Then an initial object model should be constructed which is usually called as the conceptual model of the system. Stakeholders should involve on both above-mentioned tasks to ensure correct system is being developed. Thus, the tools or diagrams used at these initial phases should be understandable to the stakeholders who are not software professionals. Additionally, these techniques must not deform or incorrectly simplify requirements of the system.

"Concept Space" is what the users believe, assume, or know while the "Articulation Space" is what the user communicates to the business analyst [3]. The analyst then creates a model to match with the mental model of the concept space of the user. The difference between this analyst's model and the user's concept space is the "Concept Gap". It is inevitable to fully diminish this gap, yet it can be reduced by utilizing ideal modelling techniques. There are many modelling techniques which can be used in this regard such as UML, BPMN and EPC-Aris. However, they have certain usability issues which apparently demotivates the users to involve them in software development especially considering agile software development [7, 9]. Objective of this paper is to propose BORM (Business Object Relation Modelling) over the other modelling techniques which will comply well with agile practices.

This paper is organized as follows. Section 2 presents an overview about the motivation of this study. Section 3 provides a brief review about the existing tools. Section 4 gives a short overview about BORM. Section 5 describes case studies which have been done using BORM as the business modelling tool. Finally, Sect. 6 provides the conclusion of the study.

2 Motivation

Agility in software development does not mean the resignation to the accuracy and quality of meeting user requirements. Creating systems in agile way does not just mean to develop anything cheap and fast without unnecessary annoying modelling. Hence, we know from practice many projects financed by various bureaucracies (for example from the governmental budget), where the true goal is to do anything quickly and cheaply, which could then be declared a successful result for just drawing money purposes. Based on many years of our experience, we are convinced that the agility must also strongly mean the quality. On one hand, of course, the simplification of the development process is required, but at the same time we need to keep and even increase the user requirements validation. The criterion for this kind of the validation, for us – the software engineers, there is not financial success in obtaining a contract, but the satisfaction of end users, so to have a good reputation not only with providers of financial resources but also the people working with the result of our work. Validation here means the usefulness of the result which gives people real added value and makes their everyday life better.

If agility is understood as a mere simplification, there is an effect that van der Aalst describes as oversimplification [1]. Such a result works (because almost anything can be functional), but it does not bring any improvements to its end users. It happened because of the used "agile method", there were omitted many important business details. In addition, there is yet another danger because various unnecessary things get into the project that end users do not need, but the "agile method" required them. This is the effect of "bias" as it was also pointed in [1]. Therefore, from both reasons, we believe that we urgently need to have an optimal and balanced ratio between the simplicity and the accuracy to honestly say we are agile. After all, the word agile has its origin in the Latin verb "agere" which means "to work". It is neither from the word "to be rapid" nor from the word "to be simple".

Wang et al. point out that even though most agile practitioners accept the importance of requirements engineering, they are not allocating enough resources for this activity due to the budget concerns [12]. They have also found out that interviewing and user stories are main requirements elicitation methods while user stories and use cases are main requirements representation methods. On the contrary in a much recent study Schon et al. mentions that there is no common process model for stakeholders to involve in an agile software development environment [8]. They further mention that only half of the projects under their study have involved users directly into the development process. Furthermore, they suggest the need of a structured process model for stakeholder and user involvement in agile development.

Therefore, agility should not merely exist in the implementation process of software, but also in the requirements engineering (business modelling, requirements elicitation, requirements validation etc.). We believe that the lack of proper requirements engineering in agile development is due to the absence of proper techniques. BORM will be a good candidate technique to overcome this issue.

3   Existing Tools

There are various tools and techniques for business modelling. Some of the well-known techniques are briefly reviewed in this section in the perspective of usage in software development.

- UML – UML is the most popular modelling language among software engineers. However, UML diagrams contain information about underlying software implementation which makes them complex for the users from the problem domain to comprehend and use [9].
- BPMN – Even though this is a proven business process modelling notation, it is less popular in the software engineering community. But it has a higher learning curve to use it for advanced process modelling [7]. This limits the usage of BPMN as a common tool between domain experts and software engineers.
- EPC-Aris – A popular tool in Europe with Aris Case tool support. It is also easy to use by domain experts. However, there is weak connection to software development with low expressiveness of large models.

According to our many years of practical experience, UML is complex, and it requires a thorough knowledge of object-oriented programming to understand. On the other hand, it has weak support for decompositions and generalisations, which are essential for understanding, formulating and verifying requirements. Of course, UML is not just for object-oriented object programming today, but it should be universal. But it is not yet. The same consortium is also working on BPMN. Should we be afraid that these two giants will merge into an even bigger and more complex giant? Of course, we follow various attempts at universal ontologies, for example [6], but this intimidates business domain experts and practitioners even more, because we force them not only to be skilled programmers, but even philosophers, to be able to explain and correctly describe their needs.

Therefore, there has been a need for a simple yet expressive tool for business modelling which can be collaboratively used by business users, domain experts, business analysts and software developers. BORM is built on the synergy of Object-Oriented Paradigm (OOP) and Finite State Machines (FSM) [4, 5]. Thanks to this synergy, we can bridge the gap between the business world and the world of software development without having to change modelling techniques. In this agile software development era, the modelling should be easier and less time consuming than ever. Hence this paper aims at offering BORM to be used as an agile modelling tool.

4   Short Overview of BORM

BORM is an approach to both process modelling and subsequent development of information systems. It provides an approach that facilitates the description of how real business systems evolve, change and behave. BORM was originally developed in 1993 and was intended to provide seamless support for the building of object-oriented software systems based on pure object-oriented languages, databases and distributed environments. Subsequently, it has been realised that this method has significant potential in business process modelling and other related business issues. For more on information on the BORM method see [4, 5].

BORM is based on the spiral model for the software development life cycle. One loop of the object-oriented spiral model contains stages which are as follows: *strategic analysis, initial analysis, advanced analysis, initial design, advanced design, implementation*, and *testing*. The typical number of these iterations is between 2 and 4, but it can also be used for separate performed 2–3 days engineering tasks as in agile XP or Scrum methods and compose the whole project from them.

The first three stages are collectively referred to as the *expansion* stages. Expansion ends with the finalizing of the detailed analysis conceptual model, which fully describes the solution to the problem from the requirements point of view. The remaining stages are called *consolidation* stages. These are concerned with the process of developing from 'expanded ideas' to a working application (or a working piece). During these stages, the conceptual model is step by step, transformed into a software design.

BORM was initially developed as an object-oriented method for the analysis and design of object-oriented software systems. The process starts from an informal problem specification and provides both methods and techniques, to enable this informal specification to be transformed into an initial set of interacting objects.

The tools and techniques developed for requirement analysis and used in the initial phases of BORM, provide an independent method for business process modelling as part of BPR. This independent method, referred to as BOBA (BORM Object Behaviour Analysis) is frequently used alone for describing *user stories* as we know from agile methods. It provides closer interactive interchange between the developers and members of the user's organization. As well as identifying initial objects, BOBA elicits from the domain experts detailed descriptions of their requirements which are fed back to them via easily understood descriptions of the proposed system's behaviour suitable for accurate and also fast formulation of assignments for agile development.

There is a list of required system functions, which are essentially *use cases*. From this list, a set of system *scenarios* is formed. BOBA scenarios always include these four sections:

1. **Initiation.** A brief verbal description of the beginning of the scenario including inputs or entry conditions. It also describes the first event or first activity of some participant within the scenario.
2. **Action.** A verbal description of the process itself (e.g., *to-do* description).
3. **Participants.** The set of those elements of the scenario, which are required for its operation. It is often the case that the same participants may be present in different roles in several processes of the same modelled system.
4. **Result.** A brief verbal description of the outcome and outputs of the scenario.

The next feature of the BOBA approach is the ability to model processes. As noted earlier, UML use-cases often requires the support of activity diagrams to fully convey the deeper meaning of any system. BOBA uses its own form of less complex diagrams to achieve such deeper understanding which performs the function of multiple UML diagrams together all in one: *state-transition, activity, communication,* and *event-state.*

The notation of our Object Relation Diagram (ORD) is very simple and easily understood by domain experts and it does not require knowledge of concepts which will only belong at subsequent programming stages in the development process.

In carrying out the real-world projects, it was found that teaching this notation and syntax has a short learning curve and does not conflict with the principles of agility. This synergy of simplicity and potency, allows domain experts to become active members of the modelling team, working with formal modelling tools and techniques.

ORD uses the graphical concepts, for representing *objects, states, activities* and *communication.* Additionally, all used concepts use the standard UML notation but only in our original combination. ORD philosophy is strictly based on the theory of communicating finite-state machines combined with the object-oriented paradigm.

It is also possible, of course, to simplify it even more and draw object activities just without any transitions between states if we do not require a detailed description of some object. Thus, we have a 'two-dimensional' style of modeling:

- The first dimension is the *sequence of communications* between activities of the objects in the system. This plays a role of UML object interaction diagrams.
- The second dimension shows internal behaviour of objects as their *sequences of states and transition.* This plays a role of UML state-transition diagrams.

5 BORM Projects

BORM has been successfully used for numerous large projects including,

- the identification of business processes in Prague city hospitals,
- the modelling of properties necessary for the general agricultural commodities wholesale sector in the Central European region,
- as a tool for business process reengineering in the electricity supply industry
- and as a tool for business process reengineering for telecommunication network management in the Central European region [4].

Table 1 gives some indication of the size of the models that were constructed for some of the projects undertaken using BOBA.

Table 1. Size of the models that were constructed using BOBA [4]

Project	System functions	Scenarios	Process diagrams	Objects (participants)	Avg. states per object	Avg. activities per object
National agrarian chamber (analysis and design of software for fruit market public information system)	4	7	7	6	4	4
Hospital complex (BPR of organization structure)	6	12	12	8	10	12
TV and radio broadcasting company (BPR and company transformation for open market)	4	9	9	14	8	8
Regional electricity distribution company (customer information system analysis)	12	19	19	23	12	12

(*continued*)

Table 1. (*continued*)

Project	System functions	Scenarios	Process diagrams	Objects (participants)	Avg. states per object	Avg. activities per object
Regional electricity distribution company (failure handling information system analysis and prototype implementation)	19	31	34	27	13	14
Regional gas distribution company (BPR of all company)	28	81	97	210	11	12
Regional gas distribution company (BPR of all company)	23	60	63	120	12	12

BOBA is fully supported by the MetaEdit© case tool developed by Metacase Ltd. (Metacase Ltd., Jüväskyllä Finland, info@metacase.com, http://www.metacase.com) and the Craft. CASE modelling tool by Craftcase Ltd. (www.craftcase.com). There is also academic research and its own open-source tool, which is being developed at the Faculty of Information Technology of the Czech Technical University in Prague (https://github.com/OpenPonk) and where experiments with modifications of the BORM method are experimented in various ways [11]. We illustrate the details of the BOBA method through two selected case studies.

5.1 EPOS Terminal

The system is the familiar one of an EPOS (Electronic POint of Sales) terminal in a supermarket. The main functional requirement of the system is to process the goods that a supermarket customer brings to the terminal and to produce the total cost of this transaction. Figure 1 shows two required system functions, together with four associated scenarios.

Using BORM, we can describe the first scenario in the following manner:

1. **Initiation.** A customer arrives at a terminal with several items to purchase.
2. **Action.** The Cashier scans each item at the terminal. The terminal reads the bar code and the stock database is consulted to determine the description of the item and its

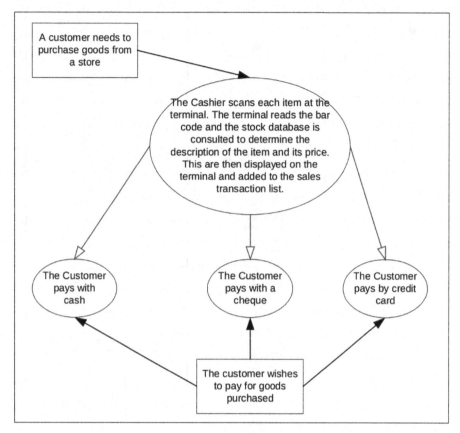

Fig. 1. System functions and scenarios

price. These are then displayed on the terminal and added to the sales transaction list.

3. **Participants.** Customer, Cashier, EPOS Terminal, Sale, Stock List
4. **Result.** The cashier prints the bill and provides it to customer.

The list of participants is the term used for what will probably become the objects in the system. In BOBA, a participant is any entity that has a role in a scenario. These may eventually correspond to either system objects or actors. If the software is to be released in a series of incremental steps, the system boundary could be dynamic. Participants might be external to the system initially, but in later releases be implemented as part of the system. Therefore, it may prove meaningful to begin identifying relevant attributes of the candidate objects. Figure 2 shows the initial process model for the customer purchasing items from the store.

Each process diagram is related to a scenario from which it has been exploded. These diagrams must be drawn, but case tools like MetaEdit support the drawing process as all the necessary information, which has been obtained in previous stages, can be imported from the repository.

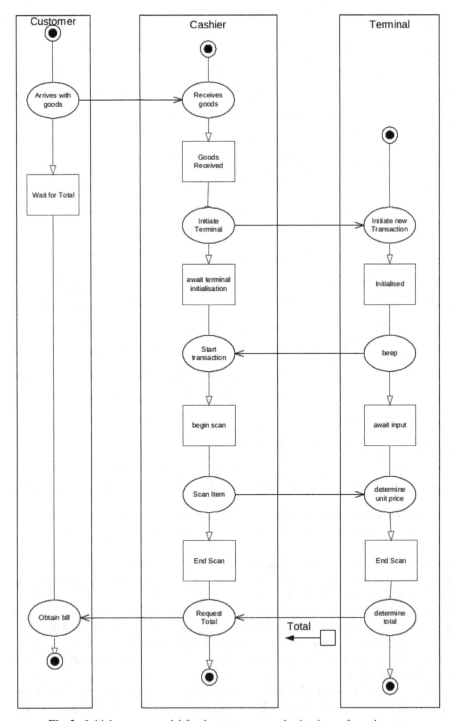

Fig. 2. Initial process model for the customer purchasing items from the store

Many aspects of the model under construction, can be reported as HTML documents or as MS Access database format files. One such report is the set of model cards for all the candidate objects as shown in Fig. 3. These are very similar to Class-Responsibility- Collaboration (CRC) cards with the exception that they do not show collaborating objects. Collaborations are however provided in Object Collaboration Tables. From these tables, we can easily construct the initial conceptual model for the proposed system using the list of objects and associations. Even automated construction of the initial model is possible.

Cashier	components:
activities	*visible properties*
iniate terminal Receive goods Request total Scan Items Start Sale	Staff Number

Fig. 3. Object modeling cards

5.2 Modelling Key Processes of Faculty of IT at CTU

We can further demonstrate the process of orchestration and choreography using BORM methodology on one of the process diagrams created for the project mapping the key processes of the Faculty of Information Technology (FIT) at the Czech Technical University (CTU - the oldest technical university in Central Europe). Output obtained from the project used for the case study are as follows.

- 63 processes
- 46 internal participants
- 7 external participants
- 72 unique dataflows

As an example, we will present the process of establishing a bilateral agreement between the FIT (or CTU as whole) and a foreign university or college.

1. **Participants.** Following participants of the process were identified based on the information obtained from the faculty staff:

    a. FIT: Vice-dean for the foreign relations – vice-dean for the foreign relations of the FIT.

b. Rector's office: Department of international relations – department of international relations of the CTU.
c. Foreign university – any foreign university or college.

2. **Initiation.** The initiator of the process is the contact person.
3. **Action.** The baseline is the need to establish a bilateral agreement allowing the teachers or students to take study trips to foreign university.
4. **Result.** The target state is a signed bilateral agreement brief verbal description of the outcome and outputs of the scenario.

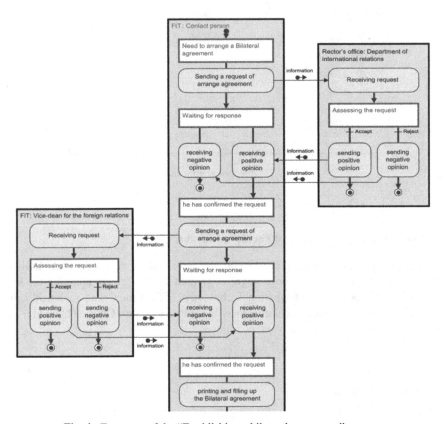

Fig. 4. Fragment of the "Establishing a bilateral agreement" process

Contact person fills in the "Request for a bilateral agreement" application form. The application must first be approved by the Department of International Relations of the CTU and then by the vice-dean for foreign relations of the FIT. After the application is approved the contact person fills in the "Bilateral Agreement" form, which again must first be approved by the Department of International Relations of the CTU and then by the vice-dean for foreign relations of the FIT. Contact person then sends the approved "Bilateral Agreement" document to the foreign university for approval. If the foreign university approves the document, new bilateral agreement is signed. The result of the process is a new bilateral agreement. As shown in Fig. 4, the process may end any time during its course if one of the documents is rejected.

From the process control perspective is the FIT: Contact Person the coordinator of the whole process and can be therefore classified as the orchestrator. Other participants, except Foreign University are internal participants. Therefore, part of the process will be orchestrated while the communication with the foreign university will be choreographed. As the original process diagram is too extensive for the purposes of this paper, in the Fig. 5 we present a simplified view of the communications in the process.

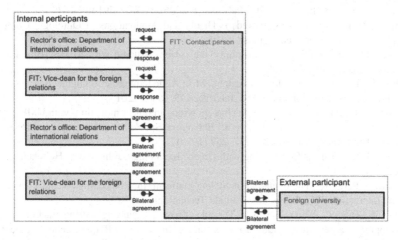

Fig. 5. Simplified view of communications in Establishing a bilateral agreement.

6   Conclusion

In UML, numerous diagrams are used to describe the system which makes the process time consuming and complex and is against the principles of agility. BORM also uses the UML concepts but only in one special diagram of communicating objects as interconnected finite-state machines efficient to model *user stories*. This is our agile solution to *fill the gap* between requirements description and the software system features.

It was also proven on our practical projects that the BORM process diagrams serve well when reengineering the business processes and work-flow yet before starting agile software development. With the experience of past projects normally one hour introduction at the start of analysis is sufficient to understand the BORM philosophy.

As per the above observations, we believe that BORM can be a promising tool for agile development. Future research will be carried out towards even greater support for modelling business agility.

References

1. Aalst, W.M.P.: Business Process Simulation Revisited, in Lecture Notes in Business Information Processing (LNBIP), vol. 63, Springer Business and Science (2010)
2. Darnton, G., Darnton, M.: Business Process Analysis, International Thomson Publishing, (1997). ISBN 1-861-52039-5
3. Goldberg, A., Rubin, K.S.: Succeeding with Objects - Decision Frameworks for Project Management. Addison Wesley, Reading Mass (1995)
4. Knott, R., Merunka, V., Polak, J.: The BORM methodology: a third-generation fully object-oriented methodology Knowl. Based Syst. **16**, 77–89 (2003)
5. Liping, L., Borislav, R., et al.: Management of the Object-Oriented Development Process - Part 15: BORM Methodology, Idea Publishing (2006). ISBN 1-59140-605-6
6. Poli, R., Healy, M., Kameas, A. (eds.): Theory and Applications of Ontology: Computer Applications. Springer, Netherlands (2010)
7. Recker, J.: Opportunities and constraints: the current struggle with BPMN. Bus. Process Manage. J. **16**(1), 181–201 (2010)
8. Schon, E.M., Thomaschewski, J., Escalona, M.J.: Agile requirements engineering: a systematic literature review. Comput. Stand. Interfaces **49**, 79–91 (2017)
9. Simons, A.J.H., Graham, I.: 30 things that go wrong in object modelling with UML 1.3. In: Kilov, H., Rumpe, B., Simmonds, I. (eds.) Behavioral Speciation of Businesses and Systems. Kluwer Academic Publishers, pp. 237–257 (1999)
10. Taylor, D.A.: Business Engineering with Object Technology, John Wiley, Hoboken (1995). ISBN 0-471-04521-7
11. Uhnák, P., Pergl, R.: The openponk modeling platform. In: Proceedings of the 11th edition of the International Workshop on Smalltalk Technologies (2016)
12. Wang, X., Zhao, L., Wang, Y, Sun, J.: The role of requirements engineering practices in agile development: an empirical study. In: Zowghi, D., Jin, Z. (eds) Requirements Engineering. Communications in Computer and Information Science, vol 432. Springer, Berlin, Heidelberg (2014). https://doi.org/10.1007/978-3-662-43610-3_15

Explanation in Multi-Stakeholder Recommendation for Enterprise Decision Support Systems

Giandomenico Cornacchia[1], Francesco M. Donini[2], Fedelucio Narducci[1],
Claudio Pomo[1]([✉]), and Azzurra Ragone[3]

[1] Politecnico di Bari, Via E. Orabona 4, 70125 Bari, Italy
{giandomenico.cornacchia,fedelucio.narducci,claudio.pomo}@poliba.it
[2] Università della Tuscia, Via S.M. in Gradi 4, 01100 Viterbo, Italy
donini@unitus.it
[3] EY, Via Oberdan 40, 70125 Bari, Italy
azzurra.ragone@it.ey.com

Abstract. Business agility requires support from recommendation systems, but explaining recommendations may yield information disclosure. We analyze how to provide explanations in the scenario of Multi-Stakeholder Recommendation where the sensible information of one stakeholder should not be disclosed in the explanation to another stakeholder. Among the several types of explanations analyzed, counterfactual explanations come off best as they allow the system to preserve each stakeholder's privacy and sensitive information in terms of preferences.

Keywords: Decision support systems · Multi-Stakeholder
Recommender Systems · Explanations · Counterfactual explanations

1 Introduction

Business Agility requires tools to support personalized information access, most notably Recommendation System. Business Decision Support System (DSS) like e-commerce or streaming platforms, social media, multimedia applications, booking systems, among others, exploit Recommendation Systems to help users find their way through the multitude of information available to them. We can consider a Recommendation System as a specific DSS, evaluated by its ability to propose appealing items to a user. However, recently, this kind of systems evolved to match a better user experience. This aspect is addressed by the latest research beyond accuracy metrics. In this direction, a significant role is played by explanation.

With the social emergence of Recommendation Systems as a well-established tool for orienting oneself in scenarios involving a choice among a substantial number of options, users became increasingly choosy. To make a user feel comfortable about the provided suggestion, it is necessary to explain why he received that recommendation from the system. Hence, explaining a recommendation

© Springer Nature Switzerland AG 2021
A. Polyvyanyy and S. Rinderle-Ma (Eds.): CAiSE 2021 Workshops, LNBIP 423, pp. 39–47, 2021.
https://doi.org/10.1007/978-3-030-79022-6_4

provides a clear tentative to engage the user, gain her trust, and give her the best user experience. Moreover, in the context of a real Recommendation System, the agents playing a role are not just the users. In the last few years, a new research field has emerged that considers different stakeholders involved in the recommendation process, leading to Multi-Stakeholder Recommendation Systems (MS-RS). This perspective is also acknowledged in the literature as Reciprocal Recommendation, and researchers have deeply investigated how to make a recommendation acceptable to both parties involved in the recommendation process. Thanks to emerging studies about the effect of recommendations on different user clusters and what impact specific groups of items have on the overall process, MS-RS attract an increasing interest. Furthermore, MS-RS are involved in many real scenarios based on transactions between a consumer who is looking for a product/service and a provider who wants to match the preferences of as many consumers as possible to sell them his items.

In this paper, we investigate the explanations that can be given to two kinds of users of an MS-RS: *consumers* and *providers*. In the MS-RS context, each agent has some personal information that should not be revealed to other agents. We review different kinds of explanations and determine that a counterfactual explanation comes off best, since it explains to a generic consumer how her preferences drive the recommendation process, and to a generic provider how a different strategy could change consumers' recommendation lists.

The rest of the paper is organized as follows: in the next section we summarize the state of the art for MS-RS, pointing to the (very few) works about explanation in this field. Then in Sect. 3 we set up some notation that formalizes profiles, utilities, and recommendations in MS-RS. In Sect. 4 we review the available methods that can be used to compute balanced recommendations in MS-RS, and then in Sect. 5, after considering several types of explanations, we focus our attention on counterfactual explanations. The final section summarizes our conclusions and draws some future directions of research.

2   Related Work

This work cuts across two main topics in the research area of Recommender Systems: Explanations and Multiple stakeholders. From a general point of view, recommender systems are linked to the idea of learning-to-rank. Ideally, a generic user would like to receive a list of recommendations of the most appealing items for her. Generally, this list ranks items in descending order, starting from the most important item to the least important one. Hence, a Recommendation System estimates the user's *utility* of a set of items by optimizing an accuracy metric. However, this kind of metrics do not take into account some other aspects of the utility score computation [19,24]. A new evaluation perspective tries to put them in the loop beyond accuracy metrics [25]. This family of metrics are helpful to estimate, for example, the novelty [7], the diversity [15], or the serendipity [19] of a recommendation with the aim of improving the user experience. In this context, a crucial role is played by explanation [22]. Explainable recommendations are a research field that emerged years ago when early models whose aim was to suggest items appeared in the scientific literature [12,21,28]. Nava *et al.* [23] provide seven different dimensions to consider when an explanation is provided: user's trust, satisfaction, persuasiveness, efficiency, effectiveness, scrutability, and transparency. Accordingly, when a Recommendation System suggests an item to a generic user, she could ask why she receives that suggestion. A good explanation could impact at least one of the above-mentioned dimensions. Related to this aspect, Gedikli *et al.* [10] study how different explanation types and strategies affect the final result of the process, and provide guidelines to evaluate each of these aspects.

However, providing an explanation is particularly challenging and difficult when more than one kind of user is involved in the recommendation process, as in the case of Multi-Stakeholder Recommender Systems (MS-RS). Such systems are useful in a real recommendation scenario like e-commerce, where also the provider of products is involved in the recommendation process. Another classical scenario is dating, in which the recommendation has to be acceptable to both kinds of users of the transaction [27]. Following this idea, group Recommendation Systems were proposed, with the aim of maximising the utility of each stakeholder in the group [18]. In this direction, it is clear that the MS-RS approach is to devise a strategy that includes the utility of different stakeholders (like in a multi-side approach) and this approach was generalised to every recommendation task [2,3]. Abdollahpouri *et al.* [6] propose a general model for MS-RSs, which considers three kinds of users in the loop: the consumer who receives the recommendation, the system that supports the recommendation process, and the provider who feeds the system catalogue. Naturally, in the MS-RS scenario, all involved kinds of users must be taken into account in the explanation process.

To the best of our knowledge, research in MS-RS did not deeply address yet such explanation aspects. Verdeaux *et al.* [26] consider counterfactual explanations in MS-RS scenario, but only from the consumer's viewpoint. In that work, the authors adopt a causality-based approach for the counterfactual explanation, but they do not consider explanations from the provider's perspective. Conversely, in our work we propose a counterfactual explanation both to the consumer and to the provider, based on each stakeholder's own utility function. In this way, the private/confidential information of each stakeholder is never revealed to the counterpart during the explanation process.

3   Notation

In this section, we formally define the viewpoint of each stakeholder, in terms of both her profile and the recommendation the MS-RS gives her. This will set our notation for a formalization of counterfactual explanations of such recommendations in Sect. 5.

In the present study, we envisage two types of stakeholders: consumers and providers (we leave the inclusion of the MS-RS utility for future work). We denote the set of all consumers as $\mathcal{C} = \{c_1, c_2, \ldots\}$, and the set of providers as $\mathcal{P} = \{p_1, p_2, \ldots\}$.

Items are enumerated into a set $\mathcal{I} = \{I_1, I_2, \ldots\}$. To simplify the formulas in the paper, we represent an item just by its index in $\mathcal{I}$, so that a list of items $\langle I_3, I_7, I_2 \rangle$ (*e.g.*, a recommendation) will be just a list of natural numbers $\langle 3, 7, 2 \rangle$. We do not delve in this paper into the characteristics of items—*i.e.*, their features.

In general, the MS-RS keeps a *profile* for each consumer c that collects her preferences or requirements. In this paper, we consider a consumer profile as a list of items in decreasing consumer preference order: $P_c = \langle i_1, i_2, \ldots \rangle$—*i.e.*, an ordered list of items the consumer has chosen (or preferred in the past) the most. The recommendation process consists of a utility function $u_c : \mathcal{C} \times \mathcal{I} \to \mathbb{R}^+$. Such a utility can be represented by an accuracy, diversity, serendipity metric, or any other consumer utility, with the constraint that u_c is such that $u_c(c, i_1) \geq u_c(c, i_2) \geq u_c(c, i_3) \geq \ldots$, *i.e.*, the utility is coherent with the consumer's profile. A *recommendation for a consumer* c is an ordered list of items, denoted by $R_c = \langle i_1, i_2, \ldots \rangle$, meaning that the MS-RS suggests the consumer the new item i_1 as most suitable, then item i_2 as a second choice, etc. The recommendation must be coherent with the consumer's utility, *i.e.*, $u_c(c, i_1) \geq u_c(c, i_2) \geq u_c(c, i_3) \geq \ldots$

Similarly, the *profile* of a provider p is a collection of her requirements. In this case, the provider's requirements represent some strategy that could maximize *e.g.*, profits, stock clearance, budget allocation, some other objectives, or a combination of some of them. Each strategy yields an ordered list of items, $P_p = \langle i_1, i_2, i_3 \ldots \rangle$, with the meaning that the provider would prefer to sell item i_1 the most, then item i_2, etc. Observe that such a set of strategies could be as large as needed, taking into account all possible choices the provider could make. Similarly to consumers, the recommender implements a utility function $u_p : \mathcal{P} \times \mathcal{I} \to \mathbb{R}^+$, giving a value to items from the provider's point of view, with the constraint that such utility is coherent with the provider's strategy, that is, $u_p(p, i_1) \geq u_p(p, i_2) \geq u_p(p, i_3) \geq \ldots$

In the next section, we summarize methods combining the above utilities into recommendations that balance between different stakeholders' objectives.

4   Computing Recommendations in MS-RS

Traditional Recommendation Systems are built to recommend to end users a ranked list of items based on the user's tastes and preferences. Accordingly, the development of conventional collaborative filtering [16] algorithms has been centred on minimising an error to maximise unilateral utility metrics (*i.e.*, the consumer's point of view). However, it is now recognized that the recommendation task is not unilateral.

Considering only the user utility in the recommendation task raises a problem called "Popularity Bias" [4] in which the Recommendation System suggests the most popular items with higher probability than less frequent ones. In this case, the problem was addressed by spreading diversity in the recommendation task [17]. Yet, approaches that promote diversity still lack the provider's perspective.

In a more recent work [1], Abdollahpouri *et al.* proposed another way to implement the recommendation task in a MS-RS setting by using learning-to-reranking methodologies. The core problem is to compose the (sometimes) diverging interests of the two principal stakeholders: consumers and providers. Consumers want a personalized recommendation list that maximizes their utility, whereas providers want their products to have a higher probability of being sold. To find a new recommendation list which reflects a possible equilibrium point between consumer and provider utility functions a possible approach is to introduce a maximization problem of log-likelihood estimation. Following the same direction adopted by Abdollahpouri *et al.* [1] the problem becomes

$$\max_{\beta} \mathcal{L}(u_p | R_c, \mathcal{I}) = \sum_{j=1}^{m} \log(u_c(c, i_j)) + \beta \times \log(u_p(p, i_j))$$

In this formulation $\mathcal{L}$ denotes the loss of the log-likelihood estimation, m is the number of items presented in the recommendation list R_c. This maximization problem aims to fine-tune the parameter β to generate the new list of recommendation R_c^* optimized for both consumer and provider utility functions. Furthermore, the idea is to provide a new recommendation list that is not disruptive from the consumer's viewpoint. Hence, R_c^* is expected to be as similar as possible to R_c and this similarity could be expressed by a distance measure like the Kendall tau. This metric operates on the relative pairwise order of the items between the two lists to measure their difference.

Considering these two aspects, it is possible to introduce a new formulation for the generation of R_c^* in the form of

$$\min_{\beta, \gamma} \mathcal{L}(u_p | R_c, \mathcal{I}) = \mathcal{L}(u_p | \mathcal{I}) + \gamma(1 - \hat{K}(R_c, R_c^*))$$

The first term is referred to the optimization problem for generation R_c^* considering both consumer- and provider utilities. The term $\hat{K}(R_c, R_c^*)$ is the kernel-ized version [14] of the Kendall tau distance that regularized the loss as a similarity-based distance of R_c^* from the original R_c, while β are the weights of the optimized functions and γ is a hyper-parameter responsible for balancing the effect between the two terms of optimization.

5   Explanations for MS-RS

This analysis does not consider *white-box* explanations, since—by exploiting the inner mechanisms implemented by the recommendation algorithm for generating the explanation—they might reveal preferences and private information that the part (*i.e.*, each stakeholder) does not desire to disclose. Hence in this section, we focus on *black-box* approaches, analyzing two of the most prominent ones, namely, counterfactual and contrastive explanations.

5.1   Counterfactual Explanations

We now discuss counterfactual explanations in the context of MS-RS. Counterfactual explanations follow the causality theory by Halpern&Pearl [11] for generating an explanation. Explanations depending on causality have not yet stood out in the Recommendation System research area, but recently they are starting to attract interest.

In their work, Halpern&Pearl identify two kinds of events, *exogenous* and *endogenous*. The former are determined by external factors and define the context. The latter are the factors an agent can change to influence a result and are in this way the expected causes of that result. In our MS-RS scenario, we consider that events are exogenous or endogenous based on a stakeholder's perspective: namely, each stakeholder sees her actions as endogenous events, while all events corresponding to other stakeholder choices are exogenous.

Clearly, in a MS-RS scenario, the only choices stakeholders can make are about their profile: a consumer might change her list of preferred items, while a provider might change his strategy. Consequently, we consider as events of our causal theory of counterfactuals the stakeholders' profiles.

We consider this kind of approach as the most suitable for MS-RS, since we can distinguish between consumer-side and provider-side explanations, where each explanation does not reveal to a stakeholder the other stakeholders' preferences—as they are seen as exogenous causes.

Depending on the granularity of events, the computation of an explanation could change considerably. In the approach by Verdeaux *et al.* [26], the events that cause a change in a consumer's recommendation list are purchases of single items; eliminating a suitable subset of such events would cause a rearrangement in the recommendation list, pushing lower items upwards. In that case, choosing a minimal set of purchases that change the consumer's preferences can be a computationally intractable problem [9]. However, for simplicity, in this preliminary paper we treat the entire profile as an event, simplifying the search for a counterfactual cause of the recommendation to a simple rearrangement of the profile—in the simplest case, just a change in the first item. In this way, we decouple our analysis from computational problems, which we will deal with in future works. Explanations from the provider's perspective follow a similar approach: the endogenous cause of a particular recommendation to the consumer is the provider's strategy, that is, his profile as an ordered list of items. A counterfactual explanation looks for another strategy the provider could have chosen, which would have changed the recommendation.

More formally, a *counterfactual explanation* of a recommendation R_c^* for a consumer c, with profile P_c, is a pair $(P_c', R_c^{*'})$, where both $P_c \neq P_c'$ and $R_c^* \neq R_c^{*'}$, to be interpreted as follows: "Had Consumer c the profile P_c', the MS-RS would recommend $R_c^{*'}$ instead of R_c^*".

In the simplest case, the recommender could focus on the first item of each list, providing an explanation of the following form: "I recommended you *Apple Phone XS* because based on your profile, you preferred *Samsung Galaxy S21* the most; if your most preferred item were *Samsung Galaxy S10*, I would suggest you *Google Pixel 5* instead".

On the provider's side, supposing the provider chose the strategy P_p, a *counterfactual explanation* of a recommendation R_c^* given to a consumer c, is a pair $(P_p', R_c^{*'})$, where both $P_p \neq P_p'$ and $R_c^* \neq R_c^{*'}$, to be interpreted as follows: "Had provider p a different strategy P_p', the MS-RS would have recommended to c the new list $R_c^{*'}$".

Again, the simplest of such explanations would be to focus on one element only; for example: "I recommended to *Early adopter #1* the item *Google Pixel 5* because *Google Pixel 5* was the first one in your priority list; had you chosen Strategy P_p', whose most prominent item is *Samsung Galaxy S10*, I would put this item in *Early adopter #1*'s recommendation".

Summarizing, counterfactual explanations never reveal to a stakeholder the other stakeholder's preferences, since they refer always to each stakeholder's own choices.

5.2   Contrastive Explanations

Exploiting the formal models of causation by Halpern& Pearl and extending the causal chain definition provided by Hilton [13], Miller [20] proposed contrastive explanations in the context of classical eXplainable Artificial Intelligence (XAI) for classification tasks. With the contrastive explanation, one wants to answer the question "Why P and not Q?". For example, a XAI system classifying pictures of animals should be able to justify its outcome by answering questions like, "Why did you classify that photo as a *spider* and not as a *crab*?" Of course, a contrastive explanation presumes that the user of the system already knows in some way the items to be contrasted.—in the previous example, the classes of spiders and crabs.

While this type of approach is claimed by Miller to be very effective in the context of XAI, when moving to the context of MS-RS, however, it seems unsuitable because it may reveal indirectly other stakeholder's preferences. To make an example, suppose that a consumer already knows items *Apple Phone XS* and *Samsung Galaxy S21*, and suppose such items are completely equivalent from the consumer's perspective; yet the MS-RS recommended *Apple Phone XS* in a privileged position over *Samsung Galaxy S21*, just because this ordering meets the preferences of the provider. A contrastive explanation to the consumer question "Why did you put *Samsung Galaxy S21* so lower than *Apple Phone XS* if I like them both?" would have in this case no reason to put forward, but the provider's preferences. No possible answer to the consumer seems both adequate and trustworthy here. The provider's side contrastive explanations suffer from the same drawback: answering about the reasons of a big discrepancy in the recommendation of very similar—from the provider's preferences—items may reveal some consumer's preferences that she might have declared as private knowledge—information that MS-RS is not authorized to reveal, adhering to EU GDPR, or other non-EU legislation.

6   Conclusion

Recommendation Systems can play an important role as a tool of Business Agility. Since a business context always presumes the existence of more than one stakeholder, we studied which kind of explanation is suitable for recommendations in an MS-RS scenario, where each stakeholder provides to the system private information that may not be disclosed to other stakeholders. It turns out that an explanation based on counterfactuals comes off best, since it can be based on the choices of each stakeholder without revealing the other's reserved information.

Our analysis leads to two future extensions: *(i)* consider items as described by a set of features, leading to Content-Based recommendation in the MS-RS scenario, where stakeholder preferences could be expressed as preferred feature values, and counterfactual explanations should be expressed in terms of such feature preferences; *(ii)* apply different optimization functions to address the recommendation list re-rank problem, following either Game Theory optimization [8] or Pareto frontier derivation [5].

References

1. Abdollahpouri, H., et al.: Beyond personalization: research directions in multistakeholder recommendation (2019)
2. Abdollahpouri, H., et al.: Multistakeholder recommendation: survey and research directions. User Modeling and User-Adap. Inter. **30**(1), 127–158 (2020). https://doi.org/10.1007/s11257-019-09256-1
3. Abdollahpouri, H., Burke, R.: Multi-stakeholder recommendation and its connection to multi-sided fairness. In: RMSE@RecSys. CEUR Workshop Proceedings, vol. 2440. CEUR-WS.org (2019)
4. Abdollahpouri, H., Mansoury, M., Burke, R., Mobasher, B.: The unfairness of popularity bias in recommendation. In: RMSE@RecSys. CEUR Workshop Proceedings, vol. 2440. CEUR-WS.org (2019)
5. Abdou, W., Bloch, C., Charlet, D., Spies, F.: Multi-pareto-ranking evolutionary algorithm. In: Hao, J.-K., Middendorf, M. (eds.) EvoCOP 2012. LNCS, vol. 7245, pp. 194–205. Springer, Heidelberg (2012). https://doi.org/10.1007/978-3-642-29124-1_17
6. Burke, R.D., Abdollahpouri, H., Mobasher, B., Gupta, T.: Towards multistakeholder utility evaluation of recommender systems. In: UMAP (Extended Proceedings). CEUR Workshop Proceedings, vol. 1618. CEUR-WS.org (2016)
7. Castells, P., Hurley, N.J., Vargas, S.: Novelty and diversity in recommender systems. In: Ricci, F., Rokach, L., Shapira, B. (eds.) Recommender Systems Handbook, pp. 881–918. Springer, Boston, MA (2015). https://doi.org/10.1007/978-1-4899-7637-6_26
8. Celli, A., Marchesi, A., Farina, G., Gatti, N.: No-regret learning dynamics for extensive-form correlated equilibrium. In: NeurIPS (2020)
9. Eiter, T., Lukasiewicz, T.: Complexity results for structure-based causality. Artif. Intell. **142**(1), 53–89 (2002). https://doi.org/10.1016/S0004-3702(02)00271-0

10. Gedikli, F., Jannach, D., Ge, M.: How should I explain? A comparison of different explanation types for recommender systems. Int. J. Hum. Comput. Stud. **72**(4), 367–382 (2014)
11. Halpern, J.Y., Pearl, J.: Causes and explanations: a structural-model approach - part II: explanations. In: IJCAI, pp. 27–34. Morgan Kaufmann (2001)
12. Herlocker, J.L., Konstan, J.A., Riedl, J.: Explaining collaborative filtering recommendations. In: CSCW, pp. 241–250. ACM (2000)
13. Hilton, D., McClure, J., Slugoski, B.: The course of events: counterfactuals, causal sequences, and explanation (2005)
14. Hofmann, T., Schölkopf, B., Smola, A.J.: Kernel methods in machine learning. Ann. Stat. **36**(3), 1171–1220 (2008)
15. Hurley, N., Zhang, M.: Novelty and diversity in top-n recommendation - analysis and evaluation. ACM Trans. Internet Technol. **10**(4), 14:1–14:30 (2011)
16. Koren, Y., Bell, R.: Advances in collaborative filtering. In: Ricci, F., Rokach, L., Shapira, B., Kantor, P.B. (eds.) Recommender Systems Handbook, pp. 145–186. Springer, Boston, MA (2011). https://doi.org/10.1007/978-0-387-85820-3_5
17. Kunaver, M., Porl, T.: Diversity in recommender systems a survey. Knowl.-Based Syst. **123**(C), 154–162 (2017)
18. Masthoff, J.: Group recommender systems: combining individual models. In: Ricci, F., Rokach, L., Shapira, B., Kantor, P.B. (eds.) Recommender Systems Handbook, pp. 677–702. Springer, Boston, MA (2011). https://doi.org/10.1007/978-0-387-85820-3_21
19. McNee, S.M., Riedl, J., Konstan, J.A.: Being accurate is not enough: how accuracy metrics have hurt recommender systems. In: CHI Extended Abstracts, pp. 1097–1101. ACM (2006)
20. Miller, T.: Explanation in artificial intelligence: insights from the social sciences. Artif. Intell. **267**, 1–38 (2019)
21. Pu, P., Chen, L.: Trust-inspiring explanation interfaces for recommender systems. Knowl.-Based Syst. **20**(6), 542–556 (2007)
22. Tintarev, N., Masthoff, J.: A survey of explanations in recommender systems. In: ICDE Workshops, pp. 801–810. IEEE Computer Society (2007)
23. Tintarev, N., Masthoff, J.: Explaining recommendations: design and evaluation. In: Ricci, F., Rokach, L., Shapira, B. (eds.): Recommender Systems Handbook, pp. 353–382. Springer, Boston, MA (2015). https://doi.org/10.1007/978-1-4899-7637-6_10
24. Vargas, S.: Novelty and diversity enhancement and evaluation in recommender systems and information retrieval. In: SIGIR, p. 1281. ACM (2014)
25. Vargas, S., Castells, P.: Rank and relevance in novelty and diversity metrics for recommender systems. In: RecSys, pp. 109–116. ACM (2011)
26. Verdeaux, W., Moreau, C., Labroche, N., Marcel, P.: Causality based explanations in multi-stakeholder recommendations. In: EDBT/ICDT Workshops. CEUR Workshop Proceedings, vol. 2578. CEUR-WS.org (2020)
27. Xia, P., Liu, B., Sun, Y., Chen, C.X.: Reciprocal recommendation system for online dating. In: ASONAM, pp. 234–241. ACM (2015)
28. Zhang, Y., Chen, X.: Explainable recommendation: a survey and new perspectives. Found. Trends Inf. Ret. **14**(1), 1–101 (2020)

Organizational Structure Reengineering Based on The Transaction Approach: Case of Construction Business

Nadezhda Blazhchuk[1], Pavel Malyzhenkov[1(✉)], and Maurizio Masi[2]

[1] Department of Information Systems and Technologies, National Research University – Higher School of Economics, Bol. Pecherskaya 25, 603155 Nizhny Novgorod, Russia
pmalyzhenkov@hse.ru
[2] Department of Economy, Engineering, Society and Business, University of Tuscia, Via Del Paradiso, 47, 01100 Viterbo, Italy
maurizio.masi@unitus.it

Abstract. The construction business is burdened by an emphasis on risk and finance. In pursuit of external changes and high income, the company may suffer large financial and quality losses. Considering that construction is characterized by cyclicity and seasonality it may seem that the problem is complex and hardly solved. To be successful and competitive in the market it is needed to have a good organizational structure, streamlined business processes and appropriate IT-structure. The aim of this paper to analyze construction business, analyze existing organizational structures and on example of company provide a possible solution for re-organization of organizational structure.

Keywords: Building · Network organizational structure · Construction

1 Introduction

In the information age, firms are increasingly organizing their activities through networks [4, 5]. In many countries several institutions have encouraged the implementation of strategic alliances to stimulate the national and regional development [7, 14] and allow companies and entrepreneurs to cooperate in the fields of their activities in order to increase their innovation capacity and competitiveness. The concept of network could be considered as an intentional, long-term alliance enabling different companies to acquire or defend the competitive advantage against competitors outside the network [5].

The subject of the strategic analysis, engineering and management of networks has come to the attention of academics and practitioners for the last years [10, 11, 17] in a broader framework of theoretical researches.

The emergence of the new business context is creating innovative systems and models of work, having a deep impact on business environment and organizational interdependencies. To define the current business landscape, some authors [2, 11–13] suggest the metaphor of the "rainforest", indicating that one of its basic feature is the intricate interdependency among companies that requires an alternative framework to be studied.

A. Polyvyanyy and S. Rinderle-Ma (Eds.): CAiSE 2021 Workshops, LNBIP 423, pp. 48–58, 2021.
https://doi.org/10.1007/978-3-030-79022-6_5

A business network can be defined as "a set of business entities, legally independent, reciprocally committed to implement a deliberate and finalized cooperation strategy, leveraging the technical and economical complementarities in achieving joint economic objectives, which indirectly benefit the individual businesses" [5].

Business literature presents several approaches to the study of networks and alliances, mainly including transaction cost economics, strategic management and institutional perspective. Transaction cost economists [16, 19, 20] have argued that networks are hybrid forms of organization between markets and hierarchy and that they occur when transaction costs associated with a specific exchange are too high for a market exchange but not high enough to mandate vertical integration [3]. In transaction cost economic literature various roles have been identified for inter-firm settings that relates to specific accounting techniques and different uses of accounting information in the selection of a potential partner, during the management of cooperation and in the monitoring and evaluation of collaborations activities.

Strategic management literature [5, 10–12, 14] recognizes business relationships as another type of resource that a company can use in the strategic game. The opportunity to mobilize others as "partners" has increasingly become an emergent issue in the strategic management literature. From a resource-based perspective [13] the importance of business relationship is emphasized by the idea that a firm's critical resources may span the boundaries of the firms. It is often claimed that a firm's network of business partners should be considered as an inimitable resource itself and as a means by which to assess others' inimitable resources. So, in these studies collaborations and networks encompass a broad range of inter-organizational relationships.

Business networks can also be analyzed as a result of an engineered process [13], where the working arrangements are fulfilled in a formal organization, the goals are planned and specified in a predetermined time horizon, the cooperation is based on "network capital" rooted in a business and economic rationality and focused on investing in relationships as a means to increase business performances. The architectural approach [13, 16, 19] helps to balance 'market-driven' perspective (focused on customer's needs) with a 'technology-driven' approach (focused on internal technology aspects).

Organizational structure describes role units, relation between units and governs responsibilities and hierarchy of roles in company. By analyzing an organizational structure a company size, its departments and divisions, the resources necessary to process company needs can be defined. It's important to analyze company as a system. An organizational structure in classical understanding has the following characteristics [6, 15]:

- the aggregate of all services, division and individual role units;
- vertical and horizontal relation between role units;
- hierarchy levels.

A well-built organizational structures have a great impact on the business functioning. A well-chosen and built organizational structure determines the development of the business and can greatly worsen the market position if the communication in the organization, responsibilities and roles are poorly defined and distributed. It should be understood that there is no ideal organizational structure that fits any company. Each company must choose an organizational structure that takes into account the goals, size, scopes, and other characteristics of the company. In dynamic word, analysis and reorganization of company structure are necessary to be competitive and successful. The steps of analysis of company structure includes [8]:

- Define aims, results and business processes of a company;
- Analyze existing company structure and make a diagram;
- Define size of a company, active role units, level of communication between roles and a hierarchy;
- Define the responsibilities between the role units;
- Prepare proposition of diagram change (make a new diagram and justifications);
- Prepare new distribution of responsibilities.
  The organizational structure affects the following parameters of the organization:
- Time and cost of work completion;
- The nature of people's behavior;
- Implementation of the company's strategy.
  While choosing an organizational structure important to consider the chain of control, scope of control and centralization [24]:
- Chain of control is a basic requirement to form the structure of organization; it governs roles, hierarchy of roles, levels of subordination;
- Scope of control define areas of responsibilities;
- Company can be centralized or decentralized. In a centralized structure, decision-making authority centralizes in one role unit; in a decentralized structure, authority allocates to several role units.

In case company works a long time with inappropriate organization structure, it can lead to following disadvantages:

- Financial losses;
- Poor communication between departments; in a case, process of communication between role units is not established it can affects the speed of work, quality of product;
- Damage company reputation; in a case organizational structure is bad-built it can also affects the quality of product that will lead to loss of trust of buyers.

Organizational structure school be appropriate with company size – structure should be more complicated when it is necessary. To choose organizational structure companies need to estimate the following parameters:

- Size of company;
- Territorial distribution of divisions;
- Variety of products;
- Dynamic of external environment;
- Adaptation to sector condition (changing sectors require a flexible organizational structure and decentralization);
- Competitive level (competitive sectors require companies to be flexible).

Organizational structures are divided in hierarchical and adaptive. Hierarchical structures a strong hierarchy in the company, formalization of the rules and procedures, and centralized decision making. A fuzzy hierarchy, flexibility of the power, formal rules and procedures and decentralization of decision-making, characterizes adaptive organizational structures. [6, 18, 24]

1. In the functional structure, employees are grouped according their skills and knowledge. Every department has vertical structure. The disadvantages of this organizational type – problems with communication between two functional departments;
2. The divisional structure implies subdivisions that are grouped by functionality. The disadvantage of divisional structure is reflected in the level of operational efficiency, which can be reduced due to division into divisions. In a most of companies with divisional structure divisions, in spite of control of central unit, make decisions;
3. The linear structure is one of the traditional vertical structures. All tasks have direction top-down. This structure usually used by small or medium companies that concentrated on one product. Linear structure allows divide task and define competence for role unit clearly;
4. The matrix structure usually mix some types of organizational structure when a company uses two lines of hierarchy (project and linear). If a company wants to use such type of structure, it is required to strongly define responsibilities for project and for linear managers.

2 Network Structure

Network structure is one of the newest forms of organization – this kind of structure is less hierarchical than other types. Network structure is focused on flexibility; the core manager coordinate and control all (external and internal) relationships. Companies that use a network structure more often actively work with external service providers, or have several divisions with different roles and functions.

The network structures is better decision for companies that pass work to outsource or to external providers. This kind of structure is based on communication between core organizations. The network exists temporarily; usually each network exists during the execution of the project: this approach is convenient for seasonal business, when the amount of required resources can increase dramatically during a certain period of the year.

Such kind of organization type allows company become more flexible and able to analyze changes and react on them, adapting, thereby maintaining competitiveness.

The disadvantage for this type of structure is the process of transforming the structure if the number and list of external service providers was changed. In addition, due to interaction with external providers, the disadvantages of this type of structure include data loss.

Network management includes a selected, permanent and structured set of autonomous firms engaged in the creation of products or services on a contract basis, adaptation to contingencies, and on coordination. The transition to this type of adaptive structure allows the organization to get rid of unnecessary management decisions [6, 18, 24] (Fig. 1).

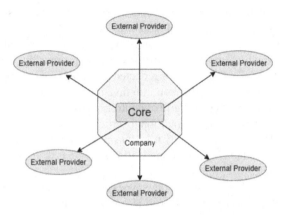

Fig. 1. Network organizational structure

3   Construction Business

The construction business represents a highly competitive environment. To receive both private and state orders, the executing company must have well-established processes, must be able to create a work plan, considering previous experience, and perform its work on time in a quality manner. The main competence of construct companies is represented by a flexibility.

Construction is one of the main sectors of economic that plays an important role in the development of the economics in Russia as well as in other countries. As a part of a study of the construction sector Gross Domestic Products (GDP) statistics published by the Federal State Statistics Service and analytical centers under the government of the Russian Federation for period from 2014–2020 (Table 1) were studied [1, 9, 22, 23].

Table 1. GDP of Russia for the period 2014–2020.

Year	2014	2015	2016	2017	2018	2019	2020
GDP, bln rub	79030,0	83087,4	85616,1	91843,2	103861,7	109193,2	106606,6

Also the GDP structure by type of economic activity and structure by sectors in 2018 was analyzed (Fig. 2).

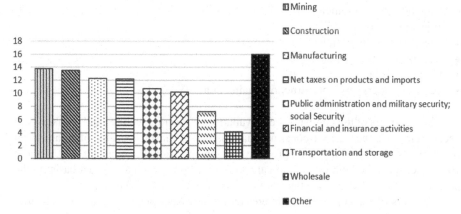

Fig. 2. GDP structure by type of economic activity, %

The last official statistic by sectors was published only on April 2019 and presents statistic for the end of 2018 year. The article publishes data on the contribution of sectors in the period 2014–2018. As it was presented construction sector rapidly grows from 2014 and in 2018 made one of the largest contributions to GDP [8]. It demonstrates the high importance of this sector of business activity for Russian national economy and, hence, underlines the relevance of the present research.

Construction is one of the key sectors of economics in different countries and in Russia. The construction industry plays a significant role in the socio-economic development of any country, being an important factor in its stability. According to the data published by the World Economic Forum in May 2016 construction contributed equal 6% of global GDP [21].

At the beginning of 2019, there were about 277 thousand construction organizations operating in the Russian market, including 268 thousand small businesses, 87.2% are micro-enterprises with an average number of employees up to 15 people. Organizations that do not belong to small businesses have completed 40.1% of the volume of construction work, mainly the result of the work of large organizations. The share of medium-sized organizations accounted for about 6.6% of the volume of construction work. Over 95% of the total volume of construction work in recent years has been carried out by private construction organizations [9, 25].

The main difference in construction business is represented by the seasonality: most percent of work should be done only during the period from May to November.

4 Practical Use

The practical part of the research was realized on the case of a construction company AtlantStroy-NN operating in the Region of a Nizhny Novgorod (Russia). The main processes in the company (as in usual construct company) are composed by:

- Collection of requirements
- Project preparation
- Procurement of materials
- Organization of logistics
- Order execution
- Technical supervision (construction quality control)

The managers of the company were available for several meetings and interviews. It became clear that the works in construct business are not constant because of organization structure and they need a special problem solving approach: the constant staff is about 10 people, since the bulk of the team are workers who work on a contract basis (in the peak month (May-November) the team of workers can reach 400 people)).

Managers of the company are interested in increasing profits, reducing lead times (by reducing downtime), using new information technologies to automate the process of managing financial flows, materials and resources, and developing the advertising department (Fig. 3 and Fig. 4).

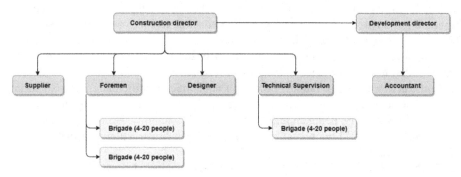

Fig. 3. Current organizational structure of «AtlantStroy-NN»

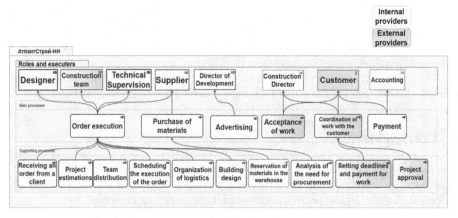

Fig. 4. Current company architecture of «AtlantStroy-NN»

The company has two directors: a construction director and a development director, they occupy the same management level, but the construction director has major authority. An important factor is that the Development Director can also manage employees which on the organizational structure are placed under the director of construction, but he needs it not for organizing the construction process, but for planning.

To choose company structure we need to analyze its' size, territorial distribution of divisions, variety of products, dynamic of external environment, competitive level.

1. Company size – small
2. Territorial distribution of divisions – the company operates in the Nizhny Novgorod region
3. Variety of products – focus on private developments
4. Dynamic of external environment – high
5. Competitive level – high

According to the analysis of organization types and company's' processes it was found out that network structure would be more appropriate. Construction business depend on seasons, the most part of works can be transferred to external providers and suppliers.

Based on the analysis of the company's work, we suppose that the network structure would be most appropriate for small construction organization. They can pass most of the work for execution to external suppliers. This solution will allow the company to focus itself mostly on coordination activities.

It is important to understand that all changes (in structure, technology, tools etc.) lead to growth or to decrease of transaction costs, so information search costs, bargaining costs will increase at the first time because of need to search external service providers, time to time to establish trust. When all re-organizational steps will be completed the same transaction will rapidly decrease because all external providers will take responsibility for searching resources. All relations, responsibilities, duties and deadlines with external providers must be concluded by agreement.

The company has two directors: the construction director deals with work with construction objects and the process of construction, and the development director who deals with planning and development of company. It was proposed to release the construction director for organizing advertising activities, since he does not have enough competence and pass this process to external marketing firms. In addition, to implement the conversion to network structure, it is necessary to have an administrator who will prepare and agree on contracts for work with external suppliers. It is proposed to transfer this activity to the development director.

After the proposed changes realization the organizational structure would be present in the following way (Figs. 5 and 6):

Here we can see that the company transfers a big part of work to external providers (law, logistic, marketing firms, realtors, providers, technical supervision, and construction team) and a company organizational structure consists of construction director, development director, designer, supplier and accountant. These roles units are important and need in them does not depend on season.

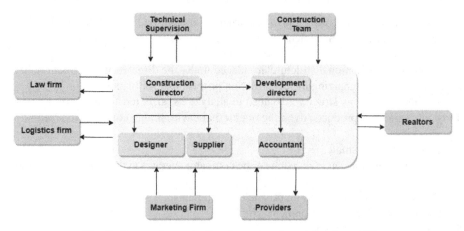

Fig. 5. Proposed organizational structure for «AtlantStroy-NN»

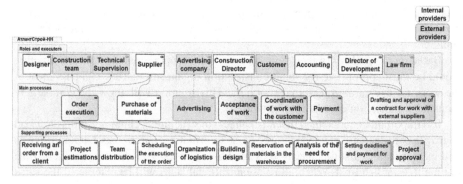

Fig. 6. Proposed company architecture for «AtlantStroy-NN»

5 Results and Effectiveness

Using network structure can help companies to become more flexible and concrete on coordination. In order to adopt a network structure it is necessary to analyze what role units can be passed to external providers and what new roles may be needed, to pay attention to the contracts that are concluded with external providers. All the operations with documents can be also passed to external providers or, if it is possible, a company can include one more role unit: a lawyer.

When introducing a network structure for managing an organization, we see the following changes:

- Technical supervision and construction team are completely transferred to external providers
- Advertising work is completely outsourced to new external providers
- A new provider "Law Firm" appears, it role unit works with the Development Director and prepares contracts for work with all external providers

- Supplier, designer and accountant remain on the staff, as their work is necessary for the construction company on a permanent basis

If we consider the changes in the company, after the implementation of the network organizational structure, from the side of the company architecture – we can see that more processes pass to external execution and more external executing agents appear (roles: construction team, technical supervision, law firm, processes: advertising).

In addition, a new process "Drafting and approval of a contract for work with external suppliers" appears, which includes the work of the Development Director and an external agent "Law Firm". This process is necessary for the mutually beneficial execution of the "Order execution" process, so that the needs of all participants and performers are taken into account and their rights are protected by agreements.

References

1. Analytical Center for the Government of the Russian Federation: Dynamics and structure of Russia's GDP. Bulletins on current trends in the Russian economy, Bulletin 62, June 2020
2. Analytical Center for the Government of the Russian Federation: Dynamics of individual housing construction in Russia and government measures aimed at developing the sector. Bulletins on current trends in the Russian economy, Bulletin 54, October 2020
3. Anderson, S., Dekker, H.: Accounting in networks. the transaction cost economics perspective. In Hakansson, H., Krauss, K., Lind, J.: Accounting in Networks. Routledge, London (2010)
4. Castells, M.: The Rise of the Network Society. Blackwell Publishers, Oxford (2000)
5. Cardoni, A.: Business planning and management accounting in strategic networks: theoretical development and empirical evidence from enterprises' network agreement. Manage. Control **3** (2012)
6. Erzhanova, S.K.: Features and possibilities of changing organizational structures when implementing the chosen strategy of a travel company (2012)
7. Etzkovitz, H.: The Triple Helix. Routledge, London (2008)
8. Federal State Statistics Service (Rosstat): Construction in Russia. Stat. Sat./ Rosstat. - M., C863 2018.– 119 s (2018)
9. Federal State Statistics Service (Rosstat): Construction in Russia – 2020 (2020)
10. Hakansson, H., Ford, D., Gadde, L.,E., Shenota, I., Waluszewski, A.: Business in Networks. John Wiley & Sons Ltd, New York (2010)
11. Hakansson, H., Krauss, K., Lind, J.: Accouting in Networks. Routledge, London (2009)
12. Huggins, R.: The evolution of knowledge clusters. Econ. Dev. Q. **22**(4), 277–289 (2008)
13. Huggins, R.: Forms of network resource: knowledge access and the role of inter-firm networks. Int. J. Manage. Rev. **12**(3), 335–352 (2010)
14. Lundberg, H., Johanson, M.: Network strategies for regional growth. In: Johanson, M., Lundberg, H. (eds.) Network Strategies for Regional Growth, pp. 1–21. Palgrave Macmillan UK, London (2011). https://doi.org/10.1057/9780230299146_1
15. Minin A.V.: Methodological approaches to the design of organizational structures of construction organizations (2009)
16. Scapens, R.W., Varoutsa, E.: Accounting in Inter-organisational relationships – the institutional theory perspective. In: Hakansson, H., Krauss, K., Lind, J.: Accounting in Networks. Routledge, London (2010)
17. Tomkins, C.: Interdependecies, trust and information in relationship, alliances and networks. Account. Organ. Soc. **26**, 161–191 (2001)

18. Tsyplenkova, M.V., Moiseenko, I.V., Guremina, N.V., Bondar, Y.A.: Fundamentals of Management: Textbook Academy of Natural Sciences (2013). ISBN: 978-5-91327-231-7

19. Vitro, R.A.: The Knowledge Economy in Development: Perspectives For Effective Partnerships. Washington, D.C (2005)

20. Williamson, O.E.: Market and Hierarchies. Free Press, New York (1975)

21. World Economic Forum in collaboration with The Boston Consulting Group: Shaping the Future of Construction: A Breakthrough in Mindset and Technology (2016)

22. Federal State Statistics Service. https://rosstat.gov.ru/accounts. Accessed 30 Mar 2021

23. Federal State Statistics Service. https://rosstat.gov.ru/folder/14458. Accessed 30 Mar 2021

24. Types of Organizational Structure Every Company Should Consider. https://blog.hubspot.com/marketing/team-structure-diagrams. Accessed 30 Mar 2021

25. Federal State Statistics Service. https://gks.ru/bgd/free/b04_03/IssWWW.exe/Stg/d02/21.htm. Accessed 30 Mar 2021

A New Approach to the Social Dimension of IT Business Alignment

Roman Khlebnikov and Pavel Malyzhenkov[✉]

Department of Information Systems and Technologies, National Research University – Higher School of Economics, Bol. Pecherskaya 25, 603155 Nizhny Novgorod, Russia
pmalyzhenkov@hse.ru

Abstract. The social dimension of IT-business inconsistency is one of the popular issues in the topic of IT-business misalignment. However, the studies that are used to develop a formalized approach use similar methodologies. Thus, the purpose of this article is to describe an approach based on the capabilities of conceptual analysis, focused on a formal search for misalignment.

Keywords: IT-business alignment · Social dimension · Conceptual analysis

1 Introduction

The problem of IT business alignment arises more actively among business problems. New technologies: artificial intelligence, bitcoin, big data only contribute to the growth of this problem. Business should understand much faster why it needs this or that technology, and IT should deliver this technology as soon as possible.

IT managers have a strong interest in aligning IT and business. According to the 2019–2020 IT trends, IT business alignment is on the 2nd place of problems of concern to managers [21]. Also, over the past 10 years, this problem did not fall below the 3rd place in the top of the worrying problems (Fig. 1).

Thus, IT and business managers have an important function: demonstrating how the IT strategy matches the Business Strategy. This can only be demonstrated when IT and business can speak the same language.

The purpose of this work is to formulate and research a new hypothesis that the terms that are found in professional artifacts of IT and business are an expression of the social aspect of reconciliation.

Further, the study is structured as follows. Section 2 summarizes the literature analysis on this topic. In Sect. 3, a hypothesis is formulated and the main points of conceptual modeling using classifiers and professional standards are presented. Section 4 summarizes the main findings and directions for future research.

A. Polyvyanyy and S. Rinderle-Ma (Eds.): CAiSE 2021 Workshops, LNBIP 423, pp. 59–68, 2021.
https://doi.org/10.1007/978-3-030-79022-6_6

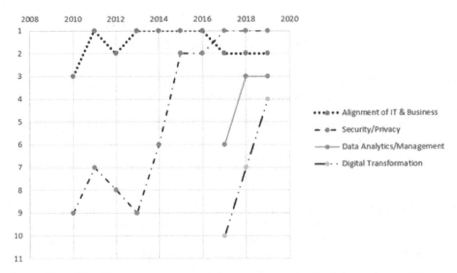

Fig. 1. Plot of Top IT management concerns/issues to your organization over the past 10 years

2　IT-Business Alignment: Main Concepts

2.1　Approaches to IT and Business Alignment

In [4], the authors explore the area of IT business misalignment versus medical sciences. Their statements are based on the fact that the study of medical diseases, as a metaphor and analogy with information systems, is that understandable approach, which is the basis for the classification scheme for the symptoms of IT-business misalignment. According to this, the authors distinguish the definition of "misalignment" - this is an abnormal condition that violates the state of the organization, as well as the architecture, which is characterized by typical symptoms and signs of interaction between the subjects of the organization. Based on this, the article provides a BISMAM (Business and Information Systems Misalignment Model) model, which systematizes possible symptoms of non-compliance, causes, and also explores the possibility of preventing them.

For example, in the modern work [5] hypotheses of IT business alignment are proposed to study the influence of the level of consistency, as well as its impact on the quality of decisions made, the time spent by them. As a result, multidimensional data analysis on a specific organization has shown that IT business consistency has a positive effect on the key characteristics of decision making. The author also proposed ways to improve business in the key characteristics of the analysis: information technology, operations, employees, customers.

The authors of [8] investigate the possibility of integrating SAM domains with domains of the TOGAF architectural methodology. Providing the definition of agreed business and IT domains, the paper provides formalized methods for assessing IT business alignment using the Alloy Analyzer software tool. As a result, the authors developed an architectural approach that proved its effectiveness in a business case.

The authors of the article [7] first introduced the SAM - The Strategic Alignment Model. This model remains one of the most cited models, as well as the most widely used in the practical and scientific communities [12].

According to SAM, an IT strategy should be formulated in terms of an internal domain - a domain that describes options for the administrative structure, design of business processes, as well as an external one that is associated with bringing a product to market.

This model consists of two fundamental blocks:

- Strategic alignment: linking external and internal domains
- Functional alignment: IT-business communication

The authors argue that alignment is impossible without cross-domain relationships. Therefore, SAM assumes 4 options for the development of alignment in an organization, using the premise that alignment in an organization can occur when at least 3 of the 4 domains are in a state of alignment: strategy execution, technology transformation, competitive potential alignment, service level.

The authors of the article [14], based on the SAM model's idea of domain matching, proposes an approach to identify symptoms of mismatch, as well as their alignment. The structure for finding and eliminating symptoms of non-compliance consists of 3 levels:

1. Level of misalignment
2. Enterprise architecture level
3. Level of analysis

The first level includes the type of activity aimed at finding and structuring symptoms using decomposition into SAM domains. Development options (perspectives) mentioned in SAM are combined with symptoms of non-compliance.

At the enterprise architecture level, an artifact catalog is created that contains possible enterprise architecture models. The necessary artifacts are associated with symptoms, from which the desired symptom can emerge, which is identified using the SAM perspective.

The analysis layer should identify those types of architecture analysis that can detect the symptom of misalignment. This paper presents a method based on analysis with XPath and Schematron. Several types of non-compliance symptoms can be detected with this method.

2.2 Social Dimension of IT-Business Alignment Problem

The authors of [3] highlight two aspects of IT-business alignment:

1. Intellectual, based on formally defined facts, methodologies, technologies, as well as information structures in the organization.
2. The social aspect concerns goals, business strategy formulations, communication methods, decision-making methods.

The existing library of IT business mismatch symptoms is widely discussed in the literature [3, 9]. However, most of the ideas are based on constructing disparity metrics based on the intelligent aspect of alignment. But the social aspect, in turn, is difficult to overestimate. With a well-structured and formally defined communicative approach, it is easy to "align" the organization.

For example, in [2, 3, 13], empirical studies are presented with a difference of more than twenty years between them, but the general meaning of the study is that interviews are conducted with various participants in the IT or business world in order to determine the consistency in understanding the goals, strategy, business management and IT professionals. Studies in [2] show that business IT alignment is a long-term process of joint development of corporate and IT strategies in order to maintain digitalization in a competitive environment.

8 proposals for effective communication between CEO/CIO (executive director/CIO) are offered by the authors of [1]. This study provides possible proposals for increasing the tightness of the social aspect of alignment based on: hierarchical positions of directors, personal characteristics, communication channels, communication style, communication frequency.

The author of article [10] explores the area of IT-business alignment, based on the proposed theoretical model. This model is a construct of four tools that affect IT business alignment:

1. Centralized organizational structure
2. Interpersonal relationships
3. Professional communications
4. Interdepartmental relations

The author puts hypotheses about the influence of these points on IT-business alignment and evaluates them with the help of data from municipalities in Sweden. The main takeaway is that interagency and interpersonal relationships have a positive effect on IT business alignment. This confirms the importance of the social aspect of alignment.

The existing literary gap between theory and practice is trying to fill with practical research [6] of the social aspect of IT-business alignment. Research based on data from web surveys of Canadian small and medium-sized businesses also helps to conclude that the social dimension is one of the main ways of developing an organization.

3 Applying Conceptual Modeling Techniques

According to John Milopolos, conceptual modeling is an activity aimed at describing aspects of the physical and social world for understanding and communication [11]. The author also points out that conceptual schemes are a description, a reflection of aspects that can be used to find points of agreement between members of a particular group in order to understand, for example, the "business world" in the same way. Conceptual schemes require the adoption of formal designations, these can be professional standards, classifiers by industry, documentation that can reflect the employee's labor functions.

According to the definition of conceptual modeling and the analysis of the literature on the social aspect of IT-business alignment, we can hypothesize:

Hypothesis: By searching for overlapping terms in business and IT artifacts, it is possible to determine the degree of social IT-business alignment.

In order to determine the level of the social aspect of alignment, it is necessary to highlight the main professions in both IT and business, assuming that each profession represents a small fraction of the areas studied. That is, fixing the profession, the boundaries of a particular type of activity are determined. Therefore, the purpose of this section is a comparative analysis of the areas of business and IT, by means of highlighting key terms, as well as searching in the description of the profession for the terms IT and business. If these terms are observable in a certain profession, then we can say that social alignment reaches the required level.

Several sources were selected for analysis, both Russian and international. From these classifiers, professional standards, descriptions of professions, tasks that are included in the profession, and goals were selected.

For the analysis of Russian sources [17], "the main goals of professional activity" were selected according to professional standards from the reference book of Russian classifiers, since the goals reflect the main and expected activities in the IT and business structures of the organization.

Social alignment requires that "language" - the set of words and terms included in the multitude of IT - have an overlap with business. That is, the goals of professional joint activities of the IT business should strive for one common goal - value creation. The hypothesis that the business does not understand IT and vice versa will be tested by means of the primary analysis of professional areas.

The terminological analysis carried out showed that, for the purposes of professional standards, there are rarely terms that reflect the participation of IT specialists in the formation of a business strategy, formalization of goals, as well as, on the contrary, an understanding of business goals in IT. However, among the professional standards stand out "Software Architect", "System Analyst", "Information Resource Specialist" among whose terms there are both IT and business terms. The conclusion that follows from this is that the objectives of these activities are aimed at aligning the IT business.

Also, a primary analysis of the following international sources of information on professions was carried out:

1. Handbook of Occupational Groups and Families [15]:

This classifier is a regularly updated source of information on the structure of occupational classification in the United States. In it, professional groups are divided by structural units, which in general is a system of classification of professions.

2. ONS Standard Occupational Classification (SOC) Hierarchy [16]:

In the hierarchy of professional classification standards, a convenient system for navigating by profession is presented. This work presents 9 main groups of professions:

1. Managers, directors, senior officials
2. Occupations requiring a narrow professional specialization
3. Professional and technical occupation
4. Administrative and secretariat groups
5. Trade specialists
6. Care, leisure and other services
7. Sales, customer service
8. Occupation related to technological skills
9. Activities that do not require classifications

As the analyzed material, a search was carried out for terms that are present both in the IT professions and in the business sector. The purpose of the initial analysis was to find intersections in terms, without making a division into business and IT. Testable hypothesis: There are terms that overlap in job descriptions to form a common language that increases the level of agreement.

This approach helps to highlight common professions, without the specifics of the organization, which have a high level of agreement. Which ultimately allows us to make the initial conclusion that the presence of such specialists in the organization leads to an increase in IT-business harmonization in the social aspect.

After the analysis was done, a pool of professions or groups with an average/high level of agreement was identified:

- Management consultant/business analyst
- IT Policy and Planning Professionals
- Enterprise architects
- IT business analyst
- System designer
- Business researcher and administrative staff
- IT managers

The professions or groups of professions with the lowest level of overlap of terms are mostly either highly specialized management industries or the most technical IT, for example:

- Software developer
- Web developer
- Corporate manager
- Financial professionals

3.1 Application of an Approach to the Bank's Business Process

Sberbank ranks first among all banks in the Russian Federation in terms of assets for 2021 [22]. Thus, this means that it is the most popular bank in the Russian Federation.

In 2017, Sberbank presented a strategy for digital transformation by 2020, which consisted of building an ecosystem [19]. Drawing an analogy with ecology, where an ecosystem is the unity of all living things in nature, from the point of view of Sberbank, this means gaining synergy between the financial, main activity, and other blocks of business and IT. In other words, for 3 years Sberbank needed to coordinate IT and business services.

One of the main business processes of the bank is the provision of a loan. Among the plans/ambitions for 2023 stands out "Creating a unified (seamless) and maximum personal customer journey with the help of unifying elements and proposals" [20]. This plan is combined with the accomplished fact of creating a single technological platform, we get that the main processes should first of all be digitalized.

In order for this process to be consistent with the digitalization and ecosystem building strategy, the stakeholders in the process must understand their role in the overall strategy. Each step of the process must be IT supported. It is necessary to test the hypothesis that the oldest business process is consistent with the IT plans (Fig. 2).

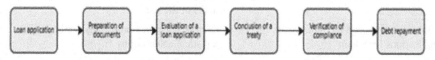

Fig. 2. Overview of a business process: "loan processing"

IT intervention is needed at every stage, for example, maintenance of AI, website/application, performance monitoring.

Possible professions involved in the process [17]:

- Professional Standard: 08.011 Mortgage Lending Specialist (Loan Officer, Loan Manager, Loan Advisor)
- Professional standard: 08.015 Corporate lending specialist
- Professional standard: 08.019 Consumer lending specialist
- Professional standard: 08.018 Risk management specialist
- Professional standard: 08.016 Credit brokerage specialist
- Professional standard: 08.014 Arrears specialist

For the implementation of IT support, according to the plans, we are also examining the pool of professions:

- Professional standard: 06.001 Programmer
- Professional standard: 06.011 Database administrator
- Professional standard: 06.025 Graphic user interface design specialist
- Professional standard: 06.035 Web and multimedia application developer
- Professional standard: 06.042 Big data specialist

At each stage, joint work of people representing certain stages of the process is possible. For example, at the stage of "filing an application", a "consumer lending specialist" and a "database administrator" work, the latter accompanying the process. Without this participation, digital transformation of the business process is impossible. Consequently, there should be a conditional interface between IT and business representatives, which

Table 1. Comparison of the terms

Loan application	
Credit manager Job function: Preliminary support of mortgage lending activities	Data base administrator Job function: Database operation monitoring, collection of statistical information about the database operation
Obtaining the client's consent to the processing of personal data	Monitoring the operation of the database, including by various automated systems
Entering into the automated banking system information about the client, as well as the parameters of the loan application	Analysis of the obtained statistical data, the formation of conclusions about the efficiency of the database
Maintaining an automated customer database	Apply automated systems of monitoring the status of the database
Analyze statistics on the number of applications for a loan	Process statistical data, apply methods of statistical calculations
Use a personal computer, software products (including an automated banking system), other organizational and technical means and equipment	
Evaluation of a loan application	
Risk management specialist Job function: Analysis of risks depending on the goals of the organization, the likelihood and volume of economic losses, the likelihood of profit stabilization, growth in asset value, the level of economic security in the context of certain types of risk based on established methodological principles and approaches	Big data analyst Job function: Conducting analytical research using big data technologies in accordance with customer requirements
Carry out calculations, forecast, test methods of risk analysis, considering industry specifics	Selection of methods and tools for big data analysis for analytical work
Apply various methods and technologies of risk analysis and modeling	Choice of tools for presenting results of big data analytics
Use software for working with information (text, graphics, tabular and analytical applications, applications for visual presentation of data) at the level of an experienced user	Program in high-level languages focused on working with big data: for statistical processing of data and working with graphics, for working with scattered pieces of data in large arrays, for working with databases of structured and unstructured data
Use specialized software and information and analytical systems for risk assessment and management	Search for information on new and promising methods of big data analysis, perform comparative analysis of methods

has terms that are understandable to each of the stakeholders. This interface improves the interaction between IT and the business, reducing transaction costs, which leads to the achievement of a common goal. After that, we can talk about the presence of social IT-business alignment in a particular process.

According to the information published on the official page of Sberbank [18], you can fill out an application using a mobile application, a free service, as well as through a face-to-face visit to the bank, with the help of a loan officer. Therefore, it confirms that this stage of the business process is accompanied by both IT and business professionals.

To test the hypothesis, it is necessary to highlight the corresponding professions and their job functions. For this, a terminological analysis has been carried out (Table 1).

4 Results and Discussion

The social aspect of it-business alignment is gaining more and more interest in the scientific community. Now, this topic requires a variety of approaches to formalize this aspect. However, the existing methodology is still relevant due to the availability of data for testing hypotheses.

We carried out a primary analysis of artifacts related to professions using job function and the goals of professions. Some of the work functions had overlaps in terms. This suggests that the degree of alignment between professions is quite high at certain stages of the business process. The hypothesis and the initial analysis provide a direction for future research. The terms are the very expression of IT-business alignment that can be represented as interfaces.

To summarize, this approach can be used as a primary analysis of their labor documents, artifacts. This analysis will allow at the stage of document development to reduce the time for the future alignment of IT and business.

Thus, future research can be continued in the context of big data analysis. And, the search for a specific manifestation of the inconsistency of the terminological base between IT and business.

A concrete future direction could be the analysis of interfaces in applications that are used by both IT professionals and business managers. Future research will test the hypothesis based on specific symptoms of IT business mismatch.

References

1. Hütter, A., Arnitz, T., Riedl, R.: Effective CIO/CEO Communication Conference Paper, August 2020
2. Becker, W., Schmid, O.: The right digital strategy for your business: an empirical analysis of the design and implementation of digital strategies in SMEs and LSEs. Bus. Res. 13(3), 985–1005 (2020). https://doi.org/10.1007/s40685-020-00124-y
3. Reich, B.H., Benbasat, I.: Measuring the linkage between business and information technology objectives. MIS Q. 20(1), 55–81 (1996). https://doi.org/10.2307/249542
4. Carvalho, R., Sousa, P.: Business and Information Systems Misalignment Model (BIS-MAM): an holistic model leveraged on misalignment and medical sciences approaches. Proc. BUSITAL 8, 105 (2008)

5. Chi, M., Huang, R., George, J.F.: Collaboration in demand-driven supply chain: Based on a perspective of governance and IT-business strategic alignment. Int. J. Inf. Manag. **52**, 102062 (2020)
6. Pelletier, C., Croteau, A.-M., Raymond, L., Vieru, D.: Achieving social IT alignment through the orchestration of IT assets: an interpretive case study. Inf. Syst. Manag. **38**(1), 42–61 (2021). https://doi.org/10.1080/10580530.2020.1733712
7. Henderson, J.C., Venkatraman, N.: Strategic alignment: leveraging information technology for transforming organizations. IBM Syst. J. **32**(1), 4–17 (1993)
8. Ivanova, M., Malyzhenkov, P.: The intellectual dimension of IT-business alignment problem: alloy application. In: Pergl, R., Babkin, E., Lock, R., Malyzhenkov, P., Merunka, V. (eds.) EOMAS 2018. LNBIP, vol. 332, pp. 153–168. Springer, Cham (2018). https://doi.org/10.1007/978-3-030-00787-4_11
9. Luftman, J.: Assessing IT/business alignment. Inf. Syst. Manag. **20**(4), 9–15 (2003). https://doi.org/10.1201/1078/43647.20.4.20030901/77287.2
10. Jonathan, G.M., Rusu, L., Perjons, E.: Organisational Structure's influence on it alignment in a public organisation: a confirmatory case study analysis. In: UK Academy for Information Systems Conference Proceedings 2020, vol. 5 (2020). https://aisel.aisnet.org/ukais2020/5
11. Mylopoulos, J.: Conceptual modeling and Telos. In: Conceptual Modelling, Databases and CASE: An Integrated View of Information Systems Development. Wiley, New York, pp. 49–68 (1992)
12. Renaud, A., Walsh, I., Kalika, M.: Is SAM still alive? A bibliometric and interpretive mapping of the strategic alignment research field. J. Strateg. Inf. Syst. **25**(2), 75–103 (2016)
13. Smajlovic, M.O., Islam, N., Buxmann, P.: How challenging is the development of digital services in an automotive environment? An empirical study of the incongruences between business and IT experts. In: Wirtschaftsinformatik 2021 Proceedings, vol. 4 (2021). https://aisel.aisnet.org/wi2021/HDigitaltransformation17/Track17/4
14. Szabó, Z., Öri, D.: On exposing strategic and structural mismatches between business and information systems: misalignment symptom detection based on enterprise architecture model analysis E-resources
15. https://www.opm.gov/policy-data-oversight/classification-qualifications/classifying-general-schedule-positions/occupationalhandbook.pdf
16. https://onsdigital.github.io/dp-classification-tools/standard-occupational-classification/ONS_SOC_hierarchy_view.html
17. https://classinform.ru/
18. https://www.sberbank.ru/ru/person/help/consumer_faq/2682
19. https://www.sberbank.com/ru/eco
20. https://www.sberbank.ru/ru/press_center/all/article?newsID=f5272ac9-b36c-4a83-a7d7-bb9441e54521&blockID=1303&regionID=77&lang=ru&type=NEWS
21. https://www.globaliim.com/global-it-trends-researc
22. https://www.sravni.ru/banki/rating/aktivy/

Problem of Semantic Enrichment of Sentences Used in Textual Requirements Specification

David Šenkýř[⊠] and Petr Kroha

Faculty of Information Technology, Czech Technical University in Prague,
Prague, Czech Republic
{david.senkyr,petr.kroha}@fit.cvut.cz

Abstract. In this paper, we describe our graph-oriented method used to find semantically similar sentences in external information sources that have a semantic enrichment potential in relation to sentences of textual functional requirements specification. Our motivation is to reduce the incompleteness of requirements that may be a source of inconsistency. We found there are some facts and rules so obvious for domain experts that they do not even mention them in requirements. We call such rules default consistency rules. These rules are often not implemented and can not be revealed from the requirements because they are not mentioned there.

Keywords: Semantic similarity of sentences · Semantic enrichment · Textual functional requirements specification · Graph-based representation of part-of-speech tagging

1 Introduction

Our project is focused on improving the quality of textual requirements specification. It is well-known that textual descriptions of requirements are very often ambiguous, incomplete, and inconsistent. This fact can result in mistakes in modeling, programming, and testing. The necessary corrections and reworks increase the costs and extend the delivery date.

In our paper [12], we discussed and proved the existence of *default consistency rules.* They represent those facts and rules that domain experts find so obvious that they do not even mention them in requirements. Therefore, we cannot find them and reveal them when we analyze the text of requirements.

Our solution is to generate specific formulations (pseudo-questions) in the form of sentence patterns based on the text of requirements. These patterns are partially filled in by fragments of textual requirements and partially contain empty containers to catch parts of texts from external sources, which can enrich the incomplete information of requirements. Then we use them to search in external sources for semantically similar sentences (pseudo-answers) that could enrich the original sentence. We use the found information to generate questions on stakeholders and analysts to warn them that there may be a forgotten

A. Polyvyanyy and S. Rinderle-Ma (Eds.): CAiSE 2021 Workshops, LNBIP 423, pp. 69–80, 2021.
https://doi.org/10.1007/978-3-030-79022-6_7

default consistency rule. We do it not automatically because the semantics is very complex and depends on context.

Unfortunately, we cannot simply use the methods of computational linguistics and text mining. The reasons are given by our specific needs. In linguistic systems, the best ranking in similarity get the sentences that have the same meaning. However, it does not bring any new information that could reduce the requirements' incompleteness. Therefore, we defined our own concept of semantic enrichment explained in Sect. 3.

In the query-answering systems, the given query is formulated by the user (e.g., a user of an application), and the answer has to be distilled from a given text (e.g., from the corresponding user guide that is available). In our case, neither the query nor the document are given. We have to generate ourselves such a query that is suitable to help us in revealing some enrichment information not contained in requirements, and we have to find ourselves documents that hopefully contain the expected answer. As we state in Sect. 8, the whole process has not a guaranteed result, i.e., it may happen that there is no suitable information in available sources that could reduce the incompleteness of our requirements, or it may exist, but we are not able to find it.

The number of similar sentences we find may be significant, and we need to define their ranking according to a measure. However, we have not found any measure that would be suitable for our purpose for the reasons given above. So, we developed our own criteria to measure the ranking of the candidate sentences found in external sources. This ranking specifies the suitability of the found sentences to provide the semantic enrichment of given requirements to reduce their incompleteness.

Our paper is structured as follows. In Sect. 2, we discuss related work. Our approach is presented in Sects. 3, 4, and 5. Our implementation, used data, experiments, and results are described in Sects. 6 and 7. In Sect. 8, we conclude.

2   Related Work

Semantic similarity of sentences measures the meaning similarity of sentences. Its applications include machine translation, text summarization, semantic search, question-answering systems, dialog and conversational systems. In paper [14], there are given four definitions of semantic similarity of sentences. They are too complex for our purpose.

Compared with our topic, these definitions have a different goal because they search after most similar sentences, in the best case, sentences with the same meaning. This is not our case because a sentence having the same meaning would bring us no additional information we are looking for.

Our approach is similar to the concept of text entailment that recognizes how much the meaning of a text entails the meaning of another text. Methods of text entailment take as input a T (a sentence)/H(a hypothesis) pair and determine automatically whether an entailment relation holds or not [3]. These methods are based on the tree edit distance algorithm. We did not use this approach because it is not suitable for our purpose. Our method of semantic enrichment is more simple.

Semantic enrichment is usually used to enrich metadata with linked open vocabularies. This process of "augmenting" the source metadata with additional terms is called semantic enrichment. The most common use case for enrichment is to support better search and browsing functionalities. So, automatic semantic enrichment is used to enrich the metadata model of stored data with some additional data and links.

The next field of semantic enrichment methods is their use in enterprise information systems. These include content management systems (CMSs) [5], customer relationship management solutions (CRMs), and also files from the company's own intranet and openly accessible sources on the Internet. The company lets find and store all data that has any connection with its products, customers, competitors, suppliers, etc.

The important concept for semantic enrichment is RDF used in the *Semantic Web* data model [1]. Its basic building block (in modeling terminology) is an object-attribute-value triple. It consists of a resource (object), a property (attribute), and a value. We use our original graph interpretation of RDF to represent a skeleton of a sentence. It is a directed graph with labeled nodes and arcs. We describe the triple ⟨**subject, predicate, object**⟩ as the RDF triple respecting the word similarity given by synonyms and antonyms with negation.

A graph-oriented approach to linguistic problems is investigated in many papers. Its complexity is discussed in [7].

3   Our Approach to Semantic Similarity and Semantic Enrichment of Sentences

In our previous paper about inconsistency [13], we clustered sentences of the requirements to find some pairs that could be in contradiction, i.e., we investigated their *semantic overlap.*

In our previous paper about default consistency rules [12], we generated patterns called pseudo-questions from specific sentences of requirements. These patterns described the conditions of sentence similarity for our purpose that are based on the RDF concept. Then we defined them as cluster seeds and clustered around them similar sentences from external information sources. The goal was to find a semantic enrichment of pseudo-questions (more details below).

In both cases, we clustered the sentences according to triples ⟨**subject, predicate, object**⟩ and their subsets, i.e., we used the word level and the structural level of similarity [6]. Even though we used the text of volume of 1000 pages in [13], the found clusters had about 20–50 members.

In our paper [12], we discussed the search of default consistency rules on Web pages. We argued that it is necessary to reduce the incompleteness of requirements. Because of that, we are not in search of the most similar sentences but sentences that could semantically enrich the sentences from requirements.

4   RDF Semantic Similarity of Sentences

The evaluation of the semantic similarity between two sentences belongs to the most important tasks in natural language processing and the derived topics like information retrieval, text mining, and query-answer systems.

We have defined the RDF semantic similarity between sentences (for our specific purposes) as a subgraph relation.

In general, the *subgraph isomorphism problem* has proven to be NP-complete [2]. Fortunately, our graph representation of sentences and the patterns of pseudo-questions makes possible a type of clustering that simplifies the subgraph search problem (see Sect. 4.1).

Based on the RDF method, we generate pseudo-questions as patterns. Some of their parts contain words taken from requirements; other parts are empty containers. The words of pseudo-questions make possible to use the pseudo-questions as cluster seeds. Corresponding to these seeds, the sentences from external sources are clustered according to their subjects (it may be expressed by a synonym or an antonym), the predicates/verbs (it may be expressed by negation or by an antonym), and the objects (it may be the same, or expressed by a synonym or by an antonym). This means that there are sentences similar (in the sense of RDF) to the cluster seed in each cluster. In our graph representation, the corresponding subgraph nodes and vertices have the same names as in the graph.

We used and applied this definition in our paper [13], in which we described how to find semantically similar sentences to test them on suspicion of being a source of inconsistency.

We accept that it is a simplified definition, but textual requirements should consist of simple formulations.

4.1   Clustering Sentences

The graphs in our method represent sentences. To make the subgraph search problem easy, we cluster the sentences from requirements and the sentences found in external sources in the same way according to their RDF structure.

We find and cluster sentences that have:

- the same triple ⟨**subject, predicate, object**⟩,
- the same tuple ⟨**subject, predicate**⟩,
- the same ⟨**subject**⟩.

These sentences obtain information about its properties and relations, i.e., about values of attributes and relations of the underlying class, given by the static model, and about actions, i.e., participation in actions given by the dynamic model.

This process is not very easy because we have to work with synonyms, the coreference of pronouns, and antonyms. This means that we are not simply looking for all sentences that have the same subject, but we have to analyze clauses in complex sentences, and additionally the following sentences that could be related using pronouns to the subject of the previous sentence. In addition, clustering sentences with respect to subjects contains another aspect of nouns, which concerns looking for opposites (antonyms) among nouns of subjects with an eventual combination of negation in the verb-part of the sentence.

Moreover, there is a style difference between sentences from requirements and sentences from external sources.

- Sentences from requirements are written by analysts. They are experienced and motivated in writing simple, close-fitting texts.
- Sentences from external sources are written by domain experts who are often using long, complex sentences.

To process the semantic similarity in the first step and the semantic enrichment analysis in the next step can be a complex task.

5 Semantic Enrichment of Sentences

As we already mentioned in Sect. 2, the semantic enrichment methods are used mostly to enrich metadata to increase the search potential or to collect additional data for enterprise information systems. This is a big topic used in software companies.

Our goal is very modest. We define the semantic enrichment of a sentence only as its extension with additional semantic information.

Exactly, we search for epithets to subject or object or both. An epithet is defined in linguistics as an adjective (it may be a compound adjective) or adjective phrase (called epithetic phrase), which may occur in place of an object's name, expressing a quality or attribute regarded as characteristic of the object mentioned. Epithets are also known as qualifiers. The complete linguistic definition includes other aspects used in epic poetry, like derogation meaning. However, this is out of the scope of requirements specification text that is in the focus of our interest.

In our case, we search for sentences from external information sources that describe the subject's or object's attributes or qualities more deeply compared with the same subjects or objects mentioned in pseudo-questions.

In Fig. 1, we can see an example of an epithet as a phrase: *"tones"* (taken from our pseudo-question) $\longrightarrow$ *"tones that sound simultaneously"* (taken from an external information source).

It is enough for our purpose of search for default consistency rules in textual requirements specifications that results in generating questions directed to domain experts and analysts.

The enrichment process can be summarized in the following steps.

Algorithm 1. The Enrichment Process

---

1. The external information sources have to be specified that are relevant to the topic of requirements.
2. The set of specific keywords (nouns) has to be selected from requirements that represent the core semantics of the application described in requirements.
3. For each of these keywords, a specific set of pseudo-questions is formulated using our question patterns that represent grammatical possibilities, how a question can be formulated. We use the term pseudo-question because it is not a question in the sense of linguistics. It is an artificial sentence containing structured information that should be expanded and enriched by using external sources. In the most simple case, it is an Is-A definition.
4. These pseudo-questions are used for search to find the corresponding pages in external documents.
5. The found pages contain sentences that have to be collected. Using our search patterns partially fulfilled by keywords, these sentences are "combed" through.
6. The lexical and structural semantic similarity of sentences is used to reduce the set of sentences from external sources.
7. The remaining sentences are analyzed by our analyzing patterns based on part-of-speech tagging. As we already mentioned in Sect. 1, we use a specific enrichment measure to compare the pseudo-questions (generated from requirements) with the selected sentences from external sources. The concept of our enrichment measure is described in Sect. 5.1.
8. The parts of sentences from external sources that have been caught in the sieve of our analyzing patterns are used to generate questions for domain experts.

5.1 Graph-Based Approach to the Semantic Enrichment of Sentences

We clustered the sentences according to methods described in Sect. 4.1. In each cluster C_i, the sentences $S\text{-}Ex_{k1,k2,...}$ from external sources are around the seed of the cluster $S\text{-}PQ_i$ which is a pseudo-question constructed from requirements.

After the sentences placed in a cluster (the pseudo-question based on requirements as a seed and sentences from external information sources) have been processed by the linguistic tools, they result in oriented (directed) graphs with marked nodes (vertices) and marked edges. The nodes carry the lexical information using triples ⟨the word itself, its tag in part-of-speech tagging, its role in the sentence⟩, e.g., ⟨**chord, noun, subject**⟩. The edges carry the structural information about the relation to other parts of the sentence. See Fig. 1.

To simplify the graphs, we eliminate some of the so-called function words that have little lexical and semantic meaning, e.g., articles. In the contrary, other words like *of, that, which, from* introduce an epithet and cannot be eliminated.

When we describe these oriented graphs using adjacency matrices, we get matrices S_{1G} and S_{2G}. Now, we ask whether the graph of the sentence S-PQ_i (pseudo-question) is a subgraph of sentences S-$Ex_{k1,k2,...}$ from external sources. In general, a subgraph G' of a graph G is a graph G' whose vertex set and edge set are subsets of those of G. If G' is a subgraph of G, then G is said to be a supergraph of G'. In general, the subgraph isomorphism problem has proven to be NP-complete [2].

However, because of the specific properties of our graphs and the previous clustering, we can find subgraphs easily. Additionally, we have found that the orientation of graph edges has no sense for our purpose because the roles of words are parts of the node information – see Fig. 2. The additional enrichment information concerns so-called open class words. In English, these are nouns, lexical verbs, adjectives, and adverbs. This means that we analyze the graph starting with nodes whose second element of the node marking tuple belongs into the set of open class words – NOUN, LEX-VERB, ADJ, ADV.

We used our methods from our previous paper concerning incompleteness [10] because the problem of missing default consistency rules can be seen as the problem of incomplete information in textual requirements.
In Fig. 1, we can see the graph of the sentence S_1 from requirements:

"*A chord is a combination of three or more tones*"
and the graph of the sentence S_2 from Wikipedia:

"*A chord is a combination of three or more tones that sound simultaneously.*"

We can see that S_1 is a subgraph of the sentence S_2 from Wikipedia. This sentence includes additional information saying that the tones of a chord "*hold simultaneously*" [12].

5.2   Our Approach to Measurement of the Semantic Enrichment of Sentences

Our approach to the measurement of semantic enrichment is specific because of our application.

Having a sentence S_1 from the requirements and the sentences S_2 from external sources, we distill the RDF skeleton of both sentences and compare the triples ⟨**subject, predicate, object**⟩ including synonyms, antonyms, etc. Then we investigate the nouns used as subject and object whether they have some adjectives or numerals, i.e., we search after edges coming from these nouns in the graph representation.

Because of the linguistic complexity, we do a simple transitive closure (see example in Fig. 2).

We denote the set of such edges in the sentence S_1 as $Edges_1$ and the set corresponding with the sentences S_2 as $Edges_2$. Then we defined our measure of semantic enrichment of the sentence S_1 by the sentence S_2 as:

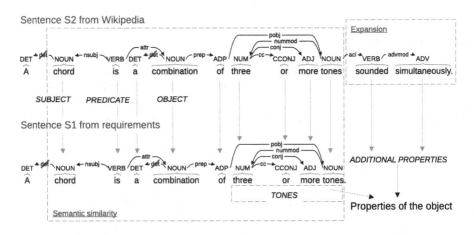

Fig. 1. Example – expansion of a chord definition.

$$M = card(Edges_2) - card(Edges_1).$$

In the following Example 1, we reduce edges (using transitive closure), and we get the semantic enrichment $M = 2$.

Example 1. Semantic enrichment of sentence graphs

Sentence S_1:   Sentence S_2:

$Edges_1$ after reduction: $Edges_2$ after reduction:

| |
| | – combination–tones
– combination–tones   – tones–three
– tones–three   – three–more
– three–more   – combination–hold
                                     – is–simultaneously

$card(Edges_1) = 3$ $card(Edges_2) = 5$

The sentence S_2 makes a semantic enrichment of the sentence S_1 by:
$M = card(Edges_2) - card(Edges_1) = 2$.

In Fig. 2, the situation is shown, when the triples ⟨**subject, predicate, object**⟩ match, and the object of the second sentence contains an enrichment – *hold*, *simultaneously*. The corresponding clustering is explained in Sect. 4.1.

In Fig. 3, the situation is shown, when the triples ⟨**subject, predicate, object**⟩ do not match completely. However, the subsets ⟨**subject, predicate**⟩ match. In such a case, a common predicate can be enriched, as shown in Fig. 3. Based on the similarity found in the matrix, questions are generated that result in decision that the adjective *harmonic* can be an expansion of *combination of tones*. The corresponding clustering is explained in Sect. 4.1.

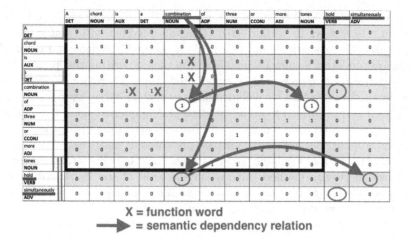

X = function word

➤ = semantic dependency relation

Fig. 2. Example – Matrix representation of a chord definition expansion – RDF complete match.

	A / DET	chord / NOUN	is / AUX	any / DET	harmonic / ADJ	set / NOUN	of / ADP	usually / ADV	three / NUM	or / CCONJ	more / ADJ	notes / NOUN
A / DET	0	1	0	0	0	0	0	0	0	0	0	0
chord / NOUN	1	0	1	0	0	0	0	0	0	0	0	0
is / AUX	0	0	0	0	0	1	0	0	0	0	0	0
any / DET	0	0	0	0	0	1	0	0	0	0	0	0
harmonic / ADJ	0	0	0	0	0	0	0	0	0	0	0	0
set / NOUN	0	0	1	1	1	0	1	0	0	0	0	0
of / ADP	0	0	0	0	0	1	0	1	0	0	0	1
usually / ADV	0	0	0	0	0	0	1	0	0	0	0	0
three / NUM	0	0	0	0	0	0	0	0	0	1	1	1
or / CCONJ	0	0	0	0	0	0	0	0	1	0	0	0
more / ADJ	0	0	0	0	0	0	0	0	1	0	0	0
notes / NOUN	0	0	0	0	0	0	1	0	1	0	0	0

Annotations: Subgraph / Subject / Verb; "No MATCH in OBJECT"

Subject – match
Verb – match
Object – NO MATCH
Match
Match
No match

Question 1:
What is a relation between a combination of tones and a set of tones

Question 2:
If a combination of tones and a set of tones are related, is "harmonic" an extension?

Fig. 3. Example – Matrix representation of a chord definition expansion – no RDF complete match.

6   Implementation and the Graph Database

Our implemented tool TEMOS (Textual Modeling System) is capable of detecting text defects (concerning ambiguity, incompleteness, and inconsistency). It delivers an internal model that should be converted to various output forms. So far, we extract the UML class diagram, a model of Normalized Systems Elements, or SHACL Shapes. On behalf of the idea of this paper, we extended our tool to reveal some missing information that can cause inconsistency through incompleteness. The current version of our tool TEMOS is written in Python, and it is powered by *spaCy*[1] NLP framework in version 3.0. We use a pre-trained model called *en_core_web_trf* in version 3.0.0 (available together with spaCy installation) to process texts written in English. Both the spaCy version and the model version are the latest versions available at the time of writing this paper.

The patterns are represented by an oriented graph. Therefore, we store them in the *Neo4j* database that we included into our tool TEMOS. Every sentence to be analyzed is transformed to an oriented graph and queried against Neo4j, too. These graphs created from sentences are clustered according to their lexical and structural content. Because the graphs are presented as matrices, we have a rich spectrum of operations available. To find the semantic enrichment, we implement the transitive closure method directly on the level of the Neo4j database in the Cypher language. In general, the *Floyd-Warshall algorithm* (Complexity: $O(Vertices^3)$) is used for computing transitive closure.

6.1   Information Sources

In our experiments, we use general information sources that should be used for various domains as follows. The condition of automatic querying requires a search engine with a public API (in our case – *Google Programmable Search Engine*). The current limitation of the free version is 10,000 requests per day. The response of a query is in JSON format and it consists of 10 results. Each result provides metadata including the web-page link. We also use *Wikidata, Wordnik, DBPedia,* and *BabelNet*.

7   Data, Experiments, Results

In our paper [12], we presented an extensive case study describing the requirements problems of a chord generation application for 4-string music instruments. Starting from the sentence *"A chord is a combination of three or more tones"*, we enhanced and enriched it with sentences from the Web saying that a chord has to be playable. This adjective means that its tones have to sound simultaneous (i.e., not more tones on one string) and that the tones of the fingering have to respect the hand span of musicians. We used our method of semantic enrichment presented in this paper, but its matrix definition and detailed description of the measure were out of the scope of our paper [12].

In this experiment, we follow the mentioned example, and we focus on the key noun *chord*. Below, we present the sentences obtained from the proposed information sources. We can see that only one definition (BabelNet) is not usable in our case because it targets a different domain.

- Wikidata: *A chord is harmonic set of three or more notes.*
- Wordnik: *A chord is a combination of three or more pitches sounded simultaneously.*
- DBPedia: *In music, a guitar chord is a set of notes played on a guitar.*

---

[1] https://spacy.io.

- BabelNet: *In computing, Chord is a protocol and algorithm for a peer-to-peer distributed hash table.*

Then, we use a custom configured instance of Google search engine. First, we search for the standalone key noun *chord*. Second, we search for all tuples where the first noun is still *chord*, and the second noun is a noun that appears together with the noun *chord* in the same sentence (we select a combination of nouns *chord* and *fingering* from the original requirements). We present the results in Table 1. The last point focused on the ratio of reasonable questions to all questions is our subjective categorization.

Table 1. Google search and our clustering: *chord* vs. *chord* + *fingering*.

	chord	chord + fingering
Sentences containing the noun *chord*	80	18
Sentences matching our pseudo-questions	30	5
Clusters	21	5
—Clusters of cardinality 1	19	5
—Clusters of cardinality 2	2	0
Sentences already used in requirements	2	0
Reasonable questions (hints)	6/19	2/5

8 Conclusions

The final goal of our project is to improve the quality of textual functional requirements. To achieve this, we analyze them and search for ambiguities [9], incompleteness [10,11], and inconsistency [4,13] using our special patterns [8]. In paper [12], we have shown that the incompleteness of requirements can be in some cases reduced if we succeed in the search for the enrichment of requirement sentences using external information sources. In this paper, we presented our graph-oriented method of enrichment search, including the enrichment measure. As we already stated, the whole process has not a guaranteed result, i.e., it may happen that there is no suitable enrichment information available in external sources that could reduce the incompleteness of our requirements, or it may exist, but we are not able to find it.

Further, we will investigate the integrity of information found in external sources because we have seen mistakes on respected Web pages. The problem is that an informed human reader can automatically filter these mistakes using common sense knowledge. Unfortunately, this is not the property of algorithms.

Acknowledgements. This research was supported by the grant of Czech Technical University in Prague No. SGS20/209/OHK3/3T/18.

References

1. Antoniou, G., van Harmelen, F.: A Semantic Web Primer. MIT Press, Cambridge (2008)
2. Gouda, K., Hassaan, M.: A fast algorithm for subgraph search problem. In: Proceedings of 8th International Conference on Informatics and Systems (INFOS) 2012, Giza, Egypt, pp. 53–59. IEEE (2012)
3. Gupta, A., Kaur, M., Mirkin, S., Singh, A., Goyal, A.: Text summarization through entailment-based minimum vertex cover. In: Proceedings of the SEM 2014, Dublin, Ireland, pp. 75–80. Association for Computational Linguistics and Dublin City University (2014)
4. Kroha, P., Janetzko, R., Labra, J.E.: Ontologies in checking for inconsistency of requirements specification. In: 2009 Third International Conference on Advances in Semantic Processing, Sliema, Malta, pp. 32–37. IEEE Computer Society Press (2009). http://ieeexplore.ieee.org/document/5291538/
5. Maass, W., Kowatsch, T.: Semantic Technologies in Content Management Systems. Springer, Berlin (2012). https://doi.org/10.1007/978-3-642-24960-0
6. Meng, L., Huang, R., Gu, J.: Measuring semantic similarity of word pairs using path and information content. Int. J. Future Gener. Commun. Netw. $7(3)$, 183–194 (2014)
7. Schluter, N.: The complexity of finding the maximum spanning DAG and other restrictions for DAG parsing of natural language. In: Proceedings of the Fourth Joint Conference on Lexical and Computational Semantics, Denver, Colorado, pp. 259–268 (2015)
8. Šenkýř, D., Kroha, P.: Patterns in textual requirements specification. In: Proceedings of the 13th International Conference on Software Technologies, Porto, Portugal, pp. 197–204. SciTePress – Science and Technology Publications (2018). https://doi.org/10.5220/0006827301970204
9. Šenkýř, D., Kroha, P.: Patterns of ambiguity in textual requirements specification. In: Rocha, Á., Adeli, H., Reis, L.P., Costanzo, S. (eds.) WorldCIST'19 2019. AISC, vol. 930, pp. 886–895. Springer, Cham (2019). https://doi.org/10.1007/978-3-030-16181-1_83
10. Šenkýř, D., Kroha, P.: Problem of incompleteness in textual requirements specification. In: Proceedings of the 14th International Conference on Software Technologies, Porto, Portugal, vol. 1, pp. 323–330. INSTICC, SciTePress – Science and Technology Publications (2019)
11. Šenkýř, D., Kroha, P.: Patterns for checking incompleteness of scenarios in textual requirements specification. In: Proceedings of the 15th International Conference on Evaluation of Novel Approaches to Software Engineering, Porto, Portugal, vol. 1, pp. 289–296. INSTICC, SciTePress – Science and Technology Publications (2020)
12. Šenkýř, D., Kroha, P.: Problem of inconsistency and default consistency rules (2021, submitted)
13. Šenkýř, D., Kroha, P.: problem of inconsistency in textual requirements specifications (2021). Accepted and presented (ENASE 2021), to be published
14. Sravanathi, P., Srinivasu, B.: Semantic similarity between sentences. Int. Res. J. Eng. Technol. (IRJET) $4(1)$, 156–161 (2017)

Adapting Domain-Specific Interfaces Using Invariants Mechanisms

Boris Ulitin$^{(\boxtimes)}$ (iD) and Tatiana Babkina (iD)

HSE University, Nizhny Novgorod, Russia
{bulitin,tbabkina}@hse.ru

Abstract. The process of implementing agile technologies in an enterprise is an example of a highly demanding and challenging topic both for practitioners and academy. Speaking about agility, we basically mean various kinds of automation. A higher degree of automation results in a more agile enterprise. However, in practice, even in the case of complete automation of the enterprise, there remains a need for user interaction with various software systems. To increase the efficiency and simplify such interactions, it is necessary to develop mechanisms, which enable adaptation of user domain-specific interfaces for actual conditions of human-machine interaction. We consider for this purpose the use of an invariant formalism based on the allocation of stable, unchanging object data structures and interface structures. Evaluation of the effectiveness of the approach proposed is carried out with the example of the analytical system of the university admissions committee.

Keywords: Organizational agility · Domain-specific interface · GUI · Object-relational schema · UML · Transformation · Invariants

1 Introduction

Engineering of digital transformations is an urgent problem for modern enterprises, especially within the Industry 4.0 paradigm [1]. This process is particularly important in the case of the 'agilisation' [18] of enterprise processes through the application of different smart components and artificial intelligence systems. As a result, the degree of autonomy of the enterprise components increases as well as the intensity of their interaction [1].

At the same time, speaking about agility, we primarily mean by this process various kinds of automation and 'smartisation'. However, as practice shows, even in the case of complete automation and agility of production, the need for user interaction with different systems remains [2]. First of all, such interaction is necessary for the accumulation of the knowledge base used during technological cycle. In addition, users may need various sorts of *ad hoc* analytical information from the system. Finally, there are situations that are not foreseen in the algorithms of behavior for the system and require the direct control by the end-user.

To increase the efficiency and simplify such interactions, it is necessary to develop mechanisms, which enable continuous adaptation of user domain-based interfaces for

© Springer Nature Switzerland AG 2021
A. Polyvyanyy and S. Rinderle-Ma (Eds.): CAiSE 2021 Workshops, LNBIP 423, pp. 81–92, 2021.
https://doi.org/10.1007/978-3-030-79022-6_8

actual conditions of human-machine interaction. Existing works [8, 10] pay more attention to automation of optimization algorithms rather than to processes of interaction with
systems. The work [9] exemplifies a common opinion that the user interface the user
interface is developed immediately as full and general as possible and subsequently it
can only be changed manually. Such a statement deprives the user interface of possible
flexibility and leads to cases when the user interface begins to contradict the conceptual
model of the domain.

In previous works we substantiated that any interface can be interpreted as a kind
of domain-specific language (DSL) [16], and an object-oriented paradigm naturally
represents the interface, since it reflects elements of the conceptual model of the domain.
Thus, when solving the problem of adapting an interface, models and methods common
to the DSL approach can be applied. This leads us to the idea that the interface also has
a model-oriented nature, which means that it is possible to automate the process of its
incremental modification during the evolution of a conceptual domain model.

Within a generic framework of DSL development this article aims at proposing a
new approach to automation of development of adaptive domain-specific interfaces using
transformations between the UML-model and Object-Relational Schema restrained by
a certain invariant formalism. In our case the UML-model is used to describe the component structure of the user interface through which an Object-Relational Schema containing domain data is filled. Invariants represent stable structures, the correspondences
between which are established at the level of both models [13]. A certain transformation
is used to shift between identified invariants of both models and to adapt the interface
components to changes in the domain model. This approach allows us to fully automate
the interface designing that results in reducing the development time of the software
system as a whole. In addition, due to the formal model of invariants [14], the interface
structure can always be consistently adapted to changes in the domain model.

In our research we evaluated the approach proposed within the task of incremental
modification and adaptation of reporting interfaces in an analytical software system for
support of admission process in a higher education institution.

Compared to previous works [16, 17], this article contains a practical implementation of the idea of using invariants for the domain-specific interfaces evolution and
presents results as follows. In Sect. 2 we observe main aspects of representation of user
interfaces by UML class-diagram and show correspondence between the UML class-
diagram and the Object-Relational Schema. Section 3 contains the description of the
proposed approach, specifies the invariants of the Object-Relational Schema and the
interface model and determines the transformations between them. Section 4 is devoted
to the application of proposed approach. We cosect.clude the article with the analysis of
the proposed approach and further research steps.

2   Key Concepts of the Research

2.1   Object-Oriented Definition of User Interface

Object-oriented representation of the Graphical user interface (GUI) in general settles
as part of the object-oriented analysis and design (OOAD) approach. It's a structured
method for analyzing, designing a system by applying the object-oriented concepts,

and develop a set of graphical system models during the development life cycle of the software [3].

From this point of view, any system is represented as a set of interconnected components (objects), characterized by their attributes and behavior.

According to this idea, we separate the system into *objects*, each of which has.

- an identity (id) which distinguishes it from other objects in the system;
- a state that determines the attributes of an object as well as each attribute values;
- behavior that represents available activities performed by an object in terms of changes in its state.

Objects containing the same attributes and/or exhibit common behavior are organized into *classes*, which contain a set of attributes for the objects that are to be instantiated from the class and operations that portray the behavior of the objects of the class.

Therefore, we can formalize any class as a combination (O, R) of some objects and relations between them, where each object is a set of its attributes (one of the attributes is unique and is considered an identifier) and operations $o_i = (Attr_i, Opp_i) = (\{attr_{i_1}, attr_{i_2}, ..., attr_{i_M}\}, \{opp_{i_1}, opp_{i_2}, ..., opp_{i_K}\}), M, K \in \mathbb{N}, i = 1, N)$.

Thus, the system is represented as a superposition of many objects of various classes. Being an integral part of the system, GUI can also be represented as a combination of the number of related objects of various classes. It is important to note that attributes may be elementary or complex [3]. Complex is an attribute that is an instance of a class (object). Elementary is an attribute containing a constant value that is not an object. Given this classification of attributes, we can argue that the system is a hierarchy of interconnected objects. At the lower level of such a hierarchy there are objects containing only elementary attributes, and at the top - the system itself. Such basic lower level objects that cannot be dissected into smaller components, make up system object invariants. Such object invariants make it possible to describe the structure as a superposition of low-level invariants. Functionals used to construct structures from object invariants form an operational invariant. These types of invariants are described in more detail in Sect. 2.2.

In this case, each object and, as a consequence, the GUI (as well as the system in general), represents a combination of many object invariants that do not change during the work on the system and can be used to automate the development process. Assuming that the GUI is tied to a certain data set, we can identify the invariants at the data level as well as at the level of the GUI. As a result, the construction of the GUI becomes nothing else than the identification of the invariant at the data level with the subsequent search and display of its equivalent at the interface level.

To better understand the mechanisms of automation through the use of invariants, it is necessary to precise their definition and develop a classification of invariants.

2.2 Definition and Classification of Invariants

First of all, it should be noted that there are at least 4 options for determining invariants depending on the context of use. This paper uses three classic forms of invariants: object-oriented (object), inductive and operational [13, 14].

Declarations of *object invariants* can appear in every class. The invariants that pertain to an object o are those declared in the classes between *object* – the root of the single-inheritance hierarchy – and *type*(o) – the allocated type of o. Each object o has a special field *inv*, whose value names a class in the range from *object* to *type*(o), and which represents the most refined subclass whose invariant can be relied upon for this object. More precisely, for any object o and class T and in any execution state of the program, if $o.inv$ is a subclass of T, which we denote by $o.inv \leq T$, then all object invariants declared in class T are known to hold for o. The object invariants declared in other classes may or may not hold for o, so they cannot be relied upon.

Inductive invariants describe the connection between components of two (or more) sets of objects and are denoted with inv_τ. The formal definition of the inductive invariants was demonstrated in [17]. An inductive invariant means, that there is a strong correspondence between elements of two sets of objects, which are connected during some relation (transformation).

In order to guarantee that the obtained set of interface invariants will be consistent and display the corresponding set of data model invariants, the third type of invariants is used. Interpreting each modification of an interface as its transformation, it can be argued that its sequential refinement is a consistent application of the transformation function. From this point of view, the process of interface development consists of the execution of the operational invariants and can be associated with a subset $\mathcal{O}.F$ of $(\Sigma, F)^w$ of (in)finite sequences of states, which were identified and analyzed in our previous work [17].

Informally, $\mathcal{O}$ consists of those sequences of states that begin with an initial state that satisfies $\mathcal{J}$ (*Neg* negative application condition in our case) and in which each state has a successor in accordance with the transition $\mathcal{W}$ (*Rule* transformation rule in our case). From this point of view, $\mathcal{O}$ can be interpreted as a transition system between various states, that satisfies $\mathcal{J}$. The set $\mathcal{O}$ is nonempty because $\mathcal{J}$ is satisfiable and $\mathcal{W}$ includes stuttering steps.

Once the computations of a transition system are built, *next* and *inv* specifications are defined as expected:

$$next_O.\,(p,q).F \triangleq \forall \sigma \in O.F : \forall i \in \mathbb{N} : p, \sigma_i \Rightarrow q, \sigma_{i+1} \tag{1}$$

$$inv_O.p.F \triangleq \forall \sigma \in O.F : \forall i \in \mathbb{N} : p, \sigma_i \tag{2}$$

Informally, $next_O.(p, q)$ means that, in any modification of the system, any state that satisfies p is immediately followed by a state that satisfies q. Although modifications include stuttering steps, $next_O.(p, q)$ does *not* imply that $[p \Rightarrow q]$. In the same way, $inv_O p$ means that any state of any modification of a system satisfies p. Naturally, $next_O$ and inv_O are related in a way similar to the relationship between $next_\tau$ and inv_τ, namely: $inv_O.p.F \equiv next_O.(p, q).F \wedge [\mathcal{J}.F \Rightarrow p]$.

The only thing is to determine the invariants at the level of the data model and interface and establish a correspondence between them. For this, it is necessary to compare the elements of the Object-Relational Schema and the object-oriented interface model.

The Object-Relational Schema looks effective in this case, since any interface involves some interaction with domain data. Taking into account the object nature of the Object-Relational Schema, this interaction can be easier to organize by establishing a correspondence between data objects and the interface.

2.3   Structural Description of UML Class Diagram and Object-Relational Schemas

Although the UML class diagrams [3] have many elements to model, we have selected the more commonly used for a database schema design, which are [4]: (1) Classes (*C*); (2) Attributes: single (*SA*), composed (*CA*), multivalued (*MA*); (3) Operations (*Op*); (4) Relationships (*Rel*) between classes: aggregation (*AG*), composition (*CM*), n-ary association (*NAS*), binary association (*BAS*), association class (*AC*), generalization-specialization (*GS*).

In defining the individual components of this diagram, we will adhere to the concepts described by M.F. Golobisky and A. Vecchietti [11].

Since we defined class *C* earlier as set of identifier, state and behavior, here we only decompose its definition as follows: $C = (id, C, SA, CA, MA, O, R)$, where: *id* is the name assigned to the class; *C* is a finite set of classes due to the fact that a class can be composed of other classes; *SA*, *CA*, *MA* are finite sets of single, composed and multivalued attributes correspondingly; *Op* is a finite set of operations and *Rel* is a finite set of relationships where the class is participating. The definition of various types of relations and their formalization are presented in more detail in [11].

After the structure of the UML class diagram is determined, we need to consider in more detail the structure of the Object-Relational Schema. Components of this model are mainly defined in the SQL standard [12]. Only the most relevant parts of this standard for this paper are considered, which are: row type, collection types (arrays and multisets) and a reference type, since they are responsible for relational object (tables) structure definition.

A row type is defined as a set of pairs $RT = (F_1: T_1, F_2: T_2, \ldots, F_n: T_n)$ where F_i is the name of a field in the row type and T_i is a built-in data type (int, float, etc.). A Reference Type called $Ref(T)$ is also a data type which contains the reference values (OID) of T. T is a row in a typed table [6].

Upon initial consideration, both models have an object-oriented nature, that results in the opportunity to establish a correspondence between them at the level of objects.

3   Description of the Approach Proposed

In our research we prove that the object-oriented model of the interface (in terms of the UML Class Diagram) can be derived through the transformations from the Object-Relational Schemas. For this, it is vital to establish a correspondence between the components of these models.

There are three layers involved in the transformation from UML class diagrams into persistent objects of the Object-Relational Schema (Fig. 1). The first one corresponds to the UML classes and relationships. The second object-relational layer contains the objects proposed by the SQL designed to implement classes and relationships. Finally, the third layer is composed of typed tables with keys, constraints, triggers (relational approach) and other elements like object identifiers (OID).

To complete the transformations, it is necessary to define several functions to translate the components from one layer to the other, using a mapping function. This function is a binary relation $f: A \rightarrow B$, where A and B are invariants from mapping models. The most important property of this function in conjunction with invariants is that each element in A maps to exactly one element in B [7].

In the case of UML classes and the Object-Relational Schema the following correspondence can be used (Table 1). The relationships cannot be transformed in the same way than the other elements of the class. Such limitations are caused by several alternatives mapping functions can be applied according to the characteristics of the relationships and the classes involved on it.

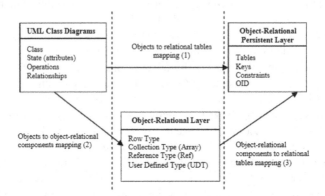

Fig. 1. Layers involved in mapping objects into the Object-Relational Schema

Since an association class is both an association and a class, the mapping function is like the one defined for a class plus the references to the classes to which the association class is linked: $f: AC = (id, Ref(C_1), Ref(C_2), ..., Ref(C_n), SA, CA, MA, Op) \rightarrow T = ('name', Ref(C_1), Ref(C_2), ..., Ref(C_n), BIT, RT, AT, T, MM)$ where the T defined for the association class contains the references to the classes related by the association plus the built-in (BIT) data types, row types, array types, Ts, and member methods of the association class.

After we have established a correspondence between the components of the UML Class diagram and the Object-Relational Schema, the only thing is to formalize the transformation between them in the form of invariants.

For this purpose, we use two types of previously reviewed invariants: object and inductive. First of all, we reveal object invariants at the level of the data model and the interface. Then, we define a function that will analyze the invariants in the data model and find the corresponding interface-level invariant for them. Such invariant is added to the set of previously found interface components and is displayed on the screen.

To identify the object invariants of both levels (Class Diagram and Object-Relational Schema) Table 1 can be used. On the Class side, attributes are invariants, which can also be simpler classes. Following this logic, we can argue that in the case of an interface, the invariant will be classes that describe its individual components and do not contain references to other classes.

Table 1. Proposed correspondence of elements of classes and tables.

Class	Table
Single attribute	Built-in type
Composed attribute	Row type
Multivalued attribute	Array type, multiset type
Operation	Member method

In the case of the Object-Relational Schema, the invariants are columns and their types, which are fully consistent with class attributes. These objects are object invariants. The transformation function between interface elements and table columns described above is an inductive invariant. Using this function, we can design the interface based on an Object-Relational Schema in the form of a complete invariant scheme.

Such a definition of the interface development process as a sequential application of the transformation function defined by inductive invariants allows us to state that the final state of the interface will fully correspond to the data model. That provides the ability to automate the process of developing interfaces and their adaptation in the case of a change in the structure of relational tables, since it is tied not to the structure of the table as a whole, but to separated invariants (columns).

As a result, the process of the interface development in form of composition of the invariants can be described in pseudo-code as follows (Fig. 2).

```
...
foreach column_invariant do
   foreach interface_invariant do
      if mapping_function(column_invariant) == interface_invariant then
         add interface_invariant onto GUI
...
```

Fig. 2. Pseudo-code description of algorithm within the approach proposed

In this case we sort through all the invariants of the columns of the Object-Relational schema and look for a correspondence among the invariants of the interface. If a match is found, the corresponding interface invariant is added to the display. Otherwise, the transition to the next interface invariant occurs.

4   Application to the Admissions Committee Domain

The application process in higher education organizations should be as simple and fast as possible and meet all the criteria for agility. The information system, which supports that process, contains about 50 relational tables (containing from 4 to 30 attributes) connected by more than 80 relationships.

The set of necessary analytical indicators expands every year according to the modification of the admission rules, that results in a change of the data set collected during the admission process.

In these conditions, it is a critical need for continuous refinement of not only the Object-Relational Schema of data collected in the admission process, but also user interfaces. In accordance with the previously described approach, it is necessary to distinguish the invariants at the level of the Object-Relational Schema, associate them with the invariants at the interface level and implement the mapping function between them.

The invariants that stand out at the level of the Object-Relational Schema were discussed in the previous section, so here we focus only on their practical implementation. It is important to note that although we have identified the table column as an invariant (namely, its type), the specific implementation of this invariant differs depending on the database management system (DBMS) chosen.

In our case, the DBMS MS SQL Server is used, therefore we will consider the main data types specific to this environment. Based on the data schema described in Fig. 1, we can identify the main types of data necessary for the task: int, float, date, etc.

After the invariants are defined at the level of the Object-Relational Schema, it is necessary to distinguish the corresponding invariants at the interface level. As noted earlier, an interface is a collection of interconnected components, each of which is tied to a corresponding data block. For the convenience of the user, it seems useful that the invariant for each individual data type contains not only the value of the corresponding data type, but also the name of the column from which this data is extracted. In this way, the user can see not only the value, but also understand which name column of which table it refers to. As a result, editing values and their processing become more understandable.

Based on this idea, a set of the object invariants was developed at the interface level in accordance with the relational invariant (Fig. 3 demonstrates the example of int invariant). These invariants are fully consistent with the previously identified structure and formalization of invariants.

NameOfElement

Fig. 3. A visual invariant at the interface layer for the int type relational invariant

The invariant system developed is complete and fully consistent with the invariants identified at the level of the Object-Relational Schema. Also, this invariant system is stable, because it is not tied to the structure of tables of the real-time model, but only to data types, which makes it easily scalable.

After the system of invariants is developed, it remains only to determine the correspondence function between them. This function determines which invariant of the Object-Relational Schema was input, and finds the corresponding interface level invariant. Taking into account that the development of the system is carried out in Java (and patterns are written in Java FX), the part of the function may look as follows (Fig. 4).

```
switch (typePattern) {
  case "boolean":
    loader.setLocation(getClass().getResource("BoolInputPattern.fxml"));
    ...
    break;
  case "date":
    loader.setLocation(getClass().getResource("DateInputPattern.fxml"));
    ...
    break;
  ...
}
```

Fig. 4. A part of the transformation function between invariants

An important result of such a structure is its adaptability. Due to the interconnection of invariants, the interface is built dynamically in real time, without the need for its design and manual programming.

In our case, the interface is a table that displays data from the corresponding database table, as well as fields for interacting with them (adding, editing). Both interface elements are built dynamically as a result of reading the structure of the corresponding table, which the user can select preliminarily (Fig. 5). Using this interface, the user can view, and also add and process data for all applicants in the database. The left part of the interface is a table showing all the data on applicants, while the right panel serves to interact with the content.

We developed a block that allows the end user to make changes to the structure of the database tables. This interface supports the following operations: creating a new table, creating a table based on existing ones (with the ability to select columns), dividing the table into several related ones, editing the structure of existing tables, etc. In the first case, the user determines the name of the table being created, as well as a list of its columns. In the second case, when creating a table, one or several existing tables are taken as the basis, from which columns are selected, the equivalents of which should be created in the new one. It is important to note that in this case the data from the linked columns of the original tables is also copied to the new one, thus the transfer of the data as well as the structure is achieved.

In the case of editing the table structure, we can change its name, as well as change the columns by adding or removing them, changing the type or name. To demonstrate the adaptability of the interface we created, let us add a new column to the table with a list of applicants: the registration code (Fig. 5).

This code contains the encoded representation of information about the applicant. It is calculated on the basis of the general data of the applicant, the number of his competitive points, etc.

After the new attribute is added, we verify that the original interface has adapted to the new table structure (Fig. 6). As we can see, the structure of the GUI has adapted to the changed structure of the database table, as well as all input fields of the interface also now correspond to the new structure. Moreover, we can interact with the modified

Fig. 5. A part of the GUI, responsible for Object-Relational Schema adaptation

table, for example, enter a value for the applicant in the added column. As a result of the input, we obtain a new state of the interface (Fig. 6).

Fig. 6. The part of the GUI after update of data in added column

As a result of the application of our approach the interface is fully adapted to the new structure. Most importantly, we did not manually make any changes to the program code or to the structure of relational tables. All changes are made through the interface. This allows users to make the system fully adaptable and customizable, without the need for special skills in programming and designing Object-Relational Schemas. Such flexibility is achieved by introducing into the software prototype mechanisms of invariants that are unchanged with any change in the system as a whole. As a result, any change in both the structure of tables and the interface is described in terms of invariants. And the interface itself is built dynamically based on an updated set of table invariants. This significantly reduces the time required to adapt a data-based system and allows end users to be involved in this process.

5   Conclusion

Lean adoption is a trend in many domains, from enterprises to small academic projects [18]. Since many enterprises are automated and use various software systems, agility results in the need for a mechanism to adapt the interfaces of these systems to the requirements of end users to improve efficiency and simplify human-cyber interaction.

This article examines the process of adapting interfaces by introducing invariant mechanisms. The approach is based on the idea that any user interface in accordance with an object-oriented paradigm can be represented as a composition of objects corresponding to individual components of the system. Each such object is an object invariant, since it is preserved when any changes are made to the system and interface. This is possible, since any interface can be considered as a special kind of domain-specific language. As a result, all methods specific to the adaptation of DSL are applicable to it.

This ability to automatically adapt the interface is important in the context of enterprise digitalization and agility. It is especially important in the case of the introduction of different smart systems and the organization of interaction with the end user [2].

On the other hand, any interface is tied to a certain set of data that can be described as an Object-Relational Schema. At the level of the Object-Relational Schema, we can also distinguish invariants that are unchanged during its evolution. Such invariants are table columns and their types.

By mapping these invariants with each other, it is possible to automate the interface development by means of a correspondence function that reads the invariant of the Object-Relational Schema and displays the corresponding interface level invariant. As a result, the need to manually create an interface disappears, since it is built as a composition of individual invariants in real time. Such automation is achieved due to the fact that the interface is constructed as a superposition of object invariants. As a result, the interface structure is dynamically built in real time based on the data structure.

In comparison with existing solutions [5, 8, 10], the approach proposed allows developers to fully automate the process of making changes to the Object-Relational Schema. This extends the adaptation capabilities described in [8], since our approach does not require the preservation of the data structure used by the interface, but allows them to be changed in real time. Our case shows that the need to interact with developers to change the data structure is completely eliminated. Furthermore, the proposed approach allows users to implement all the changes without programming skills, since all work is carried out through the interface.

In further research it is planned to expand the set of supported functions for managing the Object-Relational Schema, making it more complete. This will fully ensure the entire cycle of work with the Object-Relational Schema via the interface, without the need for preliminary database creation, even in the initial version.

References

1. Heavin, C., Power, D.J.: Challenges for digital transformation – towards a conceptual decision support guide for managers. J. Decis. Syst. **27**(1), 38–45 (2018)
2. Ruffolo, M., Sidhu, I., Guadagno, L.: Semantic enterprise technologies. In: Proceedings of the First International Conference on Industrial Results of Semantic Technologies, vol. 293, pp. 70–84 (2007)
3. Hayat, S.A.E., Toufik, F., Bahaj, M.: UML/OCL based design and the transition towards temporal object relational database with bitemporal data. J. King Saud Univ. Comput. Inf. Sci. **32**(4), 398–407 (2020)

4. Bashir, R.S., Lee, S.P., Khan, S.U.R., Chang, V., Farid, S.: UML models consistency management: guidelines for software quality manager. Int. J. Inf. Manag. **36**(6), 883–899 (2016)
5. Lazareva, O.F., McInnerney, J., Williams, T.: Implicit relational learning in a multiple-object tracking task. Behav. Proc. **152**, 26–36 (2018)
6. Wu, Y., Mu, T., Liatsis, P., Goulermas, J.Y.: Computation of heterogeneous object co-embeddings from relational measurements. Pattern Recogn. **65**, 146–163 (2017)
7. Torres, A., Galante, R., Pimenta, M.S., Martins, A.J.B.: Twenty years of object-relational mapping: a survey on patterns, solutions, and their implications on application design. Inf. Softw. Technol. **82**, 1–18 (2017)
8. Wang, N., Wang, D., Zhang, Y.: Design of an adaptive examination system based on artificial intelligence recognition model. Mech. Syst. Signal Process. **142**, 1–14 (2020)
9. Konyrbaev, N.B., Ibadulla, S.I., Diveev, A.I.: Evolutionary methods for creating artificial intelligence of robotic technical systems. Procedia Comput. Sci. **150**, 709–715 (2019)
10. Leung, Y.: Artificial Intelligence and Expert Systems. In: International Encyclopedia of Human Geography, 2nd Edn., pp. 209–215 (2020)
11. Golobisky, M.F., Vecchietti, A.: Mapping UML class diagrams into object-relational schemas. In: Proceedings of Argentine Symposium on Software Engineering, pp. 65–79 (2005)
12. Köhler, H., Link, S.: SQL schema design: foundations, normal forms, and normalization. Inf. Syst. **76**, 88–113 (2018)
13. Chen, Y., Tang, Z.: Vector invariant fields of finite classical groups. J. Algebra **534**, 129–144 (2019)
14. Carvalho, J.F., Pequito, S., Aguiar, A.P., Kar, S., Johansson, K.H.: Composability and controllability of structural linear time-invariant systems: distributed verification. Automatica **78**, 123–134 (2017)
15. SQL Standard 2016 (ISO/IEC 9075-1:2016). https://www.iso.org/committee/45342/x/catalogue/p/1/u/0/w/0/d/0
16. Ulitin, B., Babkin, E., Babkina, T.: A projection-based approach for development of domain-specific languages. In: Zdravkovic, J., Grabis, J., Nurcan, S., Stirna, J. (eds.) BIR 2018. LNBIP, vol. 330, pp. 219–234. Springer, Cham (2018). https://doi.org/10.1007/978-3-319-99951-7_15
17. Ulitin, B., Babkin, E., Babkina, T., Vizgunov, A.: Automated formal verification of model transformations using the invariants mechanism. In: Pańkowska, M., Sandkuhl, K. (eds.) BIR 2019. LNBIP, vol. 365, pp. 59–73. Springer, Cham (2019). https://doi.org/10.1007/978-3-030-31143-8_5
18. Küpper, S., Kuhrmann, M., Wiatrok, M., Andelfinger, U., Rausch, A.: Is there a blueprint for building an agile culture? In: Projektmanagement und Vorgehensmodelle 2017-Die Spannung zwischen dem Prozess und den Mensch im Projekt (2017)

Usability Evaluation of Business Process Modeling Standards – BPMN and BORM Case Study

Josef Pavlicek[1](✉) ⓘ, Martin Rod[2] ⓘ, and Petra Pavlickova[1] ⓘ

[1] Faculty of Information Technology, CTU, Thakurova 9, Prague 6–Dejvice, 166 00 Prague, Czech Republic
{Josef.Pavlicek,Petra.Pavlickova}@fit.cvut.cz
[2] Department of Information Engineering, Czech University of Life Sciences Prague, Prague, Kamycka 959, Prague 165 00, Czech Republic
rodm@pef.czu.cz

Abstract. This paper deals with the main criteria which affect the usability of business process modeling standards. This is achieved through a comparison between two of the main processes modeling standards – BPMN and BORM in the form of a usability study. Paper presents the adequate methods used to compare the usability that builds upon the ISO/IEC 25066 for usability reporting. The study is based in a suitable laboratory environment and proposes the case study model which could be then extended and generalized. The results from the two case studies performed show significant differences between the BPMN and BORM.

Keywords: BPMN · BORM · Usability study · Process modeling standards

1 Introduction

Over the years our team has addressed many issues regarding the quality of process models that have been published at EOMAS [1, 2], but also in journals and scientific articles [3–8]. We discussed the BPMN (Business Process Model and Notation) in respect to its notation part in detail [9, 10]. Our team has proposed methods to measure and qualitatively verify the quality of process models [3]. We have demonstrated the possibility of using well-known techniques to follow the classical usability study method as reported by Jacob Nielsen and his team [15, 16]. In addition to this approach, we suggested using methods published by Josef Pavlíček and Rudolf Bock [17]. Unlike conducting a usability study by Jacob Nielsen, we work with multiple concurrent participants in the study. This type of study is called collaborative and enables a new view on how to assess usability. We have designed the collaborative title and its sense [17] based on experience from our numerous studies to this date. These have demonstrated effective interaction between participants during the study.

© Springer Nature Switzerland AG 2021
A. Polyvyanyy and S. Rinderle-Ma (Eds.): CAiSE 2021 Workshops, LNBIP 423, pp. 93–104, 2021.
https://doi.org/10.1007/978-3-030-79022-6_9

1.1 On Business Process Modeling

BPMN is one of the most prominent standards for modeling the process, which also spawned multiple BPMN extensions and add-ons. However, other standards or at least notations and techniques exist, such as BPML, ARIS, or YAWL which are generally more domain specialized. The BORM (Business Objects Relation Modelling) methodology is yet another instance, which has been built, but also thoroughly utilized upon the Object-Oriented Programming paradigm (OOP). BORM development and its structure are envisioned as the solid link, which connects the domain of business process modeling to software engineering. For basic information and comparison between BPMN and BORM see Table 1.

Whereas the advantages and drawbacks could be possibly derived from the structure of those two approaches at least one aspect would be missing. BPMN and BORM could be used as enablers for Model-driven architecture, but in that aspect, it is not only about the models, it also about the people e.g. consultants, enterprise architects, software engineers who use those models. In this paper, we delve into the usability of BPMN and BORM models in correspondence to their way of usage.

Table 1. BPMN and BORM

BPMN	BORM
Very recent Business modeling technique	The quite old technique was implemented in the early 1990s, based on the OOP/ORD platform
Based on UML and XML. However, the scheme is not defined by the reference model. The fact that this scheme is implemented in some cases does not mean that it is original part of BPMN	It was showed, that stakeholders from the problem domain can understand the BORM approach very quickly, normally within an hour of introduction at the start of the analysis is enough
Designed as a graphical visualization of business processes	BORM **provides** greater **support for pure object-oriented concepts** like **refactoring** which are an integral part of the BORM development process
MDA approved and OMG standard	**Not approved** as an OMG **standard**. We can perceive this as a drawback

1.2 Usability Study as a Mean for BPMN and BORM Assessment

For the usability testing, we decided to use the collaborative approach with cognitive walkthrough. The collaborative approach focuses on the interaction of participants with the problem addressed [17]. To achieve this, the environment in which the participants are placed must be appropriately oriented. A HUBRU usability laboratory [17] located on CULS, Czechia, is provided for this purpose. The eye tracking system (which is part of HUBRU environment) also strengthens the qualitative outcome of the study, where the participants' statements obtained by the final interview are supported by a record of eye movement. Also, we have presented this practice in previous work, see for instance [1–8].

Several interesting effects could be observed during the study. These can be classified by the following scale of state of mind:

- **Uncertainty** – originates either in a wrong assignment, or a lack of participant's mental capacity during a task, or an error in usability. Uncertainty manifests itself in the effort to cooperate with "copying" from colleagues sitting side by side.
- **Disruption** – the participant is surprised by the GUI response and falls out of concentration. It manifests itself either by voice expression or very often by facial expression.
- **Block** – the participant is unable to continue. This is either due to a serious mistake in entering the test scenario, or a manifest violation of the participant's mental model by responding to the graphical interface.
- **Frustration** – its manifestation is loud commenting on the currently solved task. Furthermore, the collaborative approach allows the study to be conducted using the:
- **Heuristic** – monitoring whether the participant goes through all steps of the test scenario in the required order and is not disturbed by improper GUI behavior.
- **Cognitive** – observing if the user interface is sufficient to perform the test task. We are more interested in whether it will intuitively reveal (or whether its GUI itself will guide) the correct path and solve the task.

In the Collaborative Approach, we also find the possibility of so-called pair testing [5, 6], where one task is solved by a pair of participants. Their interaction is required. Collaborative testing or a mix of collaborative and classic testing enables us to answer our research questions, (Table 2).

Table 2. Proposed research questions.

Research question	The wording of the question
RQ1	What is the user-friendliness of business process modelling tools?
RQ2	What is the significant benefit of BPMN in terms of usability?
RQ3	What is the significant benefit of BORM in terms of usability?
RQ4	When it is appropriate to use BPMN and when BORM?

These research questions are important for the aspect of correct usage and targeting of those models and are yet to be answered. A similar problem is currently going through conceptual modeling tools such as OntoUML [12] and UML [13].

If the issue is further explored, we will probably conclude that important attributes such as usability, clarity, user-friendliness, compete with:

- availability of information on the relevant methodology,
- habits of the environment in which we implement the solution (corporate culture),
- **the size of the community using the technology,**
- **user friendliness at a glance,**
- **references to implemented solutions,**
- **market requirements for designer** certification.

Those above mentioned metrics are either based or derived as the related factors from the standard of the usability reporting, ISO/IEC 25066: for usability reporting. This concrete standard of the SQuaRE standard family was chosen as it provides the insight and common ground for qualitative usability testing.

2   Materials and Methods

To determine the scale, we can determine the quality of the BPMN and BORM standards, we must define the basic attributes of the measurement. Here we suggest inspiring the Nielsen Norman Group [15]. This approach corresponds with mentioned qualitative measurements and its reporting standardized in the ISO/IEC 25066.

Usability could be defined as [15] *"A quality attribute that assesses how easy user interfaces are to use. The word "usability" also refers to methods for improving ease-of-use during the design process".*

Usability has five attributes [15]:

- **Learnability:** How easy is it for users to accomplish basic tasks the first time they encounter the design?
- **Efficiency:** Once users have learned the design, how quickly can they perform tasks?
- **Memorability:** When users return to the design after a period of not using it, how easily can they re-establish proficiency?
- **Errors:** How many errors do users make, how severe are these errors, and how easily can they recover from the errors?
- **Satisfaction:** How pleasant is it to use the design?

The Usability test [15–17] was performed according to the Collaborative Testing Guidelines [1, 17] in the Usability Lab [17] by the method of collecting defined measurement attributes. This was successfully used to design the quality of process models [1–7]. The usability test has also been enhanced with Eye tracking, which is currently supported by Tobii Tech. The tool is part of HUBRU [17] and the results from its activities we published at previous papers on EOMAS (2016–2018).

2.1   Laboratory Measurement Architecture

The HUBRU usability lab used for research had the following architectural setup: Observation room: 4 environmental camcorders, 10 personal computers (PC) with face camcorder, screen and voice recording, 2 of the ten PC equipped with eye-tracking. Control room: Recorders for all PC, control monitors, etc.

2.2 Usability Test

The usability test was performed based on heuristic – collaborative testing. An appropriate group of participants has been selected for the prepared tasks [1]. A test of the design of a Turkish Airlines model process model was carried out with them.

2.3 Research Methods

The research method selected (usability testing) was qualitative, this method provided information on BPMN and BORM usability UI Study via the following:

- usability test according to usability testing rules [15, 16],
- collection of information from participants after the usability test

  - study the answers,
  - define the truthfulness of the statement based on the correlation of correct answers,
  - exclusion of samples due to misunderstanding by the participant,

- interview of each participant on the knowledge of usability and improvement ideas.

2.4 Participants in the Study

The method used to obtain participants was based on the snowball method. All of the referred, to-be participants for the study, were firstly asked about their experience in the field of the software engineering and system development. Only those who met the criterion of having academic background in those field or sufficient praxis were selected for the usability study.

2.5 Usability Testing Focus

The usability test was conducted in the Czech University of Life Sciences, at the collaborative Usability laboratory called HUBRU [17]. The research was based on participants running usability tests relating to typical real-life situations by focusing on documenting the processes involved in real-life testing. Two scenarios were chosen: ticket booking and reservation, on a selected airline company (Turkish airlines) and exam registration on the University information system (UIS).

The participants worked in a collaborative mode. By this, we mean the test in which they could advise each other. Interactions between them were allowed. However, everyone worked for themselves and handed over a test scenario as an individual. This method will significantly accelerate the usability study without losing qualitative power. Unlike paired usability testing [5, 6], where the result of a consensus discussion is a pair, each participant is responsible for his response. In case we need to follow the classical Jacob Nielsen [15, 16] procedure, but to be faster, the collaborative procedure of the recommendation is a good method.

The number of participants in both studies was 10. Jacob Nielsen demonstrated that the number of 8 participants is sufficiently conclusive to detect 80% of usability errors

[15]. We tested 8 participants with a collaborative (de facto-derived classical method of Jacob Nielsen), plus two workstations equipped with an eye motion-sensing system. At the end of the study, all participants in the final interview interviewed methodological questions:

1. **What was great during the study** (we are trying to positively tune the participants to the answers, often frustrating the failure of the test or unnecessary self-criticism, which then prevents objective answers and intuitively tends to more critical response.
2. **What was explicitly wrong** (we get test results and compare with assumed hypotheses).
3. **What you would recommend** (frequently, participants have recommendations, ideas, improvements, but it is neither a mistake nor great functionality. The recommendation will allow us to better understand the participant's mental model and empathize with the answer. In the case of a process model study, they can explain why a participant stopped at a specific symbol and assessed it.

Table 3. Usability task scenarios

Scenario – Turkish Airlines		Scenario – Exam registration	
Step	Task	Step	Task
1	Open any web browser, go to http://www.turkishairlines.com	1	Open any browser
2	Select book a flight, Enter your departure city as Prague and arrival destination (Lagos Nigeria)	2	Go to http://is.czu.cz (university information system, called UIS)
3	Select the date of your choice, select one adult, return ticket, economy	3	Select log in to personal administration of UIS
4	Click on the Search, Select the cheapest flights from search results, select for both going and coming back	4	Log-in using the provided student username and password
5	Click on continue, fill the form, uncheck seat reservation boxes in blue	5	Go to the section student's portal
6	Click on continue to payment	6	Select from the table Register for the examination
7	Select reserve this flight and pay later	7	If exams are available to select subject, check the date and time of the exam

(continued)

Table 3. (*continued*)

Scenario – Turkish Airlines		Scenario – Exam registration	
Step	Task	Step	Task
8	Accept terms and conditions, reservation completed	8	Register for an exam
9	Now repeat steps 5 and 6	9	If no exams are available to for registering log out
10	Select payment card. proceed to payment	10	End
11	End		

2.6 Diagrams Used for the Turkish Airlines Scenario

If we study the motion camera recording, gaze points denotes as circles, movement by linking those gaze points (Fig. 1), and we combine both participants into one graph, we can compare the passage through the test scenario. It is clear from the record that both participants in this role proceeded very similarly. However, the parallel with the graphic symbol of the database is interesting (it is not quite traditional and is missing in the general control graphs). Another interesting feature is the grey rectangle Destination, date, and airline. On it, they spent a little time on the participant.

Looking at the result of the passage of both participants through the BORM process model (Fig. 2), we notice a very natural sequence of reading the graph from left to right. This arrangement perfectly matches the mental model of users who are trained in reading from left to right. This arrangement would certainly bring several problems to readers with other additions, typically reading from right to left. The time sequence is also very natural when the first activities are located at the top of the screen and the end of the screen. While this BPMN notation does not require.

An interesting finding is the delay of the participants in directional arrows between the models. It is an atypical symbol. At the moment of its understanding by the participant, this problem is no longer necessary. Attention is also drawn to the fact that participant B progressed less conceptually and skipped the graph. That was confirmed during the study by correlating the test results and by comparing the responses in the final interview.

As can be seen on Fig. 3, both participants spend time on the decision block (diamond symbol). Participant D left the screen (top right corner). The reason is unknown. We did not encounter this problem during the interview. Participant D also did not mention this moment. The camera was exported later, and we no longer have a reference to this phenomenon. Probably the participant was disturbed by some external influence.

It is also apparent that symbols with long text (**Login in using student username and password**) take up time. Participants logically spend more time on them. Participant C probably calibrated the ophthalmic camera poorly, and his focus target was shifted down the screen. This is confirmed by the large red circle under the decision block.

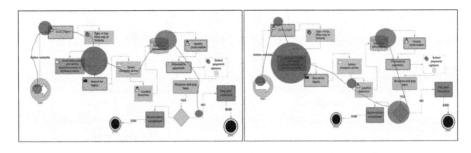

Participant A   Participant B

Fig. 1. Combined chart of eye camera record of both participants for BPMN.

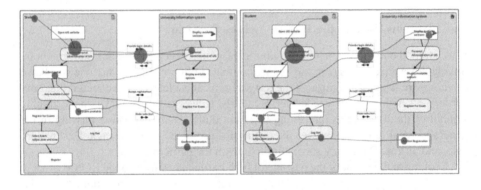

Participant A   Participant B

Fig. 2. Combined chart of eye camera record of both participants for BORM.

Another point of interest is that the black plus symbol on the edge is skipped by the participants. The hypotheses are: a) Participants at the beginning of the model did not expect complexity. b) Participants did not notice the symbol. Both of those hypotheses were then verified during the interview phase of the study.

2.7 Diagrams Used for the Exam Registration Scenario

The combined graph (Fig. 4) shows how the navigation arrows between each participating actor are complicated. In all recorded cases, the participants spent time understanding the symbol. Another interesting thing is that Participant C progressed from the top down at the University information system, but then returned to the Student back in time. The Login to Personal administration of UIS was probably not clear. Arrows to navigate the user in both directions fulfill their role in a limited or non-existent way. Participant D has misunderstood the arrow symbols and started to jump between them. Thus, he lost the natural sequence of reading the graph. In the final interview, Participant D expressed negative feelings to BORM notation. He feels BPMN is more natural.

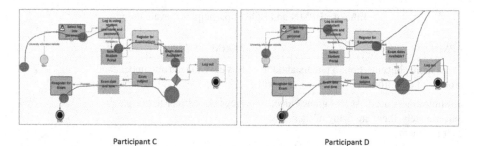

Participant C   Participant D

Fig. 3. Combined chart of eye camera record of both participants for BPMN.

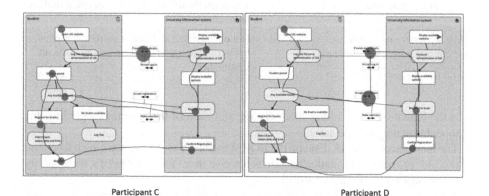

Participant C   Participant D

Fig. 4. Combined chart of eye camera record of both participants for BORM.

3   Results

The study was conducted in two days' time frame. On the first day, 10 participants were studied, and we dealt with the problem of ordering tickets. On the second day, a group of 8 participants took part in enrolling in the university system.

All information obtained from the study (Table 4) were used to evaluate those two standards. Thus, we have been able to determine and document the underlying differences between BPMN and BORM business models. These differences make the two business models unique in their way.

3.1   Limitations of the Study

The main limitations that need to be addressed with correspondence to the reliability of the study results are presented in the following list:

- One major limitation to this research was the lack of materials from different authors or previous work to help in further understanding the BORM methodology, this limited review, and research regarding the BORM methodology.
- The BORM method is mostly applied in The Czech Republic and some parts of the EU, which makes it difficult to get materials to talk on the subject as matter, as there

Table 4. BPMN and BORM participants' evaluation.

BPMN	BORM
Takes more concentration to understand the process of the information	It is easy to read and understand
Multiple colors used. At first glance nice, unfortunately, there are many of them and it distracts them	Steps were faster to grasp.
Some symbols are difficult to read, respectively understand	The chart is straightforward but may need better improvement via colors
Why is there a database symbol?	The suggestion is to add colors to make BORM more attractive
Here we focus on the process flow, why is the conceptual symbol used here?	Not complicated and can be easily interpreted, but the arrows (relations) can be a bit difficult to decipher

is the limitation to the use of the software, and most of the resources regarding this model is mainly by one author
- The majority of the work done on the BORM method was done in the Czech Republic this also proves as a limitation as it does not give room for opinions of a wide variety of scholars in the Academic world.
- A lot of other would-be good materials on the BORM method were in the Czech language, this was disadvantageous to a foreigner trying to do more research on the BORM method.

4   Discussion

Our knowledge-based hypotheses acquired and presented from past years have been confirmed by EOMAS [1, 2], below [4–8]. The fact that the more complex a graphic symbol (or a symbol that has many possible meanings) is undoubtedly a growing burden on the user to understand the symbol. Such a burden is not a problem if time and, above all, enthusiasm is to study it. Of course, basic building elements such as deciding whether parallel branching remains constant. The construction of iteration and parallel processes is more problematic. Here the difficulty increases.

Another problem of process models, in general, is their very weak physical ties to the realization of the final solution. Here BORM is certainly not a BPMN competitor. After all, some of the modern technologies (such as IBM Lombardi) allow BPMN notation and a truly real business process to be realized through BPMN and its digital conversion to the Workflow organization.

Drawbacks
The disadvantage of evaluating the quality of process models in the form of a usability study is the orientation towards the process model or final process model consumer. Thus, we always face the question of how the final process model is implemented in

the organization [14]. However, it is necessary to note: it is probably not possible to consider the process modeling tool as poor in the case when the process model was created perfectly, but its implementation was not carried out carefully in the processes of the organization. This is obvious logical nonsense. Therefore, if the process tool is easy to use and if it covers all the functions necessary for process modeling, then we can understand it as usable.

The scientific community is also not entirely open to methods of qualitative research in terms of usability. Although Jacob Nielsen [16] convincingly proves that 8 participants tested qualitatively are enough to recognize 80% of the quality of the model, the critics consider them to be a small number. This fact reduces the reliability of the test results. If we connect it with the fact that the required definition of processes according to the ISO standard is in fact only paper, then we concluded that self-improved testing will not solve the company's business problem based on ignoring the proposed processes. And another important fact is that many companies have intuitively functional processes and their model in the given methodology is only their representation, which is no longer worked with. However, the development of technologies and the development of remote testing (thanks to the current COVID-19 situation) makes it relatively easy to distribute tests. This extension can then bring significant insights into the quality of the process model versus the quantity of its testing.

5 Conclusion

The conclusions can be summarized as follows:

- BPMN It is easy to use and understandable for non-technical people.
- BPMN is intuitive and directive due to the shapes and many colors that can be applied to make it more explanatory, which can reduce communication time and fast implementation of the model.
- The BORM is popularly used by software analysts/engineers.
- BORM is a suitable tool for engineers who want to touch the process model in greater depth and follow the object paradigm. While BPMN is virtually structural, reps. imperative (command, flow, command), BORM better displays the object properties of the process model, messaging and covers the necessary refactoring.

Digitization of processes is a key point of business strategies of companies as well as organizations, both budget and contributory (schools, ministries, citizens' associations). BORM is undoubtedly a suitable candidate here. Its readability and usability from the point of view of process modelers is intuitive. Its conversion to digital form and automation is possible. The disadvantage of BORM is currently a relatively small community. Standardization of BORM at ISO level would also be beneficial.

BPMN is the notation of the present. It is implemented by various tools such as IBM Lombardi, etc.

The method of verifying the quality of process modeling tools in the form of a usability test is applicable. The results of the study show that both measured BMPN and BORM notations bring process modelers the benefits defined by authors of methodologies.

References

1. Pavlicek, J., Hronza, R., Pavlickova, R., Jelinkova, K.: The business process model quality metrics. In: Workshop on Enterprise and Organizational Modeling and Simulation, pp. 134–148, EOMAS, Springer International Publishing (2017). ISBN: 978-3-319-68184-9. https://doi.org/10.1007/978-3-319-68185-6_10
2. Pavlicek, J., Hronza, R., Pavlickova, P.: Educational Business process model skills improvement. In: Pergl, R., Molhanec, M., Babkin, E., Fosso Wamba, S. (eds.) EOMAS 2016. LNBIP, vol. 272, pp. 172–184. Springer, Cham (2016). https://doi.org/10.1007/978-3-319-49454-8_12
3. Hronza, R., Pavlíček, J., Náplava, P.: Míry kvality procesních modelů vytvořených v notaci BPMN. Acta Inform. Pragensia 4(2), 140–153 (2015)
4. Jelínková, K.: Návrh měr kvality obchodních procesních modelů, Czech Technical University in Prague (2017)
5. Lassaková, M.: Návrh a tvorba měr pro výpočet kvality procesních modelů, Czech Technical University in Prague (2016)
6. Neumann, M.: Míry kvality procesních modelů Czech Technical University in Prague (2016)
7. Hronza, R., Pavlíček, J., Mach, R., Náplava, P.: Míry kvality v procesním modelování. Acta Inform. Pragensia 4(1), 18–29 (2015)
8. Mach, R.: Návrh a tvorba nástroje pro optimalizaci procesů na základě analýzy BPM modelů, Czech Technical University in Prague (2015)
9. Bruce, S.: BPMN method and style. Cody-Cassidy Press (2011)
10. OMG, Business Process Model & Notation (BPMN) (2016). http://www.omg.org/bpmn/index.htm. Accessed 21 Mar 2017
11. Knott, R., Merunka, V., Polak, J.: The BORM methodology: a third-generation fully object-oriented. Knowl.-Based Syst. (2003). https://doi.org/10.1016/S0950-7051(02)00075-8
12. Bassetto, L.: OntoUML Specification. http://ontology.com.br/ontouml/spec/
13. OMG, Unified Modeling Language (UML) (2008). http://www.uml.org.
14. Náplava, P., Pergl, R.: Empirical study of applying the DEMO method for improving BPMN process models in academic environment. In: Proceedings of the 17th IEEE Conference on Business Informatics. IEEE Operations Center, Piscataway, pp. 18–26 (2015). ISBN 978–1–4673–7340–1
15. Nielsen Norman Group, Evidence-Based User Experience Research. https://www.nngroup.com/
16. Nielsen, J.: Why you only need to test with 5 users, 19, 1–4 (2000)
17. Pavlicek, J., Bock, R.: Collaborative Usability lab design and methodology to use that, part of HUBRU (2017). https://www.hubru.pef.czu.cz/

BC4IS

BC4IS 2021 Preface

Blockchain technology offers a wide variety of opportunities to enable new kinds of collaborations and organizations, and to improve existing ones. However, engineering blockchain-based systems is a task that is particularly complex, and that requires specific considerations, along with more traditional information systems engineering questions. In this context, research around the definition of requirements for, development, use, and evolution of blockchain-based information systems is particularly relevant.

These opportunities and challenges have generated a strong and continuously growing interest from industry and academia in the engineering of blockchain-based information systems. To help further expand knowledge around this technology and to provide relevant answers to blockchain-specific engineering questions, we organized the first edition of the International Workshop on Blockchain for Information Systems (BC4IS).

The workshop was held in conjunction with the 33rd International Conference on Advanced Information Systems Engineering (CAiSE 2021). It is a well-established and highly visible conference series, addressing contemporary topics in information systems engineering.

We invited researchers working in fields including conceptual modeling, ontology engineering, business process modeling and analysis, and information systems to submit their contributions to the workshop. Four papers were submitted, and each received two single blind reviews. A meta-review of each paper was then prepared by the workshop chairs and sent to the authors. Taking into consideration the reviews and the maximum acceptance rate of Springer (set around 50% in this case), two papers were accepted and presented during the workshop.

Considering the ongoing COVID-19 pandemic, the workshop could not be held physically and had to be organized remotely. This challenging situation didn't prevent the workshop from being a rich experience leading to interesting presentations and discussions.

As chairs of the BC4IS workshop, we would like to express our gratitude to the chairs of the CAiSE conference, to all the people that contributed to the organization of the workshop, and to the authors for their valuable contributions.

June 2021

Sarah Bouraga
Victor Amaral de Sousa

BC4IS 2021 Organization

Workshop Chairs

Sarah Bouraga   University of Namur, Belgium
Victor Amaral de Sousa   University of Namur, Belgium
Corentin Burnay   University of Namur, Belgium

Steering Committee

Monique Snoeck   KU Leuven, Belgium
Stéphane Faulkner   University of Namur, Belgium
Ivan J. Jureta   FNRS and University of Namur, Belgium
Wim Laurier   University of Saint-Louis - Brussels, Belgium

Program Committee

Pierluigi Plebani   Polytechnic University of Milan, Italy
Ghareeb Falazi   University of Stuttgart, Germany
Nicolas Six   University Paris 1 Panthéon-Sorbonne, France
Orlenys López-Pintado   University of Tartu, Estonia
Jan Mendling   Vienna University of Economics and Business,
                                   Austria
Michael Adams   Queensland University of Technology,
                                   Australia
Jean-Noël Colin   University of Namur, Belgium
Haris Mouratidis   University of Brighton, UK
Michael Verdonck   Ghent University, Belgium
Giovanni Meroni   Polytechnic University of Milan, Italy
Andreas Veneris   University of Toronto, Canada
Jan Ladleif   Potsdam University, Germany

Ontology-Driven Audit Using the REA-Ontology

Graham Gal[1]([⊠]) [iD], Monique Snoeck[2] [iD], and Wim Laurier[3] [iD]

[1] Isenberg School of Management,
University of Massachusetts Amherst, Amherst, MA 01003, USA
gfgal@isenberg.umass.edu
[2] Research Centre for Information Systems Engineering (LIRIS), KU Leuven, Leuven, Belgium
monique.snoeck@kuleuven.be
[3] NODES, Université Saint-Louis–Bruxelles, Brussels, Belgium
wim.laurier@usaintlouis.be

Abstract. While blockchains are not yet ubiquitous in business practice, they are expected to serve as a platform to handle an increasing number of business transactions in a not-too-distant future. Smart contracts can be used to code and to enforce agreements between business parties. A significant difference between traditional and smart contracts is that once the actual events of the smart contract become part of a block in the blockchain, they are almost impossible to undo. Therefore, it is important that critical validity aspects of these smart contracts are explicitly represented. As smart contracts are software products too, it is therefore also critical that the coding of these critical validity aspects guarantees a faithful implementation of the validity checks. This paper suggests applying a combination of two approaches (i.e., ontology engineering and model-driven engineering) to the design and the implementation of smart contracts, in order to facilitate their audit through a clear separation of concerns. More precisely, this paper discusses the example of the REA ontology to provide the ontological commitment of the critical validity aspects of a contract, while MDE provides a tool to unambiguously translate the REA ontology's contracting terms into a well-designed Smart Contract. This paper suggests that the resulting Smart Contract can support auditors' assertions regarding exchanges between business partners and support the audit process.

Keywords: Software audit · Model-driven engineering · Ontology · Smart contracts

1 Introduction

As part of the audit of a company's financial statements, the independent auditor conducts a substantive audit of account balances and a compliance test of controls over the processes that create these balances [1]. Auditing Statement (AS) 5 requires two types of control reviews [2]. First is the design of the controls (para. 42–43) and second is their operational effectiveness (para. 44–45). For certain types of processes, such as computer mediated processes, the testing of the design becomes crucial as deploying flawed software can result in ubiquitous errors across all of a business's operations.

© Springer Nature Switzerland AG 2021
A. Polyvyanyy and S. Rinderle-Ma (Eds.): CAiSE 2021 Workshops, LNBIP 423, pp. 109–120, 2021.
https://doi.org/10.1007/978-3-030-79022-6_10

Various software testing regimes discuss the generation and use of test cases [3–5]. As software increases in size and complexity model-based testing has been suggested [6] as way to reveal design flaws. The operational effectiveness is usually tested by statistical sampling the operations of an organization. In both cases, found errors need to be fixed. For applications which create transactions to be mined into blockchains the model-driven testing approach has some promise, particularly for the audit of the design of these blockchain applications. Flaws in a design that are related to data manipulations lead to the storage of faulty data. In 'classical' systems, the wrong data can be rectified along with the rectification of the code. In blockchain systems, once data has been stored in the blockchain, it becomes an immutable part of the chain. This presents a problem for companies and auditors as incorrect transactions cannot be "backed out" and corrected. Auditing and ensuring correctness of a blockchain application's design is thus particularly important, not only in terms of ensuring a correct data structure, but also in terms of data validation rules that ensure the validity of data before its storage in the blockchain. The use of smart contracts to create these immutable transactions becomes even more problematic as inconsistencies or errors within the smart contract itself could result in many incorrect transactions. What is needed is an approach that allows for an ex-ante audit of a smart-contracts' validity at run-time, as ex-post audits seem to lose their rationale in a world where even substantial errors are almost impossible to reverse.

This paper suggests (in response to the awareness of a problem and preceding the development of a solution as part of the high-level design research process depicted in [7]) that a particular model, the resource-event-agent (REA) ontology [8], be used to design smart contracts, and thus support the auditor's requirement to test and confirm the design of controls. Additionally, it suggests that model-driven engineering (MDE) could allow auditors to assess the design quality (i.e., ontological commitment) of smart contracts that operationalize the REA and other ontologies. While current research on the model-driven engineering of blockchain focuses on the types of models, technologies and transformations needed to create a blockchain application (more easily) [9], the approach suggested in this paper addresses two aspects related to the audit of blockchain software. First, the approach connects an ontological approach to the design of the blockchain software. Second, it also addresses the need for the ex-ante audit of the application design and the development of operational models that are consistent with the audited design.

Section 2 offers an introduction to ontology-aware MDE, with an introduction to the MDE development chain, an introduction on ontology-engineering a platform-independent model, and the need for generating ontology-aware smart contracts. Section 3 describes a concrete realization as a combination of the MERODE MDE methodology and the REA-ontology, while discussing their combined potential. Section 4 presents related work positioning this paper in the literature, and Sect. 5 concludes this paper, with the support this combination can offer auditors at three different levels.

2 Model-Driven Engineering

2.1 The MDE Development Chain

In model-driven engineering (MDE), software is created from models rather than hand-coded. The development chains start with a computation-independent model (CIM), which is *"a domain model developed by domain experts that does not show the details of the structure of the system"* [10]. A platform-independent model (PIM) is derived from this CIM, showing the structure of the system independent of the peculiarities of a specific computer platform. The PIM is the result of the analysis phase, which follows the requirements elicitation phase. Although requirements engineering [11] is a discipline in its own right, requirements are considered as given and hence outside the scope of this paper. Here, we assume that the PIM results from the assembly of domain and task ontologies into an application ontology, in which the application ontology components are determined by the requirements, as first described by Guarino [12]. Where information systems are generally tailored to a specific audience or application and thus require discovering specific requirements, we believe that in public chains requirements are of lesser importance to smart contracts as the requirements for smart contracts should be as generic as possible and supported by the largest community possible given that they are generally accessible. In private chains, we assume that a traditional MDE development chain could be applied, in which the analysis phase can still be supported by application ontologies.

In the further MDE development chain, the platform-specific model (PSM) is derived from the PIM with a set of validated model-to-model transformation rules considering platform specificities. Subsequently, the PSM is transformed in code with a set of validated model-to-code transformation rules. Direct PIM-to-code transformations are possible as well. The verification of the PIM's correctness can be done through formal verification, as well as through code generation and subsequent model-driven testing or manual testing.

2.2 Ontology Engineering a Platform Independent Model

Smart contracts (as with any other software artefact) need to reliably represent a relevant part of reality. Hence the domain model on which they are based needs to be a truthful representation of reality, preferably supported by an as large as possible community of domain experts. As it is our aim to use domain models as input for a formal transformation process, they also need to be formal. The construction of such shared and formal domain models lays in the realm of ontology engineering, since ontologies are *"formal and explicit conceptualizations of a shared conceptualization"* [13, 14]. Like requirements engineering, ontology engineering is considered outside the scope of this paper as we consider ontologies as given.

As ontology engineering is a mostly human [15] and hence costly endeavor, and because they are also validated throughout their use in practice, their reuse should be promoted through interoperability. Guarino [16] requires the formalizations of domain and task ontologies to be specializations of top-level ontologies to operationalize this interoperability and distinguish between valid and invalid combinations of domain and task ontology concepts in an application ontology. Top-level ontologies (e.g., UFO, SUMO) describe generic concepts (e.g., space and time). Domain and task ontologies (e.g., REA) capture domain knowledge about a specific domain (e.g., food) or task (e.g., sales) by specializing top-level ontology constructs. Application ontologies then combine and specialize domain and task ontology constructs to form an application-specific ontology (e.g., catering, which is food sales), while respecting the logic of the domain, task and top-level ontologies they specialize (Fig. 1).

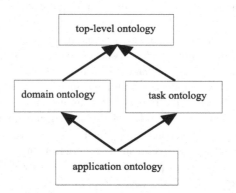

Fig. 1. Guarino's [16] ontology Aufbau principle.

As requirements engineering is an integral part of the ontology engineering process [17, 18], ontology engineers deliver and maintain ontologies that formalize expert domain knowledge. Hence, an auditor can rely on the expertise and reputation of the ontology engineer to cover the requirements engineering and analysis phase of smart-contract (and software) design that result in a CIM (i.e., the ontology) supported by a community of experts. Additionally, the auditor can rely on the respect of the formal combinatory rules coined by Guarino [16] to evaluate the face validity of the constructed application ontology, as it is virtually impossible to formulate ontologies for every possible application.

2.3 Generating Ontology-Aware Smart Contracts

In order to guarantee that the semantics of the ontology are reliably represented by the smart contract (or any other software artefact), the ontology needs to be refined into a PIM, that is then transformed into code. The transformation rules need to be transparent and reproducible. As a programmer's ways of transforming a PIM in code are not always transparent and human creativity might hamper reproducibility, it is from the perspective of the auditor better to entrust machines with this transformation, limiting the application of human creativity to the rigorous design and maintenance of a set of transformation rules that is validated and improved through repeated use.

As with the ontology, the auditor can rely on the expertise and reputation (e.g., track-record, certificates, brand) of the software engineer responsible for the design and maintenance of the code-generators and the transformation rules to evaluate the quality of the product. As the ontology engineering and PIM-to-code engineering are orthogonal (i.e. the PIM-to-code transformation is a linguistic instantiation, where the application ontology development is an ontological instantiation according to [10]), both engineers should be able to trace undesirable smart contract behavior back to either the ontology or the PIM-to-code transformation. For example, when smart contracts that are generated using the same ontology, but different code-generators, all exhibit undesirable behavior, the origin of the defect must lay in the ontology (unless in the unlikely case that all code generators exhibit the exact same error), while if different contracts generated by means of the same PIM-to-code transformation exhibit undesirable behavior, the origin of the defect must reside within the PIM-to-code transformation.

3   Generating REA-Based Smart Contracts with MERODE

3.1   MERODE

MERODE [19] is an enterprise information systems engineering method focusing on domain modelling. It uses existence dependency graphs (i.e. a sub-language of UML class diagrams) and finite state machines to model business objects and their behavior, complemented with an object-event table (i.e. a version of a CRUD matrix [20]) to model object interaction. The method has been formalized by means of process algebra [21, 22], which ensures the consistency of the existence dependency graphs and the finite state machines [23] before transforming them to code. MERODE-models are stored as XML files and can be transformed to working Java-applications in just three clicks. The transformations have been designed so as to support the transformation of high-level models by means of built-in defaults and PIM-to-PSM transformation rules [24], thus freeing the business analysts from the need of providing lots of details prior to code generation. Code-generation has proved a powerful instrument to validate models through fast prototyping [25]. While the default code generator can be used to validate an ontology (i.e. as *"a formal and explicit specification of a shared conceptualization"* [13, 14]) as has been demonstrated by the authors of [26], the generation of Smart Contracts using Blockchain technology requires an extension of the MERODE method. This extension has been developed and presented in [27], where the authors develop B-MERODE as an artefact-centric approach to smart contracts. B-MERODE adds an extension to address permissions and to distinguish between the model aspects that result in code on and off the blockchain [9]. Using these two extensions, a MERODE-model can be generated to a Hyperledger platform without any manual coding. The MERODE-method uses algebraic verification for a model's internal consistency [23]. Further validation of the model needs to be done through testing. Specific advantages of model-driven engineering and code-generation are their support for model-based testing [6] and fast turnaround times between fixing design issues and obtaining a new version of the software. This strongly reduces the cost of testing, thus allowing for a more thorough verification of the correct design of software (e.g., smart contracts) prior to its deployment. Moreover, the verification of a software's design can be based on the models used for generating the code, rather than through code inspections.

3.2 The REA Ontology

The REA Ontology [8] is a domain ontology which specifies the objects and relations for the accounting and business domain. Figure 2 provides a graphical representation of the core concepts of the ontology. The ontology is organized around three conceptual layers. The top-layer, which is color-coded yellow in REA models, incorporates a description of what could or should be. The classes in this layer are "types". These are similar to Plato's forms [28]. The middle or contracting layer, which is color-coded red in REA models, includes classes for contracts and their bundled commitments. For example, a contract to build a house includes commitments to pour the foundation, frame the house, put on the roof, etc. while the reciprocal commitments include a payment schedule. Finally, the bottom layer, which is color-coded green in REA models, includes classes for what economic events have occurred, who was involved in them, and what resources were affected.

This section looks at how smart contracts can be modeled as bundles of Economic Commitments and how their correct execution can be verified by the independent auditor examining the semantic associations of the REA ontology (e.g., specify and typify). The typify association between the Economic Event Type and Economic Event classes in conjunction with the specify association between the Economic Commitment and Economic Event classes allows auditors to check whether the Economic Event that fulfils the Economic Commitment matches the type specified in the contract. For example, the contract to build a particular type of house (e.g., two bedrooms) would include a commitment that specifies the Economic Resource Types (e.g., lumber, concrete, roofing shingles) that are to be included in the finished house. The typify association between the Economic Recourse Type and Economic Resources classes would allow for the verification that the actual components of the house are of the type specified in the contract. The association between an Economic Commitment and the Economic Event Types would specify the steps that should be used to build the house while the Typify association between the Economic Event Types and Economic Events allows for the determination that the steps specified in the contract's commitment are actually followed. In addition to these specify associations, the stock-flow association between the Economic Resources and Economic Events can allow auditors to check the materials to build the house were used in the indicated steps (Economic Events). Finally, the typify association between the Economic Agent Type and Economic Agent classes in conjunction with the specify association between the Economic Commitment and Economic Agent classes allow auditors to check whether the Economic Agent associated through an inside- or outside Participate association with the Economic Event that fulfils the Economic Commitment match the type specified in the contract. For example, before fulfilling the commitment to make the Economic Event Type of "final payment", the Economic Event Type – "final inspection" – must be completed by the Economic Agent Type of a "certified engineer." The buyer of the house could simply accept that the person actually performing the inspection Economic Event met these criteria, or they could verify this by asking for the inspector's credentials. In the development of a smart contract this could be accomplished with an oracle that examines the builder's human resources information system for example [29, 30]. This ability of a smart contract to use oracles as software connectors could allow the contract to verify that individuals fulfilling certain commitments are in fact of the type specified in the contract.

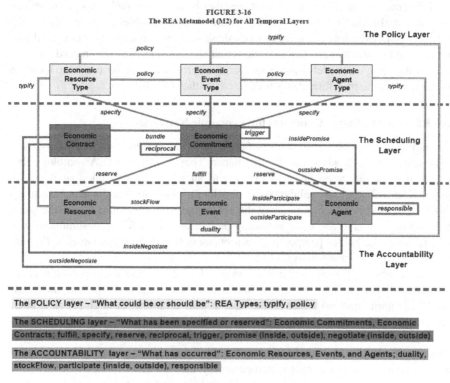

FIGURE 3-16
The REA Metamodel (M2) for All Temporal Layers

Fig. 2. REA Metamodel [8]

3.3 Support for the Audit

The outcome of an audit is an opinion on the veracity of financial statements. Auditors must come to a conclusion that the numbers contained in these financial statements are not materially different that any "true" value [1]. Here true means the value that would be about obtained if every transaction that affects these numbers was used in the calculations. In large complex organizations it has become increasingly difficult, if not impossible for the auditor to examine the complete set of transactions. Examining the transactions themselves, or a statistically significant subset, is referred to as conducting substantive test. An auditor can also use compliance testing, or testing of controls, to come to a conclusion that the processes used by the company are sufficiently controlled so that transactions with errors or irregularities do not become part of the financial record. Verifying software used in the processing of transactions is part of compliance testing. When Smart Contracts become significantly important to the exchange of assets between unrelated parties (between the firm and its customers) their transactions will be added to the financial record. Therefore, as with all other processes that impact the financial record, their accuracy needs to be verified. The output of other software products, payroll as an example, can be reviewed prior to adding the transactions to the financial record. The difference for Smart Contracts is that once they become executed and the transactions mined into the blockchain reviews of output are no longer possible. Therefore, the design of correct Smart Contracts is critical when these software products are integrated into processes of the firm that create transactions that are part of the financial record. In order to verify the design, a model-driven engineering approach allows the auditor to focus on the models and the transformations used to create the software.

3.4 REA-Aware Smart Contracts for Economic Networks

The authors of [26] published a proof-of-concept for the ontology-aware model-driven engineering approach advocated by this paper. They model the REA^2-ontology that is equivalent to the green layer in Fig. 2 and an REA^2 interpretation of the REA axioms. They subsequently validate their model with a Java-application generated using MERODE's Merlin modeling tool and the associated code generator. Where the green layer in Fig. 2 is valid for a single trading-partner at a time, REA^2 is simultaneously valid for all stake-holder perspectives in a business transaction (i.e. buyer, seller and third-party (e.g. governing body)) [31].

The authors of [32] argue that REA-aware blockchains and smart contracts could improve resilience and interoperability in economic networks, and especially in decentralized economic networks such as the peer-to-peer economy, through (1) an explicit representation of an agreed upon business vocabulary (i.e. the shared conceptualization in [13, 14]'s definition of ontology) that is an inherent characteristic of ontologies and indispensable for trade and (2) the use of the REA^2-ontology, of which the unified semantics are claimed to promote interoperability, through the elimination of stovepipe architectures for the information systems, blockchains and smart contracts that operate economic networks. The economic networks considered in [32] are value networks - defined as any set of roles and interactions by [33] - of collaboration spaces in which people participate in both tangible and intangible exchanges of economic resources (i.e. goods, services and rights) to achieve economic or social benefit. The authors of [32] also list potential application of the ontology-aware model-driven engineering approach for blockchain development for the sharing economy as an example of external-facing value networks, collaboratives of independent workers as an example of internal-facing value networks, wood and vaccine traceability. Based on these examples, we can conclude that the ontology-aware model-driven engineering approach for blockchain development and particularly the REA^2-aware model-driven engineering approach for smart contract and blockchain development has considerable potential for audit in many domains of the traditional and the new economy.

4 Related Work

The authors of [34] discuss the potential impact of blockchain technology on the accounting profession, where [35] focusses on the impact on audit, while [36] argues that smart contracts have the potential to improve audit quality and meet the information demands of various stakeholders. Dredas [37] supports this argument presenting a protocol for auditing outsourced data, where [38] presents a method for creating immutable audit trails. This paper focusses on correctness verification of smart contracts and does not consider the use of smart contracts for the creation of immutable audit trails.

In 2017, [39] published a research agenda regarding smart contract validation and verification, highlighting the need for formalization, where in 2018 [40] highlighted the importance of semantics, which are both features of the ontology-aware approach presented above. The authors of [41] distinguish between security assurance, which includes environment security, vulnerability scanning and performance, and correctness verification, which includes assessing programming correctness and formal verification, in the realm of security verification in blockchain smart contracts. [42] offers an overview of smart contract languages and verification methods. [43, 44] distinguish between theorem proving, model checking and runtime verification in the realm of formal verification. The verification through counter example generator in [45] shares characteristics with the Alloy [46] ontological analysis tool, while [47] uses semantic annotation to verify smart contracts. The authors of [48] provide a framework for run-time validation of smart contracts that could be useful for oracle integration, where [49] focuses on validation in supply chains. This paper focusses on correctness verification through model checking, abstracting from security assurance, theorem proving and runtime verification. The main advantage of the approach advocated by this paper is that is incorporates the decades of experience accumulated by the MERODE and REA communities.

5 Conclusion

In conclusion, this paper suggest that the application of ontology-aware model-driven engineering practices have the potential to enable the ex-ante (i.e., that is before they are published) audit of smart contracts. Additionally, it suggests that the REA ontology augments this potential with the ex-post (i.e., that is after the transition data have been recorded) audit of transaction data both on and off-blockchain resulting from the execution of these smart contracts. Finally, it suggests that the design of REA-aware model-driven design has the potential to enable run-time monitoring of smart-contract execution (e.g., through the use of oracles).

First, ontology-aware model-driven engineering is expected to allow auditors to achieve a clear separation of concerns through the definition of clear deliverables (i.e., ontologies and code-generators) and a clear scoping of the tasks that lead to them. The auditor can rely on ontology engineers for the design of well-formed formal top-level, domain, task and application ontologies that truthfully represent a relevant part of reality through the application of ontology engineering methods. Subsequently, the auditor can rely on software engineers and their methods to design trustworthy code-generators that transform these formal ontologies in smart contracts (and other types of software code) that truthfully reflect a relevant part of reality. Second, the work of McCarthy et al. [8] as discussed above shows the potential of the REA-ontology for ex-post auditing the transaction data both on- and off-blockchain resulting from the execution of these smart contracts. Third, the implementation of the REA axioms in [26] demonstrates the potential of the REA axioms and REA^2-aware MDE for monitoring the execution of smart-contracts at runtime.

References

1. Rittenberg, L.E., Bradley, J.: Schwieger: Auditing Concepts for a Changing Environment. Harcourt College Publishers, Orlando (2001)
2. Public Company Accounting Oversight Board: Auditing standard no. 5 – An audit of internal control over financial reporting that is integrated with an audit of financial statements. Exch. Organ. Behav. Teach. J. (2007)
3. Emam, S., Miller, J.: Test case prioritization using extended digraphs. ACM Trans. Softw. Eng. Methodol. **25**, 1–41 (2015)
4. Demillo, R.A.: Software Testing (2003)
5. Fraser, G.: Gamification of software testing. In: IEEE/ACM 12th International Workshop on Automation of Software Testing. pp. 2–7 (2017)
6. Hemmati, H., Arcuri, A., Briand, L.: Achieving scalable model-based testing through test case diversity. ACM Trans. Softw. Eng. Methodol. (2013). https://doi.org/10.1145/2430536.2430540
7. Baskerville, R., Baiyere, A., Gregor, S., Hevner, A., Rossi, M.: Design science research contributions: finding a balance between artifact and theory. J. Assoc. Inf. Syst. **19**, 3 (2018)
8. McCarthy, W.E., Geerts, G.L., Gal, G.: The REA Ontology (2021)
9. Scheynen, N.: Construction of web services using the MERODE approach, (2016)
10. Gašević, D., Djurić, D., Devedžić, V.: Model driven engineering and ontology development (2009). https://doi.org/10.1007/978-3-642-00282-3
11. Dick, J., Hull, E., Jackson, K.: Requirements engineering (2017). https://doi.org/10.1007/978-3-319-61073-3
12. Guarino, N.: Understanding, building and using ontologies. Int. J. Hum. Comput. Stud. **46**, 293–310 (1997). https://doi.org/10.1006/ijhc.1996.0091
13. Guarino, N., Oberle, D., Staab, S.: What is an ontology? Handbook on ontologies. In: Handbook on Ontologies SE - International Handbooks on Information Systems (2009)
14. Studer, R., Benjamins, V.R., Fensel, D.: Knowledge Engineering: Principles and methods. Data Knowl. Eng. 25 (1998). https://doi.org/10.1016/S0169-023X(97)00056-6
15. Iqbal, R., Murad, M.A.A., Mustapha, A., Sharef, N.M.: An analysis of ontology engineering methodologies: a literature review. Res. J. Appl. Sci. Eng. Technol. **6**, 2993–3000 (2013). https://doi.org/10.19026/rjaset.6.3684.
16. Guarino, N.: Semantic matching: formal ontological distinctions for information organization, extraction, and integration. In: Pazienza, M.T. (ed.) SCIE 1997. LNCS (including subseries Lecture Notes in Artificial Intelligence and Lecture Notes in Bioinformatics), vol. 1299, pp. 139–170. Springer, Heidelberg (1997). https://doi.org/10.1007/3-540-63438-x_8
17. Al-Arfaj, A., Al-Salman, A.: Ontology construction from text: challenges and trends. Int. J. Artif. Intell. Expert Syst. **6**, 15–26 (2015)
18. Cimiano, P., Völker, J., Studer, R.: Ontologies on demand? A description of the state-of-the-art, applications, challenges and trends for ontology learning from text. Information-wiss. und Prax. **57**, 315–320 (2006)
19. Snoeck, M.: Enterprise Information Systems Engineering: The MERODE Approach. Springer, Cham (2014). https://doi.org/10.1007/978-3-319-10145-3
20. Martin, J.: Information Engineering. Prentice Hall, Englewood Cliffs (1989)
21. Snoeck, M., Dedene, G.: Existence dependency: The key to semantic integrity between structural and behavioral aspects of object types. IEEE Trans. Softw. Eng. **24**, 233–251 (1998)

22. Dedene, G., Snoeck, M.: Formal deadlock elimination in an object oriented conceptual schema. Data Knowl. Eng. **15**, 1–30 (1995)

23. Snoeck, M., Michiels, C., Dedene, G.: Consistency by construction: the case of MERODE. In: Jeusfeld, M.A., Pastor, Ó. (eds.) ER 2003. LNCS, vol. 2814, pp. 105–117. Springer, Heidelberg (2003). https://doi.org/10.1007/978-3-540-39597-3_11

24. Monsieur, G., Snoeck, M.: PIM to PSM transformations for an event driven architecture in an educational tool. Milestones, Model. Mappings Model. Archit. 55–63 (2006)

25. Sedrakyan, G., Snoeck, M., Poelmans, S.: Assessing the effectiveness of feedback enabled simulation in teaching conceptual modeling. Comput. Educ. **78**, 367–382 (2014). https://doi.org/10.1016/j.compedu.2014.06.014

26. Laurier, W., Horiuchi, S., Snoeck, M.: An executable axiomatization of the REA2 ontology. J. Inf. Syst. ISYS-19–026 (2021). https://doi.org/10.2308/ISYS-19-026

27. Amaral de Sousa, V., Burnay, C., Snoeck, M.: B-MERODE: a model-driven engineering and artifact-centric approach to generate blockchain-based information systems. In: Dustdar, S., Yu, E., Salinesi, C., Rieu, D., Pant, V. (eds.) CAiSE. LNCS, vol. 12127, pp. 117–133. Springer, Cham (2020). https://doi.org/10.1007/978-3-030-49435-3_8

28. Tarnas, R.: The passion of the western mind: understanding the ideas that have shaped our world view. In: The Passion of the Western Mind (1991)

29. Xu, X., et al.: The blockchain as a software connector. In: 13th Working IEEE/IFIP Conference on Software Architecture (WICSA), pp. 182–191 (2016)

30. Chen, Y., Liu, J.: Distributed community detection over blockchain networks based on structural entropy. In: ACM International Symposium on Blockchain and Secure Critical Infrastructure, pp. 3–12 (2019)

31. Laurier, W., Kiehn, J., Polovina, S.: REA2: a unified formalisation of the resource-event-agent ontology. Appl. Ontol. **13**, 201–224 (2018). https://doi.org/10.3233/AO-180198

32. Laurier, W., Collet, R., Desguin, S., Fauconnier, B.: Ontology-aware Model-driven Architecture A Resource-Event-Agent implementation for the Blockchain. 日本情報経営学会誌. 41, 1–12 (2021)

33. Allee, V.: Value network analysis and value conversion of tangible and intangible assets. J. Intellect. Cap. **9**, 5–24 (2008). https://doi.org/10.1108/14691930810845777

34. CGMA, C.F.E.: Blockchain augmented audit–Benefits and challenges for accounting professionals. J. Theor. Account. Res. **14**, 117–137 (2018)

35. Raphael, J.: Rethinking the audit: Innovation is transforming how audits are conducted-and even what it means to be an auditor. J. Account. **223**, 28 (2017)

36. Rozario, A.M., Vasarhelyi, M.: Auditing with smart contracts. Int. J. Digit. Account. Res. **18**, 1–27 (2018)

37. Fan, K., Bao, Z., Liu, M., Vasilakos, A.V., Shi, W.: Dredas: decentralized, reliable and efficient remote outsourced data auditing scheme with blockchain smart contract for industrial IoT. Futur. Gener. Comput. Syst. **110**, 665–674 (2020). https://doi.org/10.1016/j.future.2019.10.014

38. Kalis, R.: Using blockchain to validate audit trail data in private business applications. Univ. Amsterdam, June 2018

39. Magazzeni, D., McBurney, P., Nash, W.: Validation and verification of smart contracts: a research agenda. Computer (Long. Beach. Calif). **50**, 50–57 (2017). https://doi.org/10.1109/MC.2017.3571045

40. Clack, C.D.: Smart Contract Templates: legal semantics and code validation. J. Digit. Bank. **2**, 338–352 (2018)

41. Liu, J., Liu, Z.: A survey on security verification of blockchain smart contracts. IEEE Access. **7**, 77894–77904 (2019). https://doi.org/10.1109/ACCESS.2019.2921624

42. Harz, D., Knottenbelt, W.: Towards safer smart contracts: a survey of languages and verification methods. arXiv Prepr. arXiv1809.09805 (2018)

43. Almakhour, M., Sliman, L., Samhat, A.E., Mellouk, A.: Verification of smart contracts: a survey. Pervasive Mob. Comput. **67**, 101227 (2020). https://doi.org/10.1016/j.pmcj.2020. 101227.

44. Tolmach, P., Li, Y., Lin, S.-W., Liu, Y., Li, Z.: A survey of smart contract formal specification and verification. arXiv Prepr. arXiv2008.02712 (2020)

45. Marescotti, M., Otoni, R., Alt, L., Eugster, P., Hyvärinen, A.E.J., Sharygina, N.: Accurate smart contract verification through direct modelling. In: Margaria, T., Steffen, B. (eds.) ISoLA. LNCS, vol. 12478, pp. 178–194. Springer, Cham (2020). https://doi.org/10.1007/978-3-030-61467-6_12

46. Braga, B.F.B., Almeida, J.P.A., Guizzardi, G., Benevides, A.B.: Transforming OntoUML into Alloy: towards conceptual model validation using a lightweight formal method. Innov. Syst. Softw. Eng. **6**, 55–63 (2010). https://doi.org/10.1007/s11334-009-0120-5

47. Petrović, N., Tošić, M.: Semantic approach to smart contract verification. Facta Univ. Ser. Autom. Control Robot. **19**, 21–37 (2020)

48. Li, A., Choi, J.A., Long, F.: Securing smart contract with runtime validation. In: Proceedings of the 41st ACM SIGPLAN Conference on Programming Language Design and Implementation, pp. 438–453 (2020)

49. Su, S., Wang, K., Kim, H.S.: Smartsupply: smart contract based validation for supply chain blockchain. In: 2018 IEEE International Conference on Internet of Things (iThings) and IEEE Green Computing and Communications (GreenCom) and IEEE Cyber, Physical and Social Computing (CPSCom) and IEEE Smart Data (SmartData), pp. 988–993 (2018). https://doi. org/10.1109/Cybermatics_2018.2018.00186

TrustSECO: A Distributed Infrastructure for Providing Trust in the Software Ecosystem

Fang Hou[1], Siamak Farshidi[2], and Slinger Jansen[1,3]([⊠])

^{1} Utrecht University, Utrecht, The Netherlands
{h.fang,slinger.jansen}@uu.nl
^{2} University of Amsterdam, Amsterdam, The Netherlands
s.farshidi@uva.nl
^{3} Lappeenranta University of Technoly, Lappeenranta, Finland

Abstract. The software ecosystem is a trust-rich part of the world. Collaboratively, software engineers trust major hubs in the ecosystem, such as package managers, repository services, and programming language ecosystems. However, trust entails the assumption of risks. In this paper, we lay out the risks we are taking by blindly trusting these hubs when using information systems. Secondly, we present a vision for a trust-recording mechanism in the software ecosystem that mitigates the presented risks. This vision is realized in TrustSECO: a distributed infrastructure that collects, stores, and discloses trust facts about information systems. If our community manages to implement this mechanism, we can create an urgently needed healthy and secure software ecosystem. Finally, we report on the current status of the project.

Keywords: Software ecosystems · Distributed ledger · Software trust · Repository mining · Software security

1 Introduction

A software ecosystem (SECO) is a set of actors functioning as a unit and interacting with a shared market for software and services, together with the relationships among them [9]. Society is entirely dependent on a healthy worldwide SECO, as every aspect of our society is dependent on information systems and other software. In addition, many worldwide actors rely on the different links in the software supply chain, which works on the basis of trust, hence, trust plays a key role in our society as well as in information systems. We identify software trust as a willingness of the information systems end-users to take risks based on a subjective belief that information system providers will exhibit reliable behavior to provide its required functionalities, operate reliably and consistently without failures, even under uncertainty. Hence the system characteristics, such as reliability, fault-tolerance, safety, or security should be considered as the factors to judge an information system's trustworthiness [2,15].

A. Polyvyanyy and S. Rinderle-Ma (Eds.): CAiSE 2021 Workshops, LNBIP 423, pp. 121–133, 2021.
https://doi.org/10.1007/978-3-030-79022-6_11

Although the worldwide SECO is a trustful environment, it presents many dangers to society. First, as information systems are malleable, they evolve constantly and are evolved by actors that may have bad intentions. Also, most information systems are used for critical infrastructure on which our society depends. In addition, when information systems end-users select a software package, they give a large dosage of trust to the package manager and language ecosystem that they are part of, most of them insufficiently think about security and trust [10].

Attackers can exploit the trust we put in software to carry out attacks. For instance, a package registry can be compromised through *Registry Exploitation*: hijacking the account of a registry maintainer or package maintainer, hacking the registry itself, or hacking the registry infrastructure. Furthermore, it is possible to *publish a package with a similar name (a.k.a. Typo-squatting) or exactly the same in another registry*, leading to downloading compromised or vulnerable packages. Also, a hacker can *transfer ownership* of an abandoned package to herself and then compromise it. There are also possibilities for open source developers to compromise packages, such as by a disgruntled insider or a malicious contributor. Attackers will use these attack vectors to insert malicious code, infect packages with viruses, provide back doors, and steal sensitive data. These attacks frequently make headlines, and the outcomes are devastating. With the constant increase in the number of detected vulnerabilities, it is time to radically rethink the worldwide SECO, and the trust we put in it.

In this paper, we present TrustSECO[1], a community-managed infrastructure that underpins the SECO with a trust layer. The infrastructure gathers data on trust in particular software packages and projects. Usually, this data is made available to the SECO hubs, such as package managers and repository websites. With this data software end-users can collectively determine whether packages (versions) are reliable, contain vulnerabilities, and are trusted by other users.

The rest of this paper is structured as follows. In Sect. 2, we outline the key components of TrustSECO: the distributed ledger technology and trust score calculation component. Section 3 describes the trust score calculation, which uses facts from the SECO about information systems to provide trust data to end-users. Section 4 shows the initial vision of the distributed ledger design, which includes ledger design, data sources, and ledger sustainability. Furthermore, we discuss the evaluation of the TrustSECO platform in Sect. 5. Finally, in Sect. 6 we summarize our work and provide a status update of the project.

2   TrustSECO Infrastructure

The TrustSECO infrastructure provides a distributed system that enables software end-users to evaluate and install the software based on its trustworthiness, intending to provide a safer SECO. The main object of interest for TrustSECO are versions of software packages, i.e., collections of components that form a coherent whole that can be deployed on a system to provide a set of features to a software end-users.

---

[1] https://secureseco.org/secureseco-introduction/trustseco/.

The main stakeholders are software end-users who install and use the software, and software providers including software producing organizations, organizations that create package managers, and software engineers who create the software or packages. These different stakeholders collect trust data about software packages, by, for instance, looking at past performance, reproducible builds, or vulnerability databases. Furthermore, the stakeholders collect trust data about software providers who have contributed to the software package. In addition, the stakeholders collect trust data about the package manager offering software packages.

To ensure that the community can evenly contribute and make use of the infrastructure, we envision it as a fully distributed system, in particular a Distributed Ledger (DL) containing trust facts. The DL collects trust facts and observations from different stakeholders who participate in the network. Trust facts can be collected from various data sources, for instance, they can be from the participants in the TrustSECO DL, or different data sets in the networks. Subsequently, ecosystem hubs can reuse the data from the TrustSECO DL, base on our trust score calculation mechanism, to establish whether a particular version of a package can be trusted.

An example of how TrustSECO works is illustrated by an example with the Node Package Manager(*npm*). When a software engineer is developing software and including existing *npm* components, she might download them through *npm*. If *npm* was integrated with TrustSECO, TrustSECO can be used to provide warnings about particular configurations. TrustSECO, before downloading and installing a package, can, for instance, automatically advise the software engineer on the trust rating of the package. If the package(version) is below a particular rating set by the software engineer's organization, *npm* can use TrustSECO to select another version of the package or even a wholly different package. Furthermore, TrustSECO can warn the software engineer, when any new vulnerabilities arise in one of the installed packages. In some scenarios, TrustSECO can be used to automatically re-configure a system to ensure that the configuration matches the organization's security requirements. The TrustSECO infrastructure consists of the following parts: the trust fact DL, the trust fact observer client, the trust score calculation mechanism, and the SECO alert service. We provide an overview of the TrustSECO infrastructure in Fig. 1.

Distributed Ledger Technology

Distributed Ledger Technology (DLT) has been most successfully applied in supply chain management, which is not surprising, as DLT concerns the interaction between multiple untrusted parties that collaboratively achieve a goal [7].

Hence, we bring DLT into the worldwide SECO, i.e., the complex network of software providers that collaboratively provide software for every computer on earth to make the SECO more secure, reliable, and trustworthy. There are two reasons to choose a distributed ledger. First, as the community needs to rely on a trustworthy source, we aim for the trust data to be collected and shared through a consensus mechanism, where the perception of the package will become more reliable and complete as more participants add data about

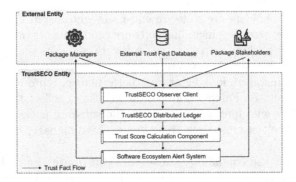

Fig. 1. The main four components of the TrustSECO infrastructure are visualized. All trust data are stored in the TrustSECO DL. Using the score calculation, the alert system notifies the stakeholders about the status in the SECO.

the package. Secondly, as the TrustSECO platform needs to outlive the duration of this academic project, we aim for the TrustSECO platform to be maintained by the community.

The DL we use includes the trust data storage structure and serves as the basis for the TrustSECO implementation. The trust data will be crawled and confirmed by the TrustSECO nodes, i.e., trusted nodes in the network that collaboratively confirm trust facts. Moreover, with the employment of the consensus mechanism, all trust facts will be validated by the nodes. Subsequently, those confirmed the trust data will be compiled into stakeholders' specific trust score calculation and reports about software packages and versions that are used by hubs in the SECO that need trust data to ensure trustful software usage. For a full discussion on the DL and its design, see Sect. 4.

Trust Fact Observer Client
Trust fact observer client will be executed by the participants in the TrustSECO DL as a mechanism for adding new trust facts to the ledger. Meanwhile it continually monitors the SECO along with package managers for new trust facts and occasionally performs jobs, such as trying to reproduce a build. When these facts are submitted, a set of items are checked, such as the submitter's trustworthiness and observation. An overview of the data stored is found in Table 1. The data must be retrievable relatively fast, even though these data are extensive.

Trust Score Calculation Component
We develop a score calculation mechanism to provide insight into the trustworthiness of the package configuration. This is especially suitable for package managers with self-contained package configurations. The score calculation can be used to ask for particular configurations, such as *"a configuration that provides Python3 and qtbitcointrader with a trust level of at least level X"*. The Configuration Trust Level Calculation can also provide a configuration where X is the highest possible. The configuration algorithm will mostly consider the weakest link principle, i.e., the package with the lowest trust level is the primary

Table 1. Each column represents a step in the software development life cycle. Each row indicates an example of a trust fact that we can read or write to the DL, with the goal of securing the worldwide SECO. For convenience, we have shaded the "writes" red, the "reads" green, and the "reads/writes" yellow. Please note that the rows in this table are an incomplete list of the technical factors described in Sect. 3.

		Source Created	Source Built	Source Tested	Source Committed to Repo	Package Built	Package Tested	Package Released	Package Published	Package Downloaded	Package Installed	Package Run	Package Removed
Software Engineer	Identity?	W	W	W	R/W	R	W	W	R/W	R	R/W	R/W	W
Internal Integrity	Syntactically correct	W	W	-	R	R	-	R	R	R	R	R	-
	Style correct	W	W	-	R	R	-	R	R	R	R	R	-
	Reproducible build	-	W	-	R	W	-	R	R	R	R	R	-
	Compiler trusted	-	W	-	R	W	-	R	R	R	R	R	-
	Package integrity	-	-	-	-	W	W	R	R	R	R	R	-
	Code complete	-	-	-	-	-	-	W	R	R	R	R	-
External Integrity	Virus scanned	-	-	-	W	W	R	W	R	R	R	R	-
	CVE free	-	-	-	W	W	W	W	W	R	R	R	-
	Most recent version	-	-	-	-	-	-	W	R	R	R	R	-
	Dependency tree up to date	-	W	W	-	W	W	W	W	R	R/W	R	-
Tested	Code tested	-	-	W	R	-	W	R	R	R	R	R	-
	Acceptance tested	-	-	-	-	-	W	R	R	R	R	R	-
License	License present	-	-	-	-	-	-	W	R	R	R	R	R
	License compliant	W	-	-	-	-	-	R/W	R	R	R	R	R
End User	Identity?	-	-	-	-	-	-	-	-	W	R/W	R/W	R/W

Checked on distributed ledger R
Added to distributed ledger W

determinant for the configuration's combined trust rating. We create a tool that supports package managers in finding the most trusted configuration of components and automatically developing a migration path. It becomes possible that configurations of which the trust rating has dropped get reconfigured automatically by their package managers by replacing one of the dependent components with a better trust rating, creating a safer SECO.

The package trust service will be somewhat intelligent: with several reproducible builds, low fix times, and few occurrences in Common Vulnerability and Exposure databases (CVEs), packages will have higher scores. This model will be designed such that it is extensible with new trust data if it becomes available. The scores will possibly be normalized to easily usable trust levels from Untrusted (T0) to Trusted (T5). One of the unique aspects of the TrustSECO is that it also uses the other package data to distribute packages over the trust levels evenly, to encourage package publishers to improve trust metrics continuously. Without action, their trust level can drop because the ecosystem is improving as a whole.

In Sect. 3, we will explore what data we can ethically gather on package software engineers, what data is available about project health.

Software Ecosystem Alert System

We build a tool that asks for data from the Trust Score Calculation Component and updates package providers and end-users on the status of their products and configurations. Additionally, the TrustSECO platform can be seen as an intrusion detection system, and if malware code is identified in a software package, we can warn both the end-users and the providers. TrustSECO uses all the data from Table 1 to secure the SECO, this can be done by running the Trust Reporting Service as a cron job on a user's system.

There are other services available that currently provide alerts to software end-users about vulnerabilities. For instance, many package managers provide some checkboxes on whether a package is vulnerable. One of the most notable commercial services is Snyk.io, which has developed its proprietary tools and database for vulnerability notification. While Snyk has been exceedingly accessible for such notifications, they insufficiently address the open-source community, its concerns, and its need for openness.

3   Trust Score Calculation

We provide information systems end-users with insight into the trust factors efficiently, by calculating a trust score for each information system and software package. Furthermore, package managers can use the trust scores to deploy reliable information systems automatically, so the trust scores should be readable by both humans and systems. The trust scores must have several properties. First, they should be *multi-dimensional*, i.e., they should give insight into the package, the package version, and the community of software engineers that produced it. Secondly, they must be *fully transparent*, such that any other stakeholder can calculate the same trust scores with the same data, which also helps build consensus about trust in the broader software engineering community. Thirdly, the scores must be *combinatorial*, in the sense that scores can be combined to calculate trust ratings for package compositions. Finally, the trust scores should be *numeric* to rapidly identify the trustworthiness of a software package version.

What are We Scoring?

When we consider what can be scored to determine the software trust, we first confirm the trust factors through a series of research to determine the dimensions of the trust score based on these factors, however, we found most literature only cover SDLC or some perspectives throughout the package selection process, instead of providing a comprehensive metrics for the whole picture, and some metrics lack practicality cannot be collected easily. We consider trustworthiness attributes will be attributed to the following aspects:

Technical Factors. Quality attributes matter most when software end-users are accepting software [12]. Here, we consider the technical factors more about the quality attributes to measure the packages and versions from the perspectives of both functional and non-functional requirements, such as if the functions align with users' requirements and original design, or if there are any outdated dependencies or numbers of open issues.

Also, we focus on vulnerability, as it negatively impacts software quality. If a vulnerability is detected in a package version, the trust referred to above is diminished appropriately, depending on the severity of the vulnerability. We are currently experimenting with a multiplier between 0 and 1 that diminishes the otherwise good trust score when a particular version contains a threatening vulnerability. In this way, other versions can keep a relatively high score, while this version is lowly rated. One of the significant upsides of TrustSECO taking care of this information is that the software end-users do not have to worry about keeping their systems up to date. If connected to a package manager that monitors the system, it can automatically reconfigure the system to include a version with a high trust score.

Ecosystem Factors. Ecosystem factors are not only the intrinsic properties to all stakeholders, but also reflect the relationship between end-users with software engineers, organizations, and communities [10]. Thus, first of all, we focus on the software engineers' experiences, knowledge, and skills; organizations or communities' reputation, popularity, and positive support; and interest from various stakeholders, e.g., packages' number of tags in Stack Overflow, or the number of downloads in npmjs. In addition, the cost is an important part of ecosystem factors, as one of our major goals in adopting software packages is to reuse the fulfilled program to speed up the coding process, and save costs. Here we emphasize the time and economic costs as the key elements to implement the software package, e.g. project time, budget, and software licenses.

A Score with Multiple Dimensions
Based on various definitions of software trust and the SECO's context, we believe that software trust does not only talk about the software package itself but also a complex and comprehensive concept about all relevant impact factors. Score calculation can be unpacked through the following dimensions:

Packages + Versions. Building trust is an ongoing process that changes over time. The same package may have different trust scores in different versions. Packages' and package versions' trust scores are influenced by several factors, such as: (a) Bug-fixing times, (b) End-users' experiences with specific package versions, (c) Known vulnerabilities, (d) Unreliable dependencies, (e) Trust in the individual software developers.

Package Managers. Package managers managing a collection of software packages, are a part of the infrastructure that enables anyone to use the software and a SECO's backbone. Unfortunately, these package managers are not as secure as users think they are. At different stages in the software life cycle, vulnerabilities [1] can enter the software, and the package managers assume no responsibility for this. Therefore the end-users' concern for package managers should be on security and continuous support. TrustSECO cares about the following facts about package managers: (a) Usage frequency, (b) Any malicious, outdated, or broken dependencies, (c) Reputation and popularity, (d) Compliance with security standards, (e) Recent compromises of the package manager.

Software Engineers. The software engineers who provide our society its critical information systems impact the trustworthiness of the packages. Factors that play a part in determining trust from individual engineers are: (a) The years of activity on well-known platforms such as Github, (b) Star ratings on development platforms, (c) Any negative experiences. We have to be careful about individuals, as TrustSECO should not function as a surveillance instrument. We do not want software engineers to get into trouble for, e.g., a bug that they introduced in an important package because their intentions were probably benign. The TrustSECO infrastructure will be developed in a way where trust facts can be used to determine the trust in a software package, but cannot lead to the individual trustworthiness of a software engineer decreased.

Software Organizations. Organizational behaviors show the ability to prevent risks and provide effective support, the following factors are considered: (a) Organizational support, e.g., fixing bugs on time and activity on the mailing list, (b) Popularity, reputation, and user reviews, e.g., number of watchers, number of contributors, user satisfaction.

4   Distributed Ledger Technology for TrustSECO

We select DLT as it enables the provision of trust knowledge as a "commons", i.e., a resource that can be generated and consumed by the community. The current vision is that the DL must be private, in order to guarantee the authenticity and validity of the data, as well as to guarantee the interests of all participants in the network. Therefore, we need to ensure that it is impossible to flood the DL with anonymous parties' trust facts.

The DL is filled by software packages providers and end-users to store events that contribute to or detract from the trust score, for instance, the confirmation of a reproducible build[2] by an end-user (positive) or the observation of an occurrence of a package version in a CVE database (negative). The trust data will be crawled and confirmed by the TrustSECO nodes, i.e., trusted nodes in the network that collaboratively confirm trust facts, even to the extent that they check for a reproducible build.

Trust facts are mined from software repositories, gathered from users and end-user organizations, and collected from third-party trusted databases. One of the challenges in this project is how we deal with such trusted *oracles* to obtain those data from the outside world to accommodate in our DL [11], i.e., data sources that can be considered as reliable or more reliable than TrustSECO itself, such as the CVE database, national vulnerability databases, and software repositories. For now, we will ensure that these databases are observed by multiple actors in the TrustSECO platform, and periodically identify which databases are trustworthy through a consensus algorithm, but in the future, we envision creating a hard connection to these trusted systems.

---

[2] https://reproducible-builds.org/.

The design of the ledger is non-trivial. We address three challenges. First, it is challenging to design or select the consensus algorithms that best fit the ledger. In particular, we will adopt the Raft [6] algorithm, to ensure that even under stress, we are guaranteed consensus. We will need to find a balance between costs to the network (of confirming data, for instance) and a healthy consensus size that leads to reliable facts in the ledger. Secondly, we need to explore what the best way is of handling the trusted third parties, such as Libraries.io and Github, who provide excellent sources for data, that is typically un-compromised. As well as the DL network must be confidential, which helps to eliminate some commercial interests from undermining trust. Finally, we need to design mechanisms that make the ledger sustained by the community, without incurring significant costs to the participants in the ecosystem.

Based on these challenges, the main requirements for the ledger are: (a) The DL must be scalable and cheap, (b) The DL must be easy and fast to search through, (c) The DL must be tamper-proof, and (d) The DL's transaction format can evolve, so new transaction types can be stored later.

Before the DL design, we first need to explore the data that is available about packages. There is a significant amount of trust data available online. For instance, we explore how existing CVE databases are used, or we can use digital signatures to ensure that a particular set of software engineers from a particular location have worked on source code. While this does not guarantee the reliability of the code, this kind of knowledge can be trusted by the software end-users. The sources of our trust data are twofold:

Online Data Sources. We will make an exploration of the data that is available about package reputation. For instance, what data we can ethically gather on package software providers, what data is available about project health, and whether we can support customers of packages to give trust ratings to packages. Our initial experiments will be primarily with the data available on Libraries.io and our own generated data. A successful build reproduction by a package end-user in the ecosystem, for instance, is a data point that adds to the trust in a particular package. A list of potential data sources are: (a) Github: project health, software developer identities, etc. (b) Libraries.io: stars, SourceRank, etc. (c) Common Vulnerabilities and Exposures Databases: (c.1) https://www.vulncode-db.com/, (c.2) https://nvd.nist.gov/vuln/search, (c.3) https://cve.mitre.org/cve/, etc. (d) Repology.org: Contains data on which package repository contains the most up-to-date package. Contains repository health statistics. (e) Owasp: Meta-data for what constitutes a trustworthy package. (f) Trustix: Reproducible build data.

Software Stakeholders. TrustSECO participants will benefit from using Trust-SECO data, accordingly, they must also provide data themselves. If a community provides data about their satisfactory usage of a particular package, it will contribute positively to the trust score. Furthermore, if end-users are not happy with a particular package (version), it may detract from the trust score.

The TrustSECO DAO for a Sustainable Infrastructure

We need a sustainable infrastructure that can independently function after the academic project ends. As trust is a phenomenon created in the SECO as a form of *digital commons*, it should also be managed by the ecosystem. The open-source community has a track record of self-cleansing through transparency and communal solution finding, so we hypothesize that the ledger can sustain itself through a contribution from the community. We envision a Distributed Autonomous Organization (DAO) [4], a distributed ledger-based system that enables people to coordinate and govern themselves mediated by a set of self-executing rules deployed on a public distributed ledger, and whose governance is decentralised (i.e., independent from central control).

To launch the DAO successfully, we take the DAO reference model of Wang et al. [14] as a starting point, who address the major design decisions as a choice in Organization Form, Incentive Mechanism, and Governance Operation. We discuss the best way to enter the DAO and make design choices with our industry partners on this basis. We aim to include incentives for participants to participate in the infrastructure, such as access to exclusive data when a participant provides hardware for the project.

5   Evaluation of the Proposed Platform and Future Work

Launching TrustSECO requires extensive evaluation before we can assume success. As we follow a design science approach [5], we must continually evaluate our approach, our intermediate products, and our potential stakeholders. The aim is to meet the needs of experts and stakeholders by progressively improving and adapting the platform so that our artifacts are rational and effective [13]. This is done by broadcasting our ideas to the different communities that are working on software engineering, software security, information systems, and distributed ledger communities. We are in discussion, for instance, with the Lisk Center in Utrecht, where multiple DLTs are under development. Meanwhile, there are multiple international commercial stakeholders who have committed to this project with both research funding and time.

Secondly, our artifacts are evaluated using technical experiments. We will evaluate the technical performance with real-world data. This approach helps us to identify and address some potential performance problems, such as response time, number of concurrent users, transactions per second or queries per second. For example, one concern is how our product handles the overhead of adding query DL to the ecosystem whenever someone builds a software system, especially when the system has dozens or even hundreds of components.

We define the following as near-future work. First, we will create a survey to establish how our stakeholders would calculate trust scores based on the impact factors identified in the SLR. Secondly, we continue developing the prototype towards a minimum viable product for early experiments with existing package managers. Thirdly, we are developing sentiment analysis techniques to extract trust facts from data sources such as Stack Overflow. Finally, we intend to deliver a prototype for the score calculation mechanism.

6   Conclusion and Status of the Project

This paper introduces the main concepts behind TrustSECO, a distributed ledger-based infrastructure that aims to provide a trustful SECO. TrustSECO targets the whole ecosystem instead of focusing on one language or package ecosystem alone. With TrustSECO, software package providers can guarantee that the software that has left software engineers' desks worldwide is the same as the software installed on the end-users' systems and that the software is maintained in a 'healthy' manner. Furthermore, TrustSECO provides users with insight into the trust levels that they can put into the software they use daily. Finally, we hope that TrustSECO can become the plumbing under the trust system that guarantees the software we use to run a modern society. In the next paragraphs, we report our progress.

Structured Literature Review into Software Trust - Several interesting models have been proposed to assist end-users in component software selection. However, most of the models aim to assess software quality, some factors they considered are difficult to collect or measure, furthermore, trust in software packages and package managers has not been studied enough. We have a team of five researchers who have are working on an SLR to determine how trust in software is defined and the factors that positively or negatively influence the perception of trust in the SECO by studying 593 scientific articles. We formulated the following research questions to guide our study: (1) How is the concept of software trust defined in literature? (2) What trust factors do end-user organizations consider when selecting software products? We uncover the trust relationships between end-user organizations and (a) software producing organizations, (b) software products and versions, (c) software developers, and (d) software package managers.

TrustSECO Infrastructure Prototype - We have developed a prototype of the TrustSECO infrastructure[3]. The prototype works as a plug-in for the npm and tells npm to avoid particular packages or package versions based on the trust data that we have stored in the DL. The DL is a database of trust facts that is currently stored in the Ethereum blockchain, but we are looking for another platform for reasons of scalability [3].

Interview Study with Software Engineers - We conducted structured interviews with twelve software engineers from different domains to explore how they perceive trust during the software package selection [8]. From the interviews, we conclude three things. (1) Technical factors and ecosystem factors are equally important. (2) Documentation, e.g. testing reports, training material, or even grey literature, can give a first impression of the software's technical capabilities. (3) Trust is subjective. Different kinds of software engineers hold different views on trust. Hence, provision of specific guidelines, reliable evidence, and customized functionalities are needed to help end-users and organizations build trust scores.

---

[3] https://github.com/SecureSECO/TrustSECO.

Business Model Exploration - We have received a research grant to explore the business model that can sustain the TrustSECO infrastructure after the academic project is finished. We are using the DAOCanvas[4] to explore how we make the TrustSECO infrastructure sustainable and self-governing with a DAO.

Acknowledgements. We thank the TrustSECO team that participated in the Odyssey Momentum Hackathon for their conceptual contributions to this paper. Specifically, we want to thank Tom Peirs, Jozef Siu, Venja Beck, Floris Jansen, and Elena Baninemeh for their inspirational ideas and their code on https://github.com/SecureSECO/TrustSECO. We also thank Swayam Shah for constructive criticism and ideas.

References

1. Cadariu, M., Bouwers, E., Visser, J., van Deursen, A.: Tracking known security vulnerabilities in proprietary software systems. In: 2015 IEEE 22nd International Conference on Software Analysis, Evolution, and Reengineering, pp. 516–519. IEEE (2015)
2. Cho, J.H., Chan, K., Adali, S.: A survey on trust modeling. ACM Comput. Surv. (CSUR) **48**(2), 1–40 (2015)
3. Farshidi, S., Jansen, S., España, S., Verkleij, J.: Decision support for blockchain platform selection: three industry case studies. IEEE TEM **67**, 1109–1128 (2020)
4. Hassan, S., Filippi, P.D.: Decentralized autonomous organization. Internet Policy Rev. **10**(2) (2021). https://doi.org/10.14763/2021.2.1556
5. Hevner, A.R., March, S.T., Park, J., Ram, S.: Design science in information systems research. MIS Q. **28**, 75–105 (2004)
6. Howard, H.: Arc: analysis of raft consensus. Tech. rep., University of Cambridge, Computer Laboratory (2014)
7. Iqbal, M., Matulevičius, R.: Blockchain-based application security risks: a systematic literature review. In: Proper, H., Stirna, J. (eds.) Advanced Information Systems Engineering Workshops. CAiSE 2019. Lecture Notes in Business Information Processing, vol. 349. Springer, Cham. https://doi.org/10.1007/978-3-030-20948-3_16
8. Jansen, F., Jansen, S., Hou, F.: TrustSECO: an interview survey into software trust. arXiv:2101.06138 (2021)
9. Jansen, S., Cusumano, M.A., Brinkkemper, S.: Software Ecosystems: Analyzing and Managing Business Networks in the Software Industry. Edward Elgar, Cheltenham (2013)
10. Larios Vargas, E., Aniche, M., Treude, C., Bruntink, M., Gousios, G.: Selecting third-party libraries: the practitioners' perspective. In: Proceedings of ESEC/FSE, pp. 245–256 (2020)
11. Lo, S.K., Xu, X., Staples, M., Yao, L.: Reliability analysis for blockchain oracles. Comput. Electr. Eng. **83**, 106582 (2020)
12. Paulus, S., Mohammadi, N.G., Weyer, T.: Trustworthy software development. In: De Decker, B., Dittmann, J., Kraetzer, C., Vielhauer, C. (eds.) CMS 2013. LNCS, vol. 8099, pp. 233–247. Springer, Heidelberg (2013). https://doi.org/10.1007/978-3-642-40779-6_23

---

[4] https://daocanvas.webflow.io/.

13. Peffers, K., Rothenberger, M., Tuunanen, T., Vaezi, R.: Design science research evaluation. In: Peffers, K., Rothenberger, M., Kuechler, B. (eds.) DESRIST 2012. LNCS, vol. 7286, pp. 398–410. Springer, Heidelberg (2012). https://doi.org/10.1007/978-3-642-29863-9_29
14. Wang, S., Ding, W., Li, J., Yuan, Y., Ouyang, L., Wang, F.Y.: Decentralized autonomous organizations: concept, model, and applications. IEEE Trans. Comput. Soc. Syst. **6**(5), 870–878 (2019)
15. Zhu, M.X., Luo, X.X., Chen, X.H., Wu, D.D.: A non-functional requirements trade-off model in trustworthy software. Inf. Sci. **191**, 61–75 (2012)

EMoBI

EMoBI 2021 Preface

There can be no question that the vital role information systems (IS) have come to assume in present-day organizations is tied to a host of moral concerns. IS are at work in almost all types of routine transactions, and they frequently facilitate the making of strategic decisions with far-reaching consequences for individuals and society. For IS system designers and engineers, there arises the need not only to study, *in situ*, the ethical ramifications of IS in organizations but also to critically reflect upon the ways in which possible detrimental effects can be recognized, and avoided, in the very design of these systems.

The workshop series *Ethics and Morality in Business Informatics* (EMoBI) is intended to provide a forum for IS academics and professionals to discuss the ethical dimensions of the design and use of IS, and to discern and tackle moral presuppositions and omissions in the methodology of the field. The 2021 edition was the third installment in the series, and the first organized at the *International Conference on Advanced Information Systems Engineering* (CAiSE). The first two editions were held at the German *Wirtschaftsinformatik* conference in 2019 and 2020. We were glad to be given the opportunity to arrange EMoBI 2021 at the renowned academic conference in systems engineering that is CAiSE.

Regrettably, with the COVID-19 pandemic still holding sway over substantial parts of societal, professional, and academic life, the number of researchers finding themselves able to make a contribution to the workshops at the conference was limited. Nonetheless, we are pleased that out of two submissions to our workshop, we were able to accept one paper. The reviews were single blind, with each submission receiving three independent reviews. The format established by the workshop organizers for the presentation was a combined super workshop, integrating contributions from several distinct workshop series.

The paper entitled *"Values in Design Methodologies for AI"* by Huib Aldewereld and Tina Mioch deals with the adoption of Value-Sensitive Design (VSD) principles in methods for systems design, with special emphasis on Artificial Intelligence (AI) projects. The analysis undertaken by the authors is thoughtful and critical, and it is revealed that despite some steps taken, more work is needed if the tenets of VSD are to become an integral and, ultimately, effective part of IS design.

We wish to express our gratitude to the authors for their contribution to our workshop, to the Program Committee members for their careful reviews, and to the organizers of the CAiSE workshops for their valuable support in organizing EMoBI 2021 under such unusual conditions.

May 2021

Jens Gulden
Alexander C. Bock
Sergio España

EMoBI 2021 Organization

Workshop Chairs

Jens Gulden — Utrecht University, the Netherlands
Alexander C. Bock — University of Duisburg-Essen, Germany
Sergio España — Utrecht University, the Netherlands

Program Committee

Fatma Başak Aydemir	Boğaziçi University, Turkey
Oliver Bendel	FHNW School of Business, Switzerland
Dominik Bork	Vienna University of Technology, Austria
Fabiano Dalpiaz	Utrecht University, the Netherlands
Hector Florez	Universidad Distrital Francisco José de Caldas, Colombia
Ulrich Frank	University of Duisburg-Essen, Germany
Waqar Hussain	Monash University, Australia
Sedef Akinli Kocak	Ryerson University, Canada
Assaf Marron	Weizmann Institute of Science, Israel
Björn Niehaves	University of Siegen, Germany
Ezio Di Nucci	University of Copenhagen, Denmark
Kai Riemer	University of Sydney, Australia
Stefan Strecker	University of Hagen, Germany

Values in Design Methodologies for AI

Huib Aldewereld[(✉)] and Tina Mioch

Department of Artificial Intelligence, University of Applied Sciences Utrecht,
Utrecht, The Netherlands
huib.aldewereld@hu.nl

Abstract. Addressing and integrating human values into AI design and development processes in research and practice can be difficult, and a clear methodological approach can clarify issues of both theory and practice. One such approach is Value Sensitive Design (VSD), an established theory for addressing issues of values in a systematic and principled fashion in the design of information technology. However, it is unclear how VSD is translated into current design practices and whether it has been integrated into existing methodologies. In this paper, we investigated whether and to what extent VSD has passed down into design methodologies used in practice. We found that the actual application of VSD in methodologies is limited, but that in the last few years, steps have been taken to bridge the gap between theory and practice.

Keywords: Value-sensitive design · System engineering · Ethics

1 Introduction

Ethics is an increasingly important topic in the current age of digitisation. With further and faster development of artificial intelligence (AI) technology, the question of what it means to be human and which parts of our daily routines we should or should not entrust to AI systems becomes ever more important [12]. It is therefore not surprising that the European Union recently launched a set of ethical guidelines to control and direct the creation of 'intelligent' systems [1][1]. These high-level design guidelines are meant to ensure the trustworthiness and safety of the complex systems that are being created. Also, the IEEE global initiative for ethical considerations in AI and autonomous systems has been launched with its mission to "ensure every technologist is educated, trained and empowered to prioritize ethical considerations". This initiative further stresses that there is a necessity to align technology to humans in terms of moral values and ethical principles [38]. Ethical discussions on technology development have a long history. However, the ethical debate has primarily focused on principles (the 'what' of AI ethics), rather than on practise (the 'how') [31].

---

[1] In contrast to the US and China, the European Union is trying to position itself as the world leader of 'human centered AI': https://www.weforum.org/agenda/2021/02/heres-what-you-need-to-know-about-the-new-ai-arms-race/.

© Springer Nature Switzerland AG 2021
A. Polyvyanyy and S. Rinderle-Ma (Eds.): CAiSE 2021 Workshops, LNBIP 423, pp. 139–150, 2021.
https://doi.org/10.1007/978-3-030-79022-6_12

As an engineer of intelligent systems it thus becomes increasingly important to be able to weigh decisions and ethical considerations in a structured way during the design process. A possible approach proposed by the IEEE initiative to guide ethical research is *Value Sensitive Design* (VSD). Originally introduced in 1996 [16], VSD is a philosophical approach to design technology that accounts for human values in a principled and systematic manner throughout the design process [18]. It can look back at over 20 years of constant development and is considered by many as the most comprehensive approach to account for human values in technology design (e.g., [29]). It also has been subject of reviews and research regarding inclusion into other methodologies, mostly intended for researchers, e.g., advice for VSD researchers on how to complete and enhance their methodological approach as the research community moves forward [45]. However, further research is needed towards translating VSD into the current AI engineering practice and how values can be integrated into existing AI engineering methodologies to make them actually usable in practice [27].

In this work we make the first step towards the translation of VSD in the AI engineering practice by revealing the adoption of VSD in current design methodologies. This leads us to the following research question:

To what extent are principles of VSD passed down into design methods for AI that are actually used in practice?

To investigate this question, we identify two sub-questions that will be investigated:

1. What AI engineering methodologies use aspects or elements of value-sensitive design?
2. What are the value-oriented AI methodologies that are used in practice?

To answer these questions, we first provide a brief overview of the principles of VSD, followed by a description of the literature review that we performed of academic papers to answer our first sub-question. Then, in Sect. 4, we describe the uses of the methodologies we have found and end this paper with answers to our research questions and a discussion of the results.

2   Values in Design

Recently much attention has been given to the ethical development of systems (e.g., through the use of VSD [16] or Design for Values [44]). These approaches focus on the integration of human values in the development of technological systems, AI systems included [12]. Based on traditional values from deontological and consequentialist moral orientations and previous work in human-computer interaction, Friedman and Kahn [17] identified 12 human values with ethical import (e.g., freedom from bias, autonomy, and accountability), which, although not being comprehensive, form a good basis for methodological investigation towards values for concrete applications.

VSD focuses on the determination of the overall values that are at stake in the development process. Through the use of the *Tripartite methodology* [36],

VSD explores the *Conceptual* design space, the *Empirical* design space, and the *Technical* design space (not necessarily in that order). The Conceptual investigation explores the stakeholders and their values that are at stake in the design (value discovery). Moreover, it tries to determine what kind of instantiation of that value is applicable. In the Empirical investigation, through discussions with stakeholders, it is identified how these values are impacted and what tensions exist between them. Through the Technical investigation, high-level design choices are made and evaluated, to ensure compliance with the identified values of the stakeholders.

It should be noted that VSD focuses on high-level value conflicts, and tries to determine the possible (technical) design space allowed by the combination of values of the stakeholders [2,43]. Tensions between the value conceptions at later stages of the development should be evaluated, according to VSD, but it is not clearly described how this should be done. It is also not clear how the values should subsequently be translated into concrete design requirements (or, in terms of software development, functional and non-functional requirements).

Building on the concepts of VSD, Aldewereld et al. [2] proposed a conceptual framework to relate the value deliberations to the engineering of sociotechnical systems. The framework, however, has not been extended with a practical methodology so far. Another attempt of relating VSD to requirements engineering focuses heavily on the value discovery phase, without providing enough concrete methodological steps to link it to the engineering practice [23]. Also, there has been effort to support skillful VSD practice, focusing on some methodological strategies and heuristics [18]. However, these attempts remained abstract also. When looking at the literature on the use of VSD in projects over the last twenty years [45], only a handful of projects reported improvements by using VSD and applied all aspects of VSD.

Points of critique are, amongst others, that VSD lacks a normative, ethical component in order for it to meet the criteria for implementing (moral) values into design in an ethically justified manner, that the integration of empirical methods with conceptual research within the methodology of VSD is obscure, and that the concept of values, as well as their realization, is left undetermined [29]. One of the other main shortcomings is that there is a gap between the theoretical framework of VSD and applying it in practice. Some attempts in that direction have been made, however. For instance, van de Poel [43] describes how to conceptually relate values into design requirements as part of the VSD approach. He introduces the notion of *value hierarchy*; a hierarchical structure of values, norms and design requirements. However, he does not specify how to include this translation activity into (AI) development. In addition, the steps that need to be taken to identify the different hierarchical elements are not further explicated.

Another attempt to integrate human values in the development of technological systems is the socio-cognitive engineering methodology that is specifically geared for the development of human-machine cooperation [33]. It combines a human-centered approach with an emphasis on technology, and consists of a foundation, specification, and evaluation component. It assumes a situated design and evaluation process, and combines methods from user-centered design, cognitive engineering, and requirements analyses. It has been successfully applied for research in various domains, e.g., to develop social robots for children with diabetes [28]. Recently, it has been extended to allow for a VSD process [34].

Approaching the problem from the other direction, some proposals towards a more inclusive manner of design can be found in the field of System Engineering as well. Methods like Soft Systems Engineering [8] were deliberately introduced to deal with the more intangible aspects of the design challenge. A rather interesting approach is that of *Value Engineering* [11]. Value Engineering (VE) is a methodological approach to system design that tries to provide a concrete measure of success. VE complements System Engineering. Through the introduction of *value functions* or by using *value criteria*, the system developer tries to define a quantifiable means to determine the desirability of the outcomes of the design decisions from the perspective of the client. With a broad enough scope, societal needs and ethical considerations might be usable in this way as well; however, we could not find examples of this, and most approaches focus on the monetary/cost type of 'value' instead.

3   Value-Sensitive Engineering Methodologies

To examine the extent to which VSD principles are being applied in generic AI methodologies, we performed two literature studies, consulted various sources (including ACM Digital Library, ScienceDirect, SpringerLink, Wiley Online Library and WorldCat.org). The first literature study was focused on finding specific value-oriented approaches integrated into design and development methodologies for AI systems. We focused on AI in general instead of its various subfields, to find generic value-oriented AI methodologies. A search on the combination of "Artificial Intelligence", "Methodology" and "Value Sensitive Design" (or synonyms) resulted in 21 papers, of which only 5 were found relevant to our topic. The relevant papers are discussed in subsection 3.1.

Due to the underwhelming number of results and the acknowledgement that AI engineering is a sub-field of the wider areas of Software and System Engineering, we broadened our scope to include these as well. We used a second key phrase *("software engineering" OR "system engineering") AND "methodology" AND ("value" OR "ethics" OR "societal" OR "norms")*, which resulted in a total of 961 papers.

A first rigorous selection of these papers was made based on the title of the paper; papers were included in this study if the title gave any indication that it concerned either a methodology or had some relation to ethics. This resulted in a selection of 45 papers. Each of those 45 papers was further examined to determine whether they indeed concerned a methodological approach with ethical aspects: 11 papers remained in that selection. During reading, it was determined that 3 of the selected papers were still irrelevant to our study because they were too marginally discussing the topics of interest. The other 8 papers are discussed in Subsect. 3.2.

3.1   VSD in AI Engineering

As stated above, we found 5 relevant papers with value-oriented approaches for the methodological design of AI systems.

One of them provides a comprehensive analysis of the spectrum of ethical values and considerations incorporated into the design of current intelligent assistive technology (IAT) for dementia [24]. A systematic literature review was performed and six main thematic families of ethical considerations were identified that had been taken into account, which were autonomy, privacy, beneficence, non-maleficence, interdependence, and justice. Also, they found that 67% of current IATs are developed without any explicit ethical considerations, and that for the IATs where ethical considerations were made, the number of different (ethical) values taken into account seem to be limited and not comprehensive. However, neither an analysis of the methodologies that were used was presented, nor any details of the process of designing for values and selecting relevant values. Although the paper is very relevant and interesting to the field itself, it looks at a subset of applications (IATs for dementia), and leaves the question regarding methodologies used open.

Umbrello [42] argues that the VSD methodology provides a principled approach to embedding common values into AI systems both early and throughout the design process. It focuses on the suitability of the VSD approach to the coordination of various stakeholders involved and implicated in AI research and development. Umbrello demonstrates this by means of an empirical investigation in which different and disparate stakeholder groups are involved in AI design and share some common values that can be used to further strengthen design coordination efforts. VSD is shown to be both able to distill these common values as well as provide a framework for stakeholder coordination.

Gazzaneo et al. [19] introduce a novel way of conceptualizing human operators in industry for emerging technologies and provide a first step of how VSD can be applied to design these emerging technologies for human values. In particular, they look at examples of values and their translation into norms as design objectives, which again can be translated into design requirements. Unfortunately, the approach is motivated by a very limited example. Therefore, it is unclear how detailed the steps have been worked out. Moreover, guidelines for the translation from values to norms and requirements are lacking. It is unclear whether any guidelines exist.

Slota et al. [35] investigate how the societal benefits and harms of AI can be understood. They found that the efforts that are taken regarding a more socially positive outcome of AI often tend to place responsibility and accountability for those outcomes at the moment of design, or at the end user of the system. However, they state that this is not sufficient. The whole ecosystem, including media representations of capacity and potential of AI, regulations and standards, and design affordances contribute to how AI is used and what its impact might be. They make a valid point, but provide no clear methodological approach.

Cawthorne and Robbins-Van Wynsberghe [6,7] are the only ones (within the articles we have found with the above mentioned search terms) that provide methodological steps with value sensitive elements. They describe the redesign process of a commercially available drone for a specific use case with high regards for the moral tensions (the drones are used for transporting blood samples). We return to this example later in Sect. 4.

As stated above, we have found a relatively small number of relevant papers regarding methodologies used for AI engineering that include VSD aspects. A number of projects do take (a limited number of) ethical considerations into account (as for example found in [24]); however, these considerations do not seem to be part of a methodology. The methodological approaches that were found (e.g., [6]) are very recent and promising applications.

3.2   VSD in System Engineering

We now turn to the relevant papers about ethics in Software and System Engineering approaches.

An relevant approach is Value-Based System Engineering and its relatives, in which for example the V-model of standard system engineering is being enhanced based on 'value-based' supportive information in the verification process [30]. However, while 'value' is considered as more than just cost and used as quantitative measures to enable a multi-decision making approach to solving issues, it is unclear how aspects such as reputation and morality are to be quantified in this process.

Kannan et al. [26] propose an extension to Value Driven Design as traditional system engineering approaches are not well enough suited for handling risks preferences of stakeholders. Because requirements, used in the design process, are surrogates of a stakeholder's true preferences, they do not provide enough guidance to the engineers to make decisions on feasible alternatives. Instead, value-functions can be used [26], a concept of Value Driven Design [10], as they represent the true preferences of stakeholders. Value-based System Engineering [26] then tries to ensure consistency in the decisions made on each of the different components of the system in relation to this central value-function. It therefore suffers from the same flaws as VBSE mentioned above.

Thew et al. [39,40] have done a current practice analysis with industry about the relevance of stakeholders values, motivations, and emotions and the impact and adoption in their work. They propose the specification of taxonomies for values, motivations, and emotions, and incorporated these into the Value-Based Requirement Engineering (VBRE) method in an iterative process. A preliminary evaluation was carried out by applying the method to the requirements analyses in two software projects. The approach is motivated by Mumford's ETHICS method [32], which provides guidance on identifying values by means of questionnaires. At the moment, the taxonomic approach in VBRE is not yet combined with VSD; however, the authors expect that it could be valuable to integrate aspects of VSD into their approach to stimulate considerations of value-oriented design implications.

Taylor and Moynihan [37] explore the use of ethics in various system engineering methodologies focused on information systems. They conclude that only a handful of methodologies applied include some elements of ethical aspects. Methodologies that include ethics are ETHICS [32] and MULTIVIEW [4]. However, as neither are used on a wide-scale commercial basis, they conclude that the vast majority of information systems methodologies used provide no guidance for ethical problems. To tackle that issue, they propose an extension to the widely used Structured Systems Analysis and Design Method (SSADM) [13], instead. SSADM is one of the most widely used methodologies in the UK, and already includes the analysis of social issues by incorporating elements of Soft Systems Methodology [8].

Systems thinking (ST) is often regarded as an holistic approach conceptually underpinning Systems Engineering [5]. It serves as a bridge between theory and practice and is deemed as essential for system engineers. By its nature it is targeted as a method to understand a system as a whole (including relations with society). Especially the theories of Soft Systems Engineering [8,9] and Critical Systems Thinking [25,41] appear relevant to our question. Soft Systems Engineering is meant to deal with soft system constraints originating from the perspective view of people; as reality is viewed through a 'subjectivist view', interrelations of such perspectives should be included in the System Engineering attempt. Critical System Thinking is an attempt to combine both the hard and soft practices. In an attempt to create a holistic system engineering approach, Camelia and Ferris [5] propose to combine the functionalist perspective (from systems dynamics [15]), the interpretative perspective (from soft systems methodology [8]) and the emancipatory perspective (from critical systems heuristics [41]). Unfortunately, the authors do not provide the necessary details of how this combination is to be used on actual system engineering challenges.

In [3], the SPADE software engineering methodology [22] is utilised to support the decision analysis process of unbiased comparison of appraisals in the acquisition of car- and passenger ferries in Norway. The interesting aspect of this example is the high amount of societal and value driven elements in the decision making process, which the authors capture in the use of a value network in the 'Problem formulation' step of the SPADE methodology. While the authors show the possibilities of incorporating values and ethical aspects in the value network, the methodology does not enforce system engineers to do so; if the engineer is mindful of the ethics, the methodology can support it, but it does not ensure it.

Génova and Gonzàlez [20] took a different approach; instead of presenting a methodology, they discuss how to teach ethics to engineers. The authors acknowledge that ethics is important to current engineering disciplines, but also argue that typical ethical education is not expected to be successful. Focusing on Virtue ethics (opposed to deontics or utilitarianism), the authors propose a course outline to attempt to incorporate ethical thinking in the engineering mindset. While an important step in getting ethics better ingrained in the engineering practice, the paper is not relevant to our question as it does not mention an engineering methodology.

All of the relevant efforts mentioned above lack a clear way to either elicit the true value-function, or miss methodological steps to transpose intangible effects, such as reputation and morality, into a clear quantitative measure. Through the examples provided, it shows that some of the methodologies have the potential to capture and use values in the engineering process, although none of them have the methodological elements needed to ensure that the inclusion of values is anything more than a coincidental exercise performed by the engineer.

4   Examples of Applications in Research

In this section we return to some of the methodologies described before, to explore them in relation to our second research sub-question. We want to determine whether the found methodologies have made the transition from science to the engineering practice. To this extent we re-examined the papers mentioned above, and selected those that mentioned either application(s) or projects in practice.

As mentioned in Sect. 2, some conceptual steps have been taken in the field of Design for Values, to align the engineering process with moral values. Attempts were made to bridge the existing gap between the philosophical aspects of VSD to the engineering reality [2,23,43]. For instance, VSD has been applied to the design of poultry farms [43], but unfortunately it was not mentioned whether the methodology can be re-used. Other only present motivational examples that lack the complexity of a project as occurring in practice [2,23].

Only recently, Harbers et al. [21] designed and built a prototype of a virtual assistant for workload harmonization in teams, using the socio-cognitive engineering methodology [33] in which value-sensitive design aspects were included. The prototype was integrated with a high-fidelity simulator and evaluated by means of focus groups of domain experts. While not originally being a part of the socio-cognitive engineering methodology, they have shown that the VSD can be integrated into this methodology in a real engineering project.

ETHICS [32], and MULTIVIEW [4] as a derivative, are actually rather old (compared to VSD). The methodology originally had its prime days in the 70s. The methodology emphasizes the incorporation of employee preferences and public opinion in the development of socio-technical (information) systems. While rather successful at first, its decline started in the 90s when the industry moved to focus on efficiency and effectiveness [14]. As systems grew more complex and started integrating large off-the-shelves solutions, ETHICS fell into decline. With the current emphasis on ethics and morality in the development of AI, a revisit to the principles of the methodology might be worthwhile.

The SPADE methodology [22] was developed with the intend of enabling sustainable development within the system engineering context. Earlier we saw the methodology applied to the evaluation of appraisals in ferry acquisitions in Norways [3]. It shows that the methodology is capable of dealing with societal constraints in a development project, but it is the only example that we could find. Other papers on the application of the methodology tend to focus on other (non-ethical) aspects of the development process.

Another recent application of the VSD methodology and ethical framework is the application to ethically evaluate and proactively guide the design of drones in healthcare contexts [7]. A commercially available drone was analysed in the context of a blood sample transportation use case; then, a redesigned drone was proposed based on the identified values [6]. VSD was used to make underlying assumptions, trade-offs, and stakeholders explicit and translate them into design requirements. A general framework for the design and implementation of drones in public healthcare is planned.

While the results on our exploration of methodologies was lacking some truly discernible results, the results of our exploration of methodologies applied in practice holds more promises. While minimal, there are some rather interesting applications of VSD in practice, all of which are very recent. There appears to still be a large gap between VSD to engineering practice.

5   Conclusion and Discussion

In this paper, we investigated whether and to what extent VSD has passed down into (AI) engineering methodologies and is actually being applied. First, we inventoried which methodologies have been extended with aspects of VSD or explicitly take values into account; then, we described examples of applications that were designed with these methodologies.

We found that the application of VSD in methodologies, at least as found in current literature, is very limited. Only a relatively small number of papers has been found that describe integration of VSD aspects into existing (AI) engineering methodologies. Several methodologies were found that have the potential to capture and use values in the engineering process; however, for most of them, no explicit integration with VSD had been done and it is unclear how this can be achieved. A number of papers has been found that describe research in which values have been identified and incorporated into the design and development of technology. Because VSD was not explicitly integrated into the methodology, this led to a more or less unstructured, incomplete, or random choice of values that were taken into account, and to no methodological support for the design, develop, and evaluation phase. For that reason, we conclude that VSD principles seem to have been passed down into design methods for AI to a limited extent, and when the case, mostly ad-hoc without explicit methodological integration.

We recognize that our choice of keywords limits the results of our literature study. Additionally to focusing on AI in general, we propose to extend the search with keywords relating to sub-fields in AI in the future, e.g., robotics and machine learning. In addition, we did not include industry or domain literature into our search; as a consequence, relevant descriptions of design methodologies in practice might have been overlooked.

Furthermore, as mentioned above, current design methodologies might be sufficiently powerful to include values; practitioners might not believe that they need additional steps in their methodology. In addition, developments regarding VSD in engineering practices might not be published at all by companies.

We have found that the first steps towards integrating VSD into design methodologies has been a very recent development and that there are a few interesting example applications that have been designed and developed in a methodological fashion. These example applications show promise towards closing the gap between the theoretical framework of VSD and engineering methodologies. In future research, we propose to inventory whether and how VSD is part of the everyday practice in companies, and the role values play in the design process in practice. Our overall goal is to further research how to integrate relevant VSD aspects into existing AI engineering methodologies, and apply these methodologies to the design and development of prototypes.

References

1. AI High-Level Expert Group. Ethics guidelines for trustworthy AI. B-1049 Brussels (2019)
2. Aldewereld, H., Dignum, V., Tan, Y.: Design for values in software development. In: van den Hoven, J., Vermaas, P.E., van de Poel, I. (eds.) Handbook of Ethics, Values, and Technological Design, pp. 831–845. Springer, Dordrecht (2015). https://doi.org/10.1007/978-94-007-6970-0_26
3. Aspen, D.M., Haskins, C., Fet, A.M.: Application of systems engineering to structuring acquisition decisions for marine emission reduction technologies. Syst. Eng. **21**(4), 388–397 (2018)
4. Avison, D.E., Wood-Harper, A.T.: Multiview - an exploration in information systems development. Aust. Comput. J. **18**(4), 174–179 (1986)
5. Camelia, F., Ferris, T.L.J.: Systems thinking in systems engineering. In: INCOSE International Symposium, vol. 26, pp. 1657–1674. Wiley Online Library (2016)
6. Cawthorne, D., Robbins-van Wynsberghe, A.: From HealthDrone to FrugalDrone: value-sensitive design of a blood sample transportation drone. In: 2019 IEEE International Symposium on Technology and Society (ISTAS), pp. 1–7. IEEE (2019)
7. Cawthorne, D., Robbins-van Wynsberghe, A.: An ethical framework for the design, development, implementation, and assessment of drones used in public healthcare. Sci, Eng. Ethics **26**(5), 2867–2891 (2020). https://doi.org/10.1007/s11948-020-00233-1
8. Checkland, P.: Systems thinking, systems practice. Wiley Chichester (1971)
9. Checkland, P.: OR and the systems movement: mappings and conflicts. J. Oper. Res. Soc. **34**(8), 661–675 (1983)
10. Collopy, P.D., Hollingsworth, P.M.: Value-driven design. J. Aircr. **48**(3), 749–759 (2011)
11. de Graaf, R., Van der Linde, G., De Jong, H., Vogt, B.: Value engineering as a specialty for systems engineering: exploring opportunities. INSIGHT **22**(1), 41–44 (2019)
12. Dignum, V.: Responsible Artificial Intelligence: How to Develop and Use AI in a Responsible Way. Springer Nature, Basingstoke, UK (2019)
13. Duncan, J.: SSADM in practice: a version 4 text. Macmillan International Higher Education, New York, USA (1995)
14. Elbanna, A., Newman, M.: The rise and decline of the ethics methodology of systems implementation: lessons for is research. J. Inf. Technol. **28**(2), 124–136 (2013)

15. Forrester, J.W.: World Dynamics. Wright-Allen Press, USA (1971)
16. Friedman, B.: Value-sensitive design. Interactions **3**(6), 16–23 (1996)
17. Friedman, B., Kahn Jr., P.H.: Human Values, Ethics, and Design. The human-computer interaction handbook, pp. 1177–1201 (2003)
18. Friedman, B., Hendry, D.G., Borning, A.: A survey of value sensitive design methods. Found. Trends Hum. Comput. Interact. **11**(2), 63–125 (2017)
19. Gazzaneo, L., Padovano, A., Umbrello, S.: Designing smart operator 4.0 for human values: a value sensitive design approach. Proc. Manuf. 42, 219-226 (2020)
20. Génova, G., González, M.R.: Teaching ethics to engineers: a socratic experience. Sci. Eng. Ethics **22**(2), 567–580 (2015). https://doi.org/10.1007/s11948-015-9661-1
21. Harbers, M., Neerincx, M.A.: Value sensitive design of a virtual assistant for workload harmonization in teams. Cogn. Technol. Work **19**(2), 329–343 (2017). https://doi.org/10.1007/s10111-017-0408-4
22. Haskins, C.: Systems engineering analyzed, synthesized, and applied to sustainable industrial park development (2008)
23. Huldtgren, A.: Design for values in ICT. In: van den Hoven, J., Vermaas, P.E., van de Poel, I. (eds.) Handbook of Ethics, Values, and Technological Design, pp. 739–767. Springer, Dordrecht (2015). https://doi.org/10.1007/978-94-007-6970-0_35
24. Ienca, M., Wangmo, T., Jotterand, F., Kressig, R.W., Elger, B.: Ethical design of intelligent assistive technologies for dementia: a descriptive review. Sci. Eng. Ethics **24**(4), 1035–1055 (2018)
25. Jackson, M.C.: Social systems theory and practice: the need for a critical approach. Int. J. Gen. Syst. **10**(2–3), 135–151 (1985)
26. Kannan, H., Mesmer, B.L., Bloebaum, C.L.: Incorporation of risk preferences in a value-based systems engineering framework. Syst. Eng. **23**(2), 237–257 (2020)
27. Leijnen, S., Aldewereld, H., van Belkom, R., Bijvank, R., Ossewaarde, R.: An agile framework for trustworthy AI. In: Proceedings of the 1st International Workshop on New Foundations for Human-Centered AI, p. 8 (2020)
28. Looije, R., Neerincx, M.A., Hindriks, K.V.: Specifying and testing the design rationale of social robots for behavior change in children. Cogn. Syst. Res. **43**, 250–265 (2017)
29. Manders-Huits, N.: What values in design? the challenge of incorporating moral values into design. Sci. Eng. Ethics **17**(2), 271–287 (2011)
30. Mastrofini, M., Cantone, G., Seaman, C., Shull, F., Diep, M., Falessi, D.: Enhancing the system development process performance: a value-based approach. In: INCOSE International Symposium, vol. 22, pp. 401–415. Wiley Online Library (2012)
31. Morley, J., Floridi, L., Kinsey, L., Elhalal, A.: From what to how. an overview of AI ethics tools, methods and research to translate principles into practices (2019). arXiv preprint arXiv:1905.06876
32. Mumford, E.: Values, Technology and Work, p. 318. Springer Science & Business Media, Netherlands (2013). https://doi.org/10.1007/978-94-009-8343-4
33. Neerincx, M.A., Lindenberg, J.: Situated cognitive engineering for complex task environments. Ashgate Publishing Limited, Aldershot (2008)
34. Neerincx, M.A.: Socio-cognitive engineering of a robotic partner for child's diabetes self-management. Frontiers Robot. AI **6**, 118 (2019)
35. Slota, S.C., et al.: Good systems, bad data?: interpretations of AI hype and failures. Proc. Assoc. Inf. Sci. Technol. **57**(1), e275 (2020)
36. Spiekermann, S.: Ethical IT innovation: a value-based system design approach. Auerbach Publications, New York (2015)
37. Taylor, M.J., Moynihan, E.: Analysing IT ethics. Syst. Res. Behav. Sci. Official J. Int. Fed. Syst. Res. **19**(1), 49–60 (2002)

38. The IEEE Global Initiative for Ethical Considerations in AI and Autonomous Systems. Ethically aligned design: A vision for prioritizing wellbeing with AI and autonomous systems. (Version 1) (2016)
39. Thew, S., Sutcliffe, A.: Value-based requirements engineering: method and experience. Requirements Eng. **23**(4), 443–464 (2018)
40. Thew, S.L.: Value based requirements engineering. The University of Manchester, UK (2014)
41. Ulrich, W.: Critical Heuristics of Social Planning: A New Approach to Practical Philosophy. Wiley, Hoboken, USA (1983)
42. Umbrello, S.: Beneficial artificial intelligence coordination by means of a value sensitive design approach. Big Data Cogn. Comput. **3**(1), 5 (2019)
43. Poel, I.: Translating values into design requirements. In: Michelfelder, D.P., McCarthy, N., Goldberg, D.E. (eds.) Philosophy and Engineering: Reflections on Practice, Principles and Process. PET, vol. 15, pp. 253–266. Springer, Dordrecht (2013). https://doi.org/10.1007/978-94-007-7762-0_20
44. Van den Hoven, J., Vermaas, P.E.: Handbook of Ethics, Values, and Technological Design, p. 871. Springer, Netherlands (2015)
45. Winkler, T., Spiekermann, S.: Twenty years of value sensitive design: a review of methodological practices in VSD projects. Ethics Inf. Technol. **23**, 17–21 (2018). https://doi.org/10.1007/s10676-018-9476-2

KET4DF

KET4DF 2021 Preface

The manufacturing industry is entering a new digital era in which ICT technologies and collaboration applications will be integrated with traditional manufacturing practices and processes to increase flexibility and sustainability in manufacturing, along with mass customization and automation, and to improve both quality and productivity.

A digital factory is defined as a multi-layered integration of the information related to various activities regarding manufacturing-related resources in the factory and along the product lifecycle. A central aspect of a digital factory is to enable stakeholders in the product lifecycle to collaborate using software solutions. The digital factory thus expands outside the actual company boundaries and offers the opportunity for the business and its suppliers to collaborate on business processes that affect the supply chain.

This translates not only into a strong technological evolution but also into an unprecedented extension of companies' information systems. Exploitation of data and services derived from disparate and distributed sources, development of scalable and efficient real-time systems, management of expert knowledge, advanced data analytics, and optimized decision making are some of the key challenges that advanced information systems can address in an effort to reach the vision of Industry 4.0.

The goal of the International Workshop on Key Enabling Technologies for Digital Factories (KET4DF) is to attract high-quality research papers focusing on technologies for Industry 4.0, with specific reference to digital factories and smart manufacturing.

The idea of the workshop was born to promote the research topics of some international projects, which have also become the supporters of the workshop: FIRST (H2020 grant # 734599), UPTIME (H2020 grant # 768634), Z-BRE4K (H2020 grant # 768869), QU4LITY (H2020 grant # 825030), BOOST 4.0 (H2020 grant # 780732), and DIH4CPS (H2020 grant #872548).

This second edition of the workshop received two submissions, both of high quality, and the Program Committee decided to propose both for presentation at KET4DF 2021 and inclusion in the CAiSE 2021 Workshops proceedings.

We thank the Workshop Chairs of CAiSE 2021, Stefanie Rinderle-Ma and Artem Polyvyanyy, for their precious support. We also thank the members of the Program Committee and the external reviewers for their hard work in reviewing the submitted papers.

May 2021

Federica Mandreoli
Giacomo Cabri
Gregoris Mentzas
Karl Hribernik

KET4DF 2021 Organization

Organizing Committee

Federica Mandreoli	Università di Modena e Reggio Emilia, Italy
Giacomo Cabri	Università di Modena e Reggio Emilia, Italy
Gregoris Mentzas	National Technical University of Athens, Greece
Karl Hribernik	Bremer Institut für Produktion und Logistik, Germany

Program Committee

Marco Aiello	University of Stuttgart, Germany
Kosmas Alexopoulos	University of Patras, Greece
Dimitris Apostolou	University of Piraeus, China
Yuewei Bai	Shanghai Polytechnic University, China
Luca Bedogni	Università di Modena e Reggio Emilia, Italy
Alexandros Bousdekis	National Technical University of Athens, Greece
Christos Emmanouilidis	University of Groningen, the Netherlands
Fabrício Junqueira	University of São Paulo, Brazil
Fenareti Lampathaki	Suite5, Greece
Alexander Lazovik	University of Groningen, the Netherlands
Joachim Lentes	Fraunhofer IAO, Germany
Marco Lewandowski	University of Bremen, Germany
Sotirios Makris	University of Patras, Greece
Massimo Mecella	Università Sapienza di Roma, Italy
Ifigeneia Metaxa	Atlantis Engineering, Greece
Michele Missikoff	IASI-CNR, Italy
Hervé Panetto	University of Lorraine, France
Pierluigi Petrali	Whirlpool Europe, Italy
Marcos André Pisching	Federal Institute of Santa Catarina, Brazil
Pierluigi Plebani	Politecnico di Milano, Italy
Zoltan Rusák	Technische Universiteit Delft, the Netherland
John Soldatos	University of Glasgow, UK, and Intrasoft International, Luxembourg
Walter Terkaj	STIIMA-CNR, Italy
Lai Xu	Bournemouth University, UK
Paul de Vrieze	Bournemouth University, UK

Real-Time Equipment Health State Prediction with LSTM Networks and Bayesian Inference

Afroditi Fouka, Alexandros Bousdekis[✉], Katerina Lepenioti, and Gregoris Mentzas

Information Management Unit (IMU), Institute of Communication and Computer Systems (ICCS), National Technical University of Athens (NTUA), Athens, Greece
{el11513,albous,klepenioti,gmentzas}@mail.ntua.gr

Abstract. Due to the emergence of sensing technology, a large number of sensors is used to monitor the health state of manufacturing equipment, thus enhancing the capabilities of predicting abnormal behaviours in (near) real-time. However, existing algorithms in predictive maintenance suffer from several limitations related to their scalability, efficiency, and reliability preventing their wide application to various industries. This paper proposes an approach for real-time prediction of the equipment health state using time-domain features extraction, Long Short-Term Memory (LSTM) Neural Networks, and Bayesian Online Changepoint Detection (BOCD). The proposed approach is applied to a real-life case in the steel industry and extensive experiments are performed. The paper also discusses the results and the conclusions drawn from the proposed approach.

Keywords: Predictive analytics · Deep learning · Changepoint detection · Prognosis · Machine learning · Predictive maintenance · Industry 4.0

1 Introduction

Predictive Maintenance has gathered an increasing interest in both literature and practice. Due to the emergence of sensing technology, a large number of sensors is used to monitor the health state of the manufacturing equipment, thus enhancing the capabilities of detecting anomalies and abnormal behaviours in (near) real-time. Anomaly detection in real-time big data processing is a well-studied research area [1, 2] with a large variety of applications in the context of predictive maintenance [3–5]. Beyond that, these technological advancements also form the basis for predicting the health state of the equipment, something which is crucial for the implementation of predictive maintenance [6, 7]. Machine learning algorithms are capable of manipulating the complex and non-linear inputs and the short-term dependencies in this time series data generated by sensors, while they are capable of modelling the complexity of the manufacturing environment [7].

However, existing algorithms in predictive maintenance suffer from the following main limitations [7–10]: (i) they are usually based on supervised learning, i.e. datasets need to be uniquely annotated; (ii) the existing unsupervised learning algorithms usually have a high computational cost, a relatively low response time, while they are sensitive to

© Springer Nature Switzerland AG 2021
A. Polyvyanyy and S. Rinderle-Ma (Eds.): CAiSE 2021 Workshops, LNBIP 423, pp. 155–166, 2021.
https://doi.org/10.1007/978-3-030-79022-6_13

sensor noise; (iii) they mainly rely on laboratory-created or publicly available datasets, with the works analysing data from the actual operation being rare, thus posing challenges to reach a mature application level; (iv) the implementation of appropriate feature engineering approaches is challenging; and, (v) existing deep learning algorithms use massive amounts of data to train large neural networks, thus causing challenges to their accuracy, efficiency, scalability and applicability to some application domains.

In order to tackle these challenges, in this paper, we propose an approach for real-time prediction of the equipment health state using time-domain features extraction, Long Short-Term Memory (LSTM) Neural Networks, and Bayesian Online Changepoint Detection (BOCD). The proposed approach aims at predicting the changepoint from the normal state into a deteriorating state of the equipment in (near) real-time and was applied to a case study from the steel industry. The rest of the paper is organized as follows: Sect. 2 describes the theoretical background of the proposed approach. Section 3 presents the proposed approach for real-time equipment health state prediction. Section 4 shows the results from its application to a real-life scenario in the steel industry. Section 5 concludes the paper and presents our plans for future work.

2 Related Work

Due to the rapid development of sensing technology, a huge variety of sensors are used to monitor the health condition of the manufacturing equipment. Manufacturing systems usually undergo gradual degradation rather than failing abruptly making it possible to detect and predict their degradation behaviour [11]. This fact has led to a large number of research works dealing with data-driven detection and prediction of the equipment health state. Existing literature moves beyond traditional statistical approaches and increasingly adopts machine learning methods [7]. In this context, the need for sequential data processing in health state detection and prediction has made unsupervised learning methods, such as Hidden Markov Models (HMM), to be considered as the most suitable approach [12–14]. Feature engineering in order to tackle with the sensor signal non-stationarity, especially in vibration condition monitoring, is an aspect of outmost importance for the effective processing of raw data [11, 15, 16].

One of the most common sequential modelling techniques is the Recurrent Neural Networks (RNN). The main advantage of RNNs over HMMs is that HMMs have a finite, discrete set of states to represent the system. RNN has no such limitations, while, at the same time, they are able to capture complex non-linear relationships [13]. However, RNN usually underperform when learning long-term dependencies of time series due to the vanishing and exploding gradient problems [7]. Recently, a growing number of deep learning research has been reported in manufacturing industry [6, 7]. The LSTM network, a deep learning extension of RNN, has been designed to prevent the vanishing and exploding gradient problems. LSTM has been applied in several prognostics problems [6, 17, 18]. More advanced LSTM architectures are able to deal with more complex conditions and degradation behaviours [7, 13, 19–21].

Manufacturing systems start at the normal operation and begin to degrade at an uncertain changepoints [7]. The sensor measurements acquired before the changepoint provide very limited information about the degradation process while they occupy the most part of equipment lifetime, thus decreasing the accuracy and efficiency of RUL estimation algorithms. Moreover, most of the existing LSTM networks developed for prognostics assume that no changepoint exists or they assign a fixed changepoint for any unit regardless of the operational conditions, thus decreasing their reliability. There are few research efforts that apply change point detection prior to RUL prediction using LSTM. For example, [18] used the Support Vector Machine (SVM) to detect the change point, while [7] proposed a dual-LSTM for both change point detection and RUL prediction by predicting a health index beyond the changepoint. On the other hand, applying LSTM for predicting the future equipment health state through the identification of changepoints is a direction that has not been explored.

3   The Proposed Approach for Real-Time Equipment Health State Prediction

The proposed approach aims at anticipating changepoints in equipment behaviour in order to predict its health state in real-time. Following the concept of the P-F curve, we define two health states: (i) normal state, in which the equipment performs its operation as expected; and, (ii) dangerous state, in which the equipment is subject to degradation which will lead to a failure. The P-F curve is a well-established representation of asset's behaviour. The condition of an asset deteriorates over time leading to functional failure. Therefore, the failure is considered as a process instead of an instant event. As shown in Fig. 1, this approach provides an opportunity time window, between the time of the potential failure (P), i.e. the point that the equipment starts failing, and the functional failure (F), i.e. the point when the equipment actually fails. With the advancements in sensor technology and machine learning algorithms in the context of predictive maintenance, the point P can be predicted much earlier than the time it becomes visible to the expert.

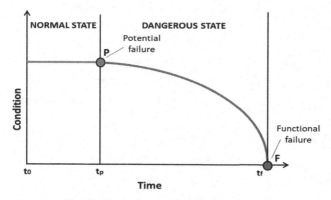

Fig. 1. The P-F curve of equipment health.

The proposed approach consists of 3 main building blocks, as shown in Fig. 2: LSTM (Sect. 3.1), time-domain features extraction (Sect. 3.2), and BOCD (Sect. 3.3).

The sensor measurements are acquired in real-time by the LSTM which generates the predicted sensor measurements over a pre-defined time frame. These predicted sensor data feed into the features extraction building block. Since BOCD is sensitive to noise, in this way, we transform the predicted raw dataset to a rolling feature dataset in order to achieve a higher level of information and thus, eliminate uncertainty. The rolling features extracted from the predicted sensor data feed into the BOCD algorithm, which indicates the log likelihood of having a changepoint and predicts the future health state within the aforementioned time frame.

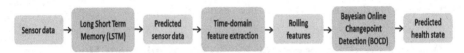

Fig. 2. The data processing in the proposed approach.

3.1 Long Short-Term Memory

The structure of LSTM's cell consists of three gates, which protect and control the cell state allowing information to be removed or added. Each gate, is comprised of a sigmoid layer (σ) and a pointwise multiplication operation, handles the input data and previous hidden state [9]. Sigmoid layer outputs numbers between 0 and 1, describing the percentage of information that is important to be kept. The first one is the forget gate and decides what information is useless for the cell state. Similarly, the input gate decides which new information is going to be stored in cell state. Lastly, the output gate defines the next hidden state, which contains information on previous inputs. Another component in LSTM cell is a tanh layer. In conclusion, the output of LSTM cell is the

Table 1. LSTM's description by equations.

Equations	Description
$f_t = \sigma(W_f * [h_{t-1}, x_t] + b_f)$	Output vector of forget gate
$i_t = \sigma(W_i * [h_{t-1}, x_t] + b_i)$	Output vector of input gate
$\tilde{C_t} = tanh(W_C * [h_{t-1}, x_t] + b_C)$	New candidate values that could be added to the state
$C_t = C_{t-1} * f_t + i_t * \tilde{C_t}$	New cell state
$o_t = \sigma(W_o * [h_{t-1}, x_t] + b_o)$	Output vector of output gate
$h_t = o_t * tanh(C_t)$	New hidden state
x_t	Input data
h_{t-1}	Previous hidden state
$W_{f,i,c,o}, b_{f,i,c,o}$	LSTM parameters that need to be updated during training process

new hidden state and an updated and filtered version of the cell state. Table 1 presents the mathematical background of LSTM.

3.2 Time-Domain Features Extraction

Sensor-generated raw data usually requires a pre-processing phase in order to eliminate uncertainty caused by the sensor noise so that the data analytics models are able to generate reliable outcomes. However, choosing the right techniques and combining them for optimal performance remains a challenge [9, 22]. Statistical time-domain features such as mean, Root Mean Square (RMS), and Standard Deviation (SD) were usually used to identify the differences between vibration signals. More advanced statistical-based features such as skewness and kurtosis can be applied to the signal which is not purely stationary [23].

These features examine the Probability Density Function (PDF) of the signal. In particular, skewness is used to measure whether the signal is negatively or positively skewed, while kurtosis measures the peak value of the PDF and indicates if the signal is impulse in nature. In addition, kurtosis is obtained from the peak of the PDF of the vibration signal, while skewness is obtained from the mean value of the PDF of the vibration signal [15]. Table 2 presents the aforementioned features that have been extensively applied for condition monitoring. In real-time data processing, the features are calculated in a rolling way in order to achieve real-time higher level of information and computational efficiency [24].

Table 2. Statistical time-domain features for condition monitoring.

Feature	Formula	Description
Mean	$m = \frac{\sum_{i=1}^{N} x_i}{N}$	Mean measures the sum of the signal values divided by the number of values
SD	$SD = \sqrt{\frac{\sum_{i=1}^{N}(x_i-m)^2}{N}}$	SD measures the square root of the signal dispersion around their reference mean value
RMS	$RMS = \sqrt{\frac{1}{N}\sum_{i=1}^{N} x_i^2}$	RMS measures the square root of the signal mean square. The RMS value increase gradually as fault developed
Skewness	$Sk = \frac{\sum_{i=1}^{N}(x_i-m)^3}{(N-1)\sigma^3}$	Skewness quantifies the asymmetry behavior of signal through its PDF
Kurtosis	$Ku = \frac{\sum_{i=1}^{N}(x_i-m)^4}{(N-1)\sigma^4}$	Kurtosis quantifies the peak value of the PDF

3.3 Bayesian Online Changepoint Detection

Efficient changepoint detection requires appropriate processing of streaming data to ensure that the delay time between a true change and its detection, as well as the rate of

Table 3. Notation of the BOCD algorithm.

Notation	Description
$x_{a:b}$	The contiguous set of observations between time a and b inclusive
r_t	The length of the current run at time t
$X_{t+1}^{(r+1)}$	The set of observations associated with the run r_t
H	The hazard function
$P(x_{t+1}|x_{1:t})$	The marginal predictive distribution over the posterior one on the run length
$P(r_t, x_{1:t})$	The joint distribution over run length and observed data recursively
$P(x_{t+1}|r_t)$	The predictive distribution, conditional on the length of the current run
$v_t^{(r)}, X_t^{(r)}$	Statistical parameters for the predictive distribution of a current run length

missed change events, are kept minimal. Depending on the availability of data annotated with labelled events, changepoint detection methods can apply supervised, unsupervised, and semi-supervised learning and a range of optimisation methods [25]. Unsupervised learning methods do not operate on labelled data and are therefore a more natural choice in practice, especially in streaming data analytics [25]. This choice depends on the nature of the problem and the involved data characteristics.

Table 4. The BOCD algorithm.

Algorithm 1: Bayesian Online Changepoint Detection

Initialize $P(r_0) = \tilde{S}(r)$ or $P(r_0 = 0) = 1, v_1^{(0)} = v_{prior}, X_1^{(0)} = X_{prior}$

Observe new measurement x_t

Evaluate predictive probability $\pi_t^{(r)} = P(x_t|v_t^{(r)}, X_t^{(r)})$

Calculate growth probabilities $P(r_t = r_{t-1} + 1, x_{1:t}) = P(r_{t-1}, x_{1:t-1})\pi_t^{(r)}(1 - H(r_{t-1}))$

Calculate changepoint probabilities $P(r_t = 0, x_{1:t}) = \sum_{r_{t-1}} P(r_{t-1}, x_{1:t-1})\pi_t^{(r)} H(r_{t-1})$

Calculate evidence $P(x_{1:t}) = \sum_{r_t} P(r_t, x_{1:t})$

Determine run length distribution $P(r_t|x_{1:t}) = \frac{P(r_t, x_{1:t})}{P(x_{1:t})}$

Update parameters $v_{t+1}^{(0)} = v_{prior}, X_{t+1}^{(0)} = X_{prior}, v_{t+1}^{(r+1)} = v_t^{(r)} + 1, X_{t+1}^{(r+1)} = X_t^{(r)} + u(x_t)$

Predict state $P(x_{t+1}|x_{1:t}) = \sum_{r_t} P(x_{t+1}|x_t^{(r)}, r_t)P(r_t|x_{1:t})$

Return to *Observe new measurement* x_t

BOCD belongs to unsupervised learning and, instead of a retrospective segmentation, it implements causal predictive filtering by generating a distribution of the next unseen datum in the sequence, given only data already observed [26]. In other words, the BOCD applies online Bayesian reasoning by estimating for each current observation in a time series the probability (log likelihood) to be a changepoint based on the data observed so far. The underlying assumption is that the generated data are independent and identically distributed (i.i.d.) random variables and the change point segments are not overlapping.

Table 3 presents the notation of the BOCD equations, and Table 4 presents the BOCD algorithm as executed for each measurement.

BOCD adopts an incremental approach in order to learn or predict new pieces of coming data without restarting everything. It is computationally efficient since its average time complexity is $O(n)$ [22]. In addition, it has the ability to forget past data in order to limit its influence in the coming change points. BOCD has been proved to have a low mean time delay and a high accuracy, especially when changes of shorter duration occur; however, it generates high false alarm rates in the presence of noise, thus suffering from low robustness [22, 25].

4 Case Study in the Steel Industry

In this Section, we demonstrate our proposed approach in a case study from the steel industry. Section 4.1 briefly describes the manufacturing process and the sensor infrastructure. Section 4.2 presents an illustrative scenario. Section 4.3 presents further experiments and outlines the results. Finally, Sect. 4.4 performs a comparative analysis in order to validate the need for the proposed approach.

4.1 The Manufacturing Process and the Infrastructure Setup

The case under examination is a cold rolling process of a steel processing manufacturer. Cold rolling is a process of reduction of the cross-sectional area or shaping a metal piece through the deformation caused by a pair of rotating in opposite directions metal rolls. Given an entry steel coil of 4 tons weight and thickness of 2 mm, the rolling mill produces steel strips over the whole thickness spectrum until 0.4 mm. During the operation, the rolls are continuously being sprayed by soap oil in order to reduce heat and friction. Figure 3a depicts the raw materials that are inserted to the cold rolling process, while Fig. 3b depicts the milling station which includes the metal rolls.

Fig. 3. (a) The raw materials; (b) An overview of the rolling mill.

The sensor infrastructure consists of: 10 accelerometers, measuring a set of four variables for vibration-related data (overall acceleration, overall velocity, shock finder and overall bearing defect), 1 tachometer, and 1 current sensor. The sensor measurements are exposed from the PLC to the DB port and can thus be collected external modules that have access to the PLC via network. An adapter samples the DB Port. The sampling rate can be configured and they generally depend on the variable. The data are then processed via a Storm-Kafka pipeline. The system implementing the proposed approach is connected to the sensor infrastructure.

Before the installation of sensors, maintenance was performed on a time-based mode. The rolls were replaced every 8 h (i.e. when there was a shift change) regardless their health state. According to their condition, identified with visual inspection, the removed rolls either were subject to repair or they were sent to waste. In this way, on the one hand, replacement took place even if it was not necessary and, on the other hand, unexpected failures occurred between successive replacements.

4.2   Illustrative Scenario

In this Section, we present an indicative walkthrough of the proposed approach in the context of the steel industry case study. The results for this scenario are depicted in Fig. 4: (1) represents the raw sensor data related to the overall acceleration; (2) represents the predicted sensor data for the next 1 h as derived from the LSTM; (3) represents the rolling kurtosis data; (4) represents the log likelihood evolution for a changepoint occurrence.

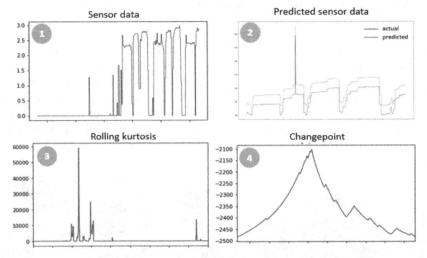

Fig. 4. A walkthrough of the proposed approach in the context of the cold rolling case study.

The LSTM was trained with the 80% of the dataset and was tested with the rest 20% and includes 1 neuron. The batch size has been set to 1, and the number of epochs is equal to 50. The loss was measured through the mean squared error and the implemented optimizer was Adam [27]. The selected measure for the evaluation of the predicted values is the Root Mean Squared Error (RMSE). In this scenario, RMSE is equal to 0.077. On LSTM output trigger, the rolling features related to the predicted sensor measurements are extracted according to the pre-defined rolling time window. In this scenario, after a trial-and-error procedure, the rolling window has been set to 6. Finally, the BOCD, which is applied on the predicted rolling features, provides the log likelihood of having a changepoint in equipment health state within next 1 h.

4.3 Experiments and Results

We performed extensive experiments on vibration sensor data generated in a time period of 9 months. In order to better validate the proposed approach, we labelled the sensor data according to the information stored in a Computerized Maintenance Management System (CMMS): start timestamp of the roll operation, end timestamp of the roll operation, and reason of replacement (failure mode or planned maintenance). In this Section, we present some indicative and representative results for the failure modes "Roll Break" and "Roll Stuck". Both of them occurred at 10th December 2019. The lifetime of the roll subjected to the "Roll Break" failure mode was from 02:20 to 07.30, while the lifetime of the roll subjected to the "Roll Stuck" failure mode was from 09.30 to 15.20.

Table 5 shows the predicted times of changepoints from a normal to a dangerous state for these failure modes as derived from each one of the sensors under examination (acceleration, overall bearing, and velocity) and for each one of the 5 adopted features (kurtosis, skewness, mean, SD, RMS). The experiments revealed that the suitability of the features depend on the application domain, the measured parameter, and the upcoming failure mode. Moreover, the selection of the most appropriate features in each case depends on the tradeoff between the time delay (between the actual changepoint and the predicted one) and the uncertainty (i.e. the log likelihood of having a changepoint).

Table 5. The predicted changepoint times for the failure modes "Roll Break" and "Roll Stuck".

Features	Acceleration		Overall bearing		Velocity	
	Roll break	Roll stuck	Roll break	Roll stuck	Roll break	Roll stuck
Kurtosis	05:21:48	15:00:25	07:04:14	11:22:58	07:02:50	15:11:30
Skewness	04:57:17	14:53:09	07:03:01	12:48:16	03:51:03	13:44:31
Mean	07:19:37	10:27:46	04:59:18	10:44:56	05:29:25	10:41:17
SD	07:17:43	10:46:39	05:43:28	10:46:39	05:30:17	13:19:11
RMS	07:19:37	10:46:29	05:00:20	10:45:47	05:30:17	13:19:11

4.4 Comparative Analysis

Although in some applications the BOCD algorithm may be applied directly on the raw data, its sensitivity to sensor noise poses challenges to the reliability and accuracy of its outcomes. For example, in the case study under examination, which incorporates vibration sensors, it rarely achieves to identify the changepoint within an acceptable level of confidence. Most of the times, the application of the BOCD algorithm directly on raw data generated results like the ones shown in Fig. 5.

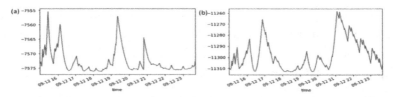

Fig. 5. An example of the log likelihood of a changepoint occurrence for (a) acceleration raw data; (b) overall bearing raw data.

Therefore, there are several timestamps with a high log likelihood that could be potential changepoints. With the application of time-domain rolling features, the BOCD is able to identify the changepoint. As shown in Fig. 6, each feature leads to a different behavior of the BOCD algorithm, thus providing different changepoint timestamps with the highest log likelihood. As already mentioned in Sect. 4.3, different features are appropriate for different sensors and degradation behavior, so the right configuration and model training at design time is of outmost importance.

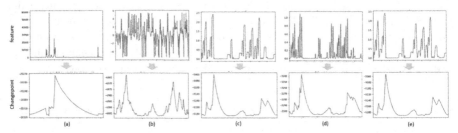

Fig. 6. Examples from the application of the rolling features and the associated results of the BOCD algorithm: (a) kurtosis; (b)skewness; (c) mean; (d) SD; (e) RMS.

In general, deep learning algorithms, such as LSTM, do not usually require a feature extraction processing and achieve an end-to-end learning manner, which is implemented by adding deep layers between the raw data and the prediction result [9]. Thus, the deep models can be deemed as a "black box," which output the prediction result directly from the input. However, our approach proposes a combination of feature extraction and deep learning for two main reasons: (i) there are several challenges related to deep learning transparency and trustworthiness [28], the investigation of which is still at its infancy; (ii) deep neural networks architectures usually take as inputs data from several diverse sources that are combined in order to derive the predictions. To that end, there is the need for huge amount of training data in order to develop more accurate and reliable predictive models. In our proposed approach, the adopted LSTM simplicity, dealing only with the raw sensor data of each sensor to predict the next measurements, leads to a higher accuracy making it suitable for the time-intensive and short timescale of the case under examination.

5   Conclusions and Future Work

With the advancements of sensing technology, lots of sensors are used to monitor the health state of the manufacturing equipment, thus enhancing the capabilities of predicting abnormal behaviours in (near) real-time. However, existing algorithms in predictive maintenance suffer from several limitations related to scalability, efficiency, and reliability preventing their wide application to various industries. In this paper, we proposed an approach for real-time prediction of the equipment health state using time-domain features extraction, LSTM, and BOCD. The proposed approach was applied in a case study from the steel industry and several experiments were performed to validate its effectiveness.

Our future work will move towards four main directions. First, we will develop a multi-sensor fusion approach in order to combine the outcomes derived from different sensors and other data sources. Second, we will develop and compare more complex deep neural network architectures in order to incorporate and process several input parameters. Third, we will develop predictive analytics models about Remaining Useful Life (RUL) that will be triggered when a changepoint is predicted. Fourth, we will develop augmented analytics algorithms [29] in order to facilitate the human-machine collaboration.

Acknowledgements. This work was partly funded by the European Union's Horizon 2020 projects: UPTIME "Unified Predictive Maintenance System" (Grant agreement No. 768634) and COALA "Cognitive Assisted agile manufacturing for a Labor force supported by trustworthy Artificial Intelligence" (Grant agreement No. 957296). The work presented here reflects only the authors' view and the European Commission is not responsible for any use that may be made of the information it contains.

References

1. Habeeb, R.A.A., Nasaruddin, F., Gani, A., Hashem, I.A.T., Ahmed, E., Imran, M.: Real-time big data processing for anomaly detection: A survey. Int. J. Inf. Manage. **45**(1), 289–307 (2019)
2. Fahim, M., Sillitti, A.: Anomaly detection, analysis and prediction techniques in IoT environment: A systematic literature review. IEEE Access **7**(1), 81664–81681 (2019)
3. Xu, Y., Sun, Y., Wan, J., Liu, X., Song, Z.: Industrial big data for fault diagnosis: Taxonomy, review, and applications. IEEE Access **5**(1), 17368–17380 (2017)
4. Liu, R., Yang, B., Zio, E., Chen, X.: Artificial intelligence for fault diagnosis of rotating machinery: a review. Mech. Syst. Signal Process. **108**(1), 33–47 (2018)
5. Angelopoulos, A., et al.: Tackling faults in the industry 4.0 era—a survey of machine-learning solutions and key aspects. Sensors 20(1), 109 (2020)
6. Zhang, J., Wang, P., Yan, R., Gao, R.X.: Long short-term memory for machine remaining life prediction. J. Manuf. Syst. **48**(1), 78–86 (2018)
7. Shi, Z., Chehade, A.: A dual-LSTM framework combining change point detection and remaining useful life prediction. Reliab. Eng. Sys. Saf. **205**(1), 107257 (2021)
8. Hribernik, K., von Stietencron, M., Bousdekis, A., Bredehorst, B., Mentzas, G., Thoben, K.D.: Towards a unified predictive maintenance system-a use case in production logistics in aeronautics. Procedia Manuf. **16**(1), 131–138 (2018)

 9. Zhang, W., Yang, D., Wang, H.: Data-driven methods for predictive maintenance of industrial equipment: a survey. IEEE Syst. J. **13**(3), 2213–2227 (2019)
10. Bousdekis, A., Apostolou, D., Mentzas, G.: Predictive Maintenance in the 4th Industrial Revolution: Benefits, Business Opportunities, and Managerial Implications. IEEE Eng. Manage. Rev. **48**(1), 57–62 (2019)
11. Ma, M., Mao, Z.: Deep-Convolution-Based LSTM Network for Remaining Useful Life Prediction. IEEE Trans. Industr. Inf. **17**(3), 1658–1667 (2020)
12. Kumar, A., Chinnam, R.B., Tseng, F.: An HMM and polynomial regression based approach for remaining useful life and health state estimation of cutting tools. Comput. Ind. Eng. **128**, 1008–1014 (2019)
13. Elsheikh, A., Yacout, S., Ouali, M.S.: Bidirectional handshaking LSTM for remaining useful life prediction. Neurocomputing **323**, 148–156 (2019)
14. Yang, T., Zheng, Z., Qi, L.: A method for degradation prediction based on Hidden Semi-Markov models with mixture of Kernels. Comput. Ind. **122**, 103295 (2020)
15. Caesarendra, W., Tjahjowidodo, T.: A review of feature extraction methods in vibration-based condition monitoring and its application for degradation trend estimation of low-speed slew bearing. Machines **5**(4), 21 (2017)
16. Wang, T., Han, Q., Chu, F., Feng, Z.: Vibration based condition monitoring and fault diagnosis of wind turbine planetary gearbox: a review. Mech. Syst. Sig. Process. **126**(1), 662–685 (2019)
17. Zheng, S., Ristovski, K., Farahat, A., Gupta, C.: Long short-term memory network for remaining useful life estimation. In: 2017 IEEE International Conference on Prognostics and Health Management (ICPHM), pp. 88–95. IEEE (2017)
18. Wu, Y., Yuan, M., Dong, S., Lin, L., Liu, Y.: Remaining useful life estimation of engineered systems using vanilla LSTM neural networks. Neurocomputing **275**(1), 167–179 (2018)
19. Song, Y., Shi, G., Chen, L., Huang, X., Xia, T.: Remaining useful life prediction of turbofan engine using hybrid model based on autoencoder and bidirectional long short-term memory. J. Shanghai Jiaotong Univ. (Sci.) **23**(1), 85–94 (2018)
20. Li, J., Li, X., He, D.: A directed acyclic graph network combined with CNN and LSTM for remaining useful life prediction. IEEE Access **7**, 75464–75475 (2019)
21. Miao, H., Li, B., Sun, C., Liu, J.: Joint learning of degradation assessment and RUL prediction for aeroengines via dual-task deep LSTM networks. IEEE Trans. Industr. Inf. **15**(9), 5023–5032 (2019)
22. Namoano, B., Starr, A., Emmanouilidis, C., Cristobal, R.C.: Online change detection techniques in time series: An overview. In: 2019 IEEE International Conference on Prognostics and Health Management (ICPHM), pp. 1–10. IEEE (2019)
23. Caesarendra, W., Kosasih, B., Tieu, K., Moodie, C.A.: An application of nonlinear feature extraction-a case study for low speed slewing bearing condition monitoring and prognosis. In: 2013 IEEE/ASME International Conference on Advanced Intelligent Mechatronics, pp. 1713–1718. IEEE (2013)
24. Ying, Y., Li, J., Chen, Z., Guo, J.: Study on rolling bearing on-line reliability analysis based on vibration information processing. Comput. Electr. Eng. **69**(1), 842–851 (2018)
25. Namoano, B., Emmanouilidis, C., Ruiz-Carcel, C., Starr, A. G.: Change detection in streaming data analytics: a comparison of Bayesian online and martingale approaches. IFAC-PapersOnLine, **53**(3), 336–341 (2020)
26. Adams, R.P., MacKay, D.J.: Bayesian online changepoint detection. arXiv preprint arXiv: 0710.3742 (2017)
27. Kingma, D. P., Ba, J.: Adam: A method for stochastic optimization. arXiv preprint arXiv: 1412.6980 (2014)
28. Bousdekis, A., Apostolou, D., Mentzas, G.: A human cyber physical system framework for operator 4.0–artificial intelligence symbiosis. Manuf. Lett. **25**(1), 10–15 (2020)
29. Prat, N.: Augmented analytics. Bus. Inf. Syst. Eng. **61**(3), 375–380 (2019)

XAI-KG: Knowledge Graph to Support XAI and Decision-Making in Manufacturing

Jože M. Rožanec[1,2,3(✉)] 🄳, Patrik Zajec[1,2] 🄳, Klemen Kenda[1,2,3] 🄳,
Inna Novalija[2] 🄳, Blaž Fortuna[2,3] 🄳, and Dunja Mladenić[2] 🄳

[1] Jožef Stefan International Postgraduate School,
Jamova 39, 1000 Ljubljana, Slovenia
`joze.rozanec@ijs.si`
[2] Jožef Stefan Institute, Jamova 39, 1000 Ljubljana, Slovenia
[3] Qlector d.o.o., Rov šnikova 7, 1000 Ljubljana, Slovenia

Abstract. The increasing adoption of artificial intelligence requires accurate forecasts and means to understand the reasoning of artificial intelligence models behind such a forecast. Explainable Artificial Intelligence (XAI) aims to provide cues for why a model issued a certain prediction. Such cues are of utmost importance to decision-making since they provide insights on the features that influenced most certain forecasts and let the user decide if the forecast can be trusted. Though many techniques were developed to explain black-box models, little research was done on assessing the quality of those explanations and their influence on decision-making. We propose an ontology and knowledge graph to support collecting feedback regarding forecasts, forecast explanations, recommended decision-making options, and user actions. This way, we provide means to improve forecasting models, explanations, and recommendations of decision-making options. We tailor the knowledge graph for the domain of demand forecasting and validate it on real-world data.

Keywords: Explainable artificial intelligence (XAI) · Knowledge base · Knowledge graph · Smart manufacturing · Demand forecasting

1 Introduction

The increasing digitization of manufacturing enables data-driven decision-making and wider adoption of Artificial Intelligence (AI). AI models can learn from past data and predict future outcomes. Though making forecasts more accurate is important, the lack of transparency on how such forecasts are achieved can undermine trust in the AI models. To mitigate this issue, techniques were developed to identify which variables were most influential to a given forecast [1,10]. While such information is valuable, it is equally important to convey such information appealingly and clearly to the user [12]. Though much research focused on techniques to identify influential forecasts, there are few validated

© Springer Nature Switzerland AG 2021
A. Polyvyanyy and S. Rinderle-Ma (Eds.): CAiSE 2021 Workshops, LNBIP 423, pp. 167–172, 2021.
https://doi.org/10.1007/978-3-030-79022-6_14

measurements for user evaluations on explanations' quality and how do such explanations influence decision-making [19,21].

Of central concern to achieve user evaluations on explanations' quality and their influence on decision-making is collecting, modeling, and storing related data. Such data are the predictive models, their forecasts, the main features influencing such forecasts, the use cases they relate to, and users' feedback. Such data can be used to complete the missing information in the knowledge graph and assess the quality of current forecast explanations. It also provides means to enhance future models' explanations and decision-making options presented to the user.

Though AI models and decision-making options differ between the different use cases, there are many common entities. We consider a generic knowledge graph to support collecting user feedback on given model forecast explanations, how those explanations influenced decision-making, and users' decisions while encoding meaningful context.

This research develops an ontology and knowledge graph for manufacturing to collect feedback regarding forecasts, XAI, and decision-making options. We also design a domain-specific ontology, which provides relevant concepts that must be taken into account to create such a knowledge graph regardless of the use case. Finally, we test our approach for the domain of demand forecasting and validate it on a real-world case study, using models we developed as part of the European Horizon 2020 projects FACTLOG[1] and STAR[2].

As part of this research, we published an ontology with the concepts and relationships we considered to build the knowledge graph. To provide insights regarding the dimension and interconnectedness of the knowledge graph, we computed a set of metrics presented in Sect. 5.

The rest of this paper is structured as follows: Sect. 2 presents related work, Sect. 3 describes the ontology we used and evolved, and the knowledge graph we designed, Sect. 4 describes the use case we used and implementation we created to test our concept, Sect. 5 provides the results we obtained and evaluates the knowledge graph. Finally, in Sect. 6, we provide our conclusions and outline future work.

2   Related Work

The increasing digitalization of the manufacturing domain [20] enables the development and usage of knowledge graphs in manufacturing. [3] found that knowledge graphs are most required for knowledge fusion and frequently considered enablers for other use cases. Ontologies can be used to guide the knowledge graph construction, helping to define formal terminology and transfer knowledge into graphical form [7]. Though many sources of data exist, conversational interfaces provide a flexible medium to gather locally observed collective knowledge [2,13].

---

[1] https://www.factlog.eu/.
[2] http://www.star-ai.eu/.

Though approaches were developed to query existing knowledge in manufacturing systems [4], we found no literature using such interfaces to gather data in a manufacturing setting. Such an interface can be useful to assess the quality of forecast explanations [6], extended to decision-making options, and help enhance their quality over time.

In this research, we dedicate particular attention to integrating knowledge modeling techniques in manufacturing with XAI, decision-making options, persisting knowledge, and feedback we aim to obtain through a question-answering interface.

3   Ontology and Knowledge Graph

In our research, the ontology defines important concepts that later guide the development of a knowledge graph. When developing the ontology, we defined its scope and level of formality required [8,17]. In particular, we require a domain-specific ontology that supports conversational interfaces to collect knowledge regarding manufacturing processes and feedback regarding explanations provided for AI models forecasts (XAI) and decision-making options. Such a knowledge graph provides ground to assess users' perceived quality of forecast explanations, a yet little researched aspect in XAI [19]. To reuse existing ontology concepts [5,18], we use Basic Formal Ontology (BFO) [16] and Industrial Ontologies Foundry (IOF) specifications [9] and import concepts from [15]. Among new concepts we introduced in our ontology are *Feature relevance, Forecast explanation*, and *Feedback*. We implemented the Knowledge Graph using Neo4j[3]. We developed an ontology with general concepts that can be reused in any use case, and an extended version with concepts related to the demand forecasting use case[4].

4   Use Case

To ensure our knowledge graph meets the goals described in Sect. 1, we instantiated it for the demand forecasting use case with data obtained from partners related to the aforementioned EU Horizon 2020 projects. Demand forecasting is a critical component of supply change management. It guides operational and strategic decisions regarding resources, workers, manufactured products, and logistics. The increasing digitalization and information sharing in the manufacturing sector accelerate the information flow. It provides means to create frequent and timely forecasts, which can consider the latest context, improving the quality of forecasts. Though increasing the quality of forecasts will always remain a priority, it is equally important to provide some forecast explanations. Such explanations provide insights into elements relevant to specific forecasts

---

[3] https://neo4j.com/.

[4] We published both ontologies at the Harvard Dataverse. They are accessible from the following link: https://doi.org/10.7910/DVN/UGYHLP.

and allow the user to judge if such a forecast can be trusted. Forecasts and forecast explanations are needed to guide decision-making. Forecasts provide ground to suggest decision-making options to the users, which can alleviate user decision-making over time. Collecting feedback on provided forecasts, explanations, and decision-making options is of utmost importance to improve forecasting models, XAI techniques, forecast explanations display, and recommended decision-making options.

For this research, we created an ontology and implemented a knowledge graph following concepts and relationships elicitated in the ontology. The knowledge graph was implemented with the Neo4j graph database. Ingested data included three years of shipment information daily, a month of demand forecasts for material and clients at a daily level, feature relevance for every forecast (computed with LIME [14] library), forecast explanations created based on those feature rankings, and decision-making options created based on demand forecasts and heuristics. We did not collect feedback from the users. However, we created synthetic data to simulate expected feedbacks on forecasts, decision-making options, and feature relevance obtained from the LIME library.

5   Results

We developed and published a domain-specific ontology that aims to represent relevant entities regarding forecasts, their explanations, decision-making options, and feedback we collect. We also published an extended version, in which we include concepts related to the demand forecasting use case.

To assess the knowledge graph structure, we adopted five metrics suggested in [11]: # nodes (number of nodes), # paths (number of paths), Total Path Lenght (TPL - the sum of relationships traversed while traveling from each node to every other node), Maximum Path Length (MPL - the maximum length among shortest paths between the nodes), and Average Path Length (APL - the average of shortest path lengths between nodes). The number of nodes and relationships provide an insight into the Knowledge Graph dimensions, while TPL, MPL, and APL measure the nodes' interconnectedness. We measured 80.948 nodes and 156.485 paths in our implementation. To estimate the rest of the metrics, we randomly sampled 0,05% of graph nodes and paths, and measured TPL: 435.943.206, MPL: 8, and APL: 5,99.

6   Conclusions

The increasing level of digitalization and AI adoption in manufacturing require developing mechanisms to provide users insights into reasons driving AI model forecasts. An increasing body of research is developing mechanisms to provide transparency to black-box models. In addition to these techniques, users' feedback is of utmost importance to understand how explanations influence users' behavior and improvement opportunities. Though much information regarding the manufacturing process is captured by software such as Enterprise Resource

Planning or Manufacturing Execution System platforms, specific details cannot be captured through regular interfaces. The use of conversational interfaces can help bridge the gap, collecting situational knowledge that is otherwise lost. Such knowledge can provide insights into demand forecasting model biases and guide further development of XAI by providing insight into the perceived value of forecast explanations and their influence on decision-making, guide further development of decision-making recommendations and ranking, and help enrich the knowledge graph with locally observed collective knowledge. In particular, for demand forecasting, such enrichment involves registering new decision-making options, provide knowledge regarding logistics (transport types, pallet sizes, rationales behind logistics decision-making, and other data and criteria that are missing in the knowledge graph).

In this work, we introduced a domain-specific ontology and built a knowledge graph to support storing and relating feedback of explanations and recommended decision-making options and collect feedback of the users' actions. We tested our approach on the demand forecasting use case with real-world data. We demonstrate how the knowledge graph can support the aforementioned requirements, benefiting from the data's semantic representation.

As future work, we will use this knowledge graph to support and develop services with conversational interfaces to collect feedback regarding AI model forecasts and their explanations and decision-making options. We envision developing an active learning module, which will guide conversations to acquire meaningful and yet unlabeled data labels. Finally, data acquired through these services will develop AI-based recommender systems for decision-making options and research users' perception of XAI and its influence on decision-making.

Acknowledgement. This work was supported by the Slovenian Research Agency and the European Union's Horizon 2020 program projects FACTLOG under grant agreement H2020-869951, and STAR under grant agreement number H2020-956573.

References

1. Adadi, A., Berrada, M.: Peeking inside the black-box: a survey on explainable artificial intelligence (XAI). IEEE Access **6**, 52138–52160 (2018)
2. Bradeško, L., Witbrock, M., Starc, J., Herga, Z., Grobelnik, M., Mladenić, D.: Curious cat-mobile, context-aware conversational crowdsourcing knowledge acquisition. ACM Trans. Inf. Syst. (TOIS) **35**(4), 1–46 (2017)
3. Buchgeher, G., Gabauer, D., Martinez-Gil, J., Ehrlinger, L.: Knowledge graphs in manufacturing and production: a systematic literature review (2020)
4. Bunte, A., Diedrich, A., Niggemann, O.: Integrating semantics for diagnosis of manufacturing systems. In: 2016 IEEE 21st International Conference on Emerging Technologies and Factory Automation (ETFA), pp. 1–8. IEEE (2016)
5. Fernández-López, M., Gómez-Pérez, A., Juristo, N.: Methontology: from ontological art towards ontological engineering (1997)
6. Ghai, B., Liao, Q.V., Zhang, Y., Bellamy, R., Mueller, K.: Explainable active learning (XAL): toward AI explanations as interfaces for machine teachers. Proc. ACM Hum.-Comput. Interact. 4(CSCW3) (2021). https://doi.org/10.1145/3432934

7. He, L., Jiang, P.: Manufacturing knowledge graph: a connectivism to answer production problems query with knowledge reuse. IEEE Access **7**, 101231–101244 (2019). https://doi.org/10.1109/ACCESS.2019.2931361
8. Kim, H.M., Fox, M.S., Gruninger, M.: An ontology of quality for enterprise modelling. In: Proceedings 4th IEEE Workshop on Enabling Technologies: Infrastructure for Collaborative Enterprises (WET ICE 1995), pp. 105–116. IEEE (1995)
9. Kulvatunyou, B., Wallace, E., Kiritsis, D., Smith, B., Will, C.: The Industrial Ontologies Foundry Proof-of-Concept Project. In: IFIP Advances in Information and Communication Technology, pp. 402–409 (2018). https://doi.org/10.1007/978-3-319-99707-0_50
10. Li, X.H., et al.: A survey of data-driven and knowledge-aware explainable AI. IEEE Trans. Knowl. Data Eng. (2020)
11. Mathieson, J.L., Summers, J.D.: Complexity metrics for directional node-link system representations: theory and applications. Int. Design Eng. Tech. Conf. Comput. Inf. Eng. Conf. **44137**, 13–24 (2010)
12. Pedreschi, D., Giannotti, F., Guidotti, R., Monreale, A., Pappalardo, L., Ruggieri, S., Turini, F.: Open the black box data-driven explanation of black box decision systems (2018). arXiv preprint arXiv:1806.09936
13. Preece, A., et al.: Sherlock: Simple human experiments regarding locally observed collective knowledge. Technical Report, US Army Research Laboratory Aberdeen Proving Ground, USA (2015)
14. Ribeiro, M.T., Singh, S., Guestrin, C.: "why should i trust you?" explaining the predictions of any classifier. In: Proceedings of the 22nd ACM SIGKDD International Conference on Knowledge Discovery and Data Mining, pp. 1135–1144 (2016)
15. Rožanec, J.M., Lu, J.: Actionable Cognitive Twins for Decision Making in Manufacturing Ontology (2021). https://doi.org/10.7910/DVN/DVZH81
16. Smith, B., Grenon, P.: Basic Formal Ontology. Draft (2002). Downloadable at http://ontology.buffalo.edu/bfo
17. Uschold, M.: Building ontologies: Towards a uni ed methodology. In: Proceedings of 16th Annual Conference of the British Computer Society Specialists Group on Expert Systems. Citeseer (1996)
18. Uschold, M., King, M.: Towards a methodology for building ontologies. Citeseer (1995)
19. van der Waa, J., Nieuwburg, E., Cremers, A., Neerincx, M.: Evaluating XAI: A comparison of rule-based and example-based explanations. Artif. Intell. **291**, 103404 (2021)
20. Xu, L.D., Xu, E.L., Li, L.: Industry 4.0: state of the art and future trends. Int. J. Prod. Res. 56(8), 2941–2962 (2018)
21. Zhou, J., Gandomi, A.H., Chen, F., Holzinger, A.: Evaluating the quality of machine learning explanations: a survey on methods and metrics. Electronics **10**(5), 593 (2021)

NeGIS

NeGIS 2021 Preface

The amount of data and services supported by Information Systems (ISs) has increased exponentially during the last few years. To improve their efficiency and reduce costs, modern organizations have been shifting their services, with part of their ISs, to the Cloud. More recent developments have shown an inversion towards decentralization and distribution of applications and services in the huge pool of devices and computing facilities available nearer to the customers. This shift is due to the impact of the Internet of Things (IoT), which is further increasing the amount of data to be stored and computed. The next generation of information systems will further push these trends to create seamless and pervasive systems. Fog computing, in particular, is the last frontier for ISs, where data and services can be moved in the continuum of resources between the cloud and the edge. In this context, the management of ISs can exploit the diversification of the resources available, but at the same time it is getting more and more complex and challenging. The management of next generation ISs should, therefore, take into consideration the heterogeneity of the Cloud/Fog infrastructure. Such complex architecture is posing new challenges in the management of modern applications, especially in reference to enhancement of quality of service, security, privacy, and energy efficiency. In particular, security and privacy need to be considered for the amount of sensitive data possibly produced, while energy efficiency is central, due to the high amount of computational nodes involved. Universally accepted solutions for next generation ISs are yet to be found.

The Next Generation Information Systems: Emerging Challenges in Fog and Cloud Computing (NeGIS) workshop, organized in conjunction with the 33rd International Conference on Advanced Information Systems Engineering (CAiSE 2021), aims to tackle the challenges arising from information systems in heterogeneous environments and to promote collaboration between scholars interested in the topic. The workshop received four submissions from researchers in different fields of the Information Systems and Business Process Management communities. Each paper was peer-reviewed by three members of the Program Committee. Out of these submissions, the Program Committee selected one high-quality paper for presentation at the workshop, which is included in this proceedings volume. The selected paper, titled "Declarative Osmotic Application Placement", proposes a declarative methodology for an adaptive deployment in the Cloud-IoT continuum of IoT microelements, taking into account resource capabilities of the infrastructure and QoS requirements of the application.

We thank all authors of the submitted papers for their contributions to the NeGIS 2021 workshop. We are grateful to all Program Committee members and the organizers of the CAiSE 2021 conference for their trust and support.

May 2021

Mattia Salnitri
Monica Vitali
Tong Li

NeGIS 2021 Organization

Workshop Chairs

Mattia Salnitri   Politecnico di Milano, Italy
Monica Vitali   Politecnico di Milano, Italy
Tong Li   Beijing University of Technology

Program Committee

Marco Aiello   University of Stuttgart, Germany
Achim Brucker   University of Exeter, UK
Georges Da Costa   IRIT, University of Toulouse, France
Vasiliki Diamantopoulou   University of the Aegean, Greece
Christina Herzog   IRIT, University of Toulouse, France
Carlo Mastroianni   ICAR-CNR, Italy
Giovanni Meroni   Politecnico di Milano, Italy
Haris Mouratidis   University of Brighton, UK
John Mylopoulos   University of Ottawa, Canada
Pierluigi Plebani   Politecnico di Milano, Italy
Patricia Stolf   IRIT, University of Toulouse, France
Haiyang Yu   Beijing University of Technology, China

Declarative Osmotic Application Placement

Stefano Forti$^{(\boxtimes)}$ and Antonio Brogi

Department of Computer Science, University of Pisa, Pisa, Italy
stefano.forti@di.unipi.it

Abstract. Encompassing Cloud-IoT paradigms, Osmotic Computing features the management of IoT microelements (MELs), i.e. computation units (e.g. services, programs) that are available in different versions to compose adaptive IoT applications. New techniques are then needed to decide where to place MELs and which of the available versions to deploy, considering both infrastructure resource availability and Quality of Service (e.g. latency, costs) of the whole application. In this article, we tackle such an open challenge by proposing a declarative methodology in support of the placement of osmotic MELs.

Keywords: Osmotic computing · Fog · Cloud · Application placement

1 Introduction

The widespread development and deployment of Internet of Things (IoT) applications for a plethora of different new verticals has shown many limitations of the Cloud paradigm, especially when low latencies need to be met at runtime [2] (e.g. in online gaming, remote surgery, virtual reality). To tame such limitations, various paradigms are emerging that exploit computing, storage and networking resources closer to application end-users or to where IoT data is produced, e.g. Fog Computing and Multi-access Edge Computing [25]. Osmotic Computing [23] aims at encompassing all different emerging Cloud-IoT paradigms under the umbrella of a generic and adaptive application management approach, seeking to optimise different Quality of Service (QoS) parameters, like processing costs and network latencies [22]. Such unifying paradigm relies on the concept of *microelements* (MELs), heterogeneous computation units (e.g. services, microservices, IoT firmware) that can be composed into complex IoT applications. MELs can adaptively run in multiple available versions (and level of complexity) across Cloud, Edge and IoT resources so to match QoS constraints defined through context-aware policies.

The following parallel from chemistry holds: as *solvent* molecules in a solution at different concentration levels separated by a *semi-permeable membrane* move

Work partly supported by project *CONTWARE* funded by the Conference of Italian University Rectors (CRUI). The Authors wish to thank L. Dinelli for his testing activities on a first version of the code presented in this work.

© Springer Nature Switzerland AG 2021
A. Polyvyanyy and S. Rinderle-Ma (Eds.): CAiSE 2021 Workshops, LNBIP 423, pp. 177–190, 2021.
https://doi.org/10.1007/978-3-030-79022-6_15

from the less concentrated to the more concentrated part to reach a concentration equilibrium, so *MELs* move from the Cloud all through the IoT according to specified *software-defined membranes* (i.e. policies) to ensure the needed QoS. Differently from solvent molecules, when passing through software-defined membranes, migrating MELs can also adapt and reconfigure to run on less or more powerful devices. Those membranes can be implemented by suitable interactions of a centralised *MEL Orchestration Engine*, interfacing with application operators, and local *MEL Engines*, interfacing with devices at the edge of the network. The MEL Orchestration Engine must centrally decide on (*i*) *how to place different MELs* composing IoT applications and (*ii*) *which version of those MELs to deploy*. This adds an interesting new dimension to consider (i.e. configure the version to deploy) when solving the well-known NP-hard problem of application placement in Cloud-IoT scenarios [3].

In this article, we contribute to enabling decision-making on (*i*) and (*ii*) at the MEL Orchestration Engine by proposing a first declarative solution and its open-source Prolog prototype osmolog. The proposed solution models different versions of MEL-based applications along with their requirements in terms of needed hardware and software capabilities, and end-to-end latencies. Based on those requirements, on the preferred deployment version, on target operational costs, and on the available infrastructure capabilities and costs, osmolog computes eligible placements for each application MEL along with the version to be deployed. Both an exhaustive and a heuristic versions of osmolog are proposed, which can be alternatively used for long and short term placement of IoT applications in Osmotic computing settings, respectively, as illustrated over a lifelike application example, over infrastructures at varying sizes.

osmolog features two desirable properties to achieve Osmotic application management. On one hand, it is *declarative*, hence more concise, easier to understand, modify and maintain when compared to existing procedural solutions, and it also offers a high level of flexibility and extensibility, which suits the ever-changing needs of Cloud-IoT scenarios. On the other hand, it is intrinsically *explainable* as it derives proofs for input queries by relying on Prolog state-of-the-art resolution engines, and it can be easily extended to justify *why* a certain placement decision was made, in the spirit of explainable AI [13].

The rest of this article is organised as follows. After describing a lifelike motivating example and stating the considered placement problem (Sect. 2), we describe the osmolog methodology and prototype with the aid of small examples (Sect. 3). An experimental assessment of both the heuristic and exhaustive versions of osmolog (Sect. 4) is followed by a discussion of closely related work (Sect. 5), and concluding remarks pointing to directions for future work (Sect. 6).

2   Motivating Example and Problem Statement

Consider the osmotic *Augmented Reality* (AR) application sketched in Fig. 1. Such an application requires deploying four interacting MELs, namely:

- an AR Driver MEL, connected with IoT devices – a smartphone and, possibly, an ambient light sensor – to collect data and render AR footage by processing incoming video streams from the smartphone,
- a Movement Processing MEL, to process information and video samples from the AR Driver, predicting user movements and pre-fetching data coming from
- a Video Storage MEL containing video, graphics and information to be embedded in the AR footage shown on the smartphone,
- a Users Data MEL that is used to collect profiling information and statistics on the application usage and functioning by its users.

As shown in Fig. 1, some of those MELs exist in more than one version, each with different IoT, software and hardware requirements. Versions range from the less demanding `light` version (represented by a triangle) suited for resource constrained IoT devices, to a `medium` version (represented by a square) suited for more powerful edge devices, to a `full` version (represented by a circle) targeting public or private Cloud servers.

For instance the AR Driver MEL can be alternatively deployed in its `light` version (requiring 1 hardware unit, the availability of the GCC compiler, and reachability of the target smartphone), in its `medium` version (requiring 2 hardware units, the availability of the GCC compiler and of the Caffe deep learning library, and reachability of both the target smartphone and the ambient light sensor), or in its `full` version (requiring 4 hardware units, the availability of Docker, and reachability of both the target smartphone and the ambient light sensor). Finally, interacting MELs should be deployed to the same node – if possible – or to nodes distancing at most the latencies indicated over the vertical dashed lines in Fig. 1. For instance, the AR Driver MEL should be at most at a 20 ms distance from the Movement Processing MEL.

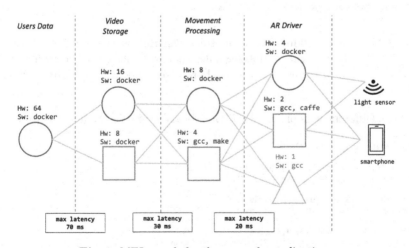

Fig. 1. MEL graph for the example application.

Running the above application requires the MEL Orchestration Engine to jointly solve a placement (*where to deploy each MEL?*) and a configuration (*which MEL version to deploy?*) problem on top of a Cloud-IoT infrastructure made of heterogeneous computing nodes, interconnected via various networking technologies featuring different latencies.

As different MEL versions might offer different Quality of Experience to the end-users, solving the above mentioned problems should also consider which version the application operator prefers to deploy – *trying to maximise the number of MELs configured in such a preferred version*. Besides, as deploying software artefacts on virtualised infrastructure involves leasing resources from Cloud, Edge and IoT providers, placing and configuring the MEL graph described before, also requires to avoid exceeding maximum target operational costs – *trying to minimise such costs as much as possible*.

3 Methodology and Prototype

In this section, after describing the application and infrastructure models of osmolog and defining eligible application placements (Sect. 3.1), we detail the objective function devised for optimising MEL placement (Sect. 3.2), and present an exhaustive (Sect. 3.3) and a heuristic (Sect. 3.4) declarative solution to the considered osmotic placement problem.

3.1 Model

Application. As building blocks of Osmotic IoT applications, MEL versions are denoted by facts like

```
mel((MelName, Version), SwReqs, HwReqs, IoTReqs).
```

where `MelName` is a unique MEL identifier, `Version` is the considered version among `full`, `medium`, `light`, and `SwReqs`, `HwReqs` and `IoTReqs` are the requirements of such a version in terms of software, hardware[1] and IoT capabilities, respectively.

Example. Different versions of the MELs described in Sect. 2 are declared as in

```
mel((usersData,full), [docker], 64, []).

mel((videoStorage,full), [docker], 16, []).
mel((videoStorage,medium), [docker], 8, []).

mel((movementProcessing,full), [docker], 8, []).
mel((movementProcessing,medium), [gcc, make], 4, []).

mel((arDriver,full), [docker], 4, [phone, lightSensor]).
mel((arDriver,medium), [gcc,caffe], 2, [phone, lightSensor]).
mel((arDriver,light), [gcc], 1, [phone]).
```

---

[1] For simplicity, we represent generic hardware units as integers, as in [12].

◇

Latency constraints on interactions among MELs are denoted by facts like

```
mel2mel(MelName1, MelName2, MaxLatency).
```

where `MelName1` and `MelName1` identify two interacting MELs and `MaxLatency` is the maximum end-to-end latency (in milliseconds) that their interaction tolerates.

Example. Latency requirements between MELs of Sect. 2 are declared as in:

```
mel2mel(usersData, videoStorage, 70).
mel2mel(videoStorage, movementProcessing, 30).
mel2mel(movementProcessing, arDriver, 20).
```

◇

Finally, different versions of an application made from N MELs are denoted by facts like

```
application((AppName, Version), [(MelName1, Version1), ..., (MelNameN, VersionN)]).
```

where `AppName` is the unique application identifier, `Version` is the considered application version, and the pairs `(MelNameK, VersionK)` indicate the version of the MELs composing the considered application version.

Example. Two versions of the application of Sect. 2 can be declared as in:

```
application((arApp, full),
            [(usersData,full), (videoStorage,full), (movementProcessing,full), (arDriver,full)]).

application((arApp, adaptive),
            [(usersData,full), (videoStorage,_), (movementProcessing,_), (arDriver,_)]).
```

The `full` version of `arApp` requires deploying all MELs as `full`. On the contrary, the `adaptive` version only specifies the version of the Users Data MEL (viz. `full`), leaving unbound those of all other MELs. This corresponds to delegating the configuration of those MELs to the MEL Orchestration Engine.   ◇

Infrastructure. Nodes in the infrastructure along with the costs[2] for using them can be declared by facts like

```
node(NodeId, [(SwCap1, SwCost1), ..., (SwCapS,SwCostS)],
             (HwCaps, UnitHwCost),
             [(IoTCap1, IoTCost1), ..., (IoTCapT, IoTCostT)]).
```

where `NodeId` is a unique node identifier, the pairs `(SwCapK, SwCostK)` are the software capabilities it features and their cost, `(HwCaps, UnitHwCost)` are the available hardware capabilities and their unitary cost, and the pairs `(IoTCapK, IoTCostK)` are the IoT devices reached out by the node and their cost.

---

[2] We model estimated (monthly) costs for leasing resources, as in [5].

Example. An `edge42` node, featuring `gcc` at no cost, `caffe` at 4 euro per month, 6 free hardware units at a unitary cost of 3 euro, and both the `phone` and the `lightSensor` at 1 euro per month each, and a `cloud42` node with Docker at 5 euro per month and 100 hardware resources at 1 euro per month each, can be declared as in:

```
node(edge42, [(gcc,0),(caffe,4)], (6, 3), [(phone,1),(lightSensor,1)]).
node(cloud42, [(docker, 5)], (100, 1), []).
```

Finally, the latency associated with links between nodes is declared as in   ◇

```
link(NodeId1, NodeId2, Latency).
```

where `NodeId1` and `NodeId2` identify two nodes and `Latency` is the monitored end-to-end latency between them.

Example. The monitored end-to-end latency of 20 ms between nodes `edge42` and `cloud42` can be declared as in:

```
link(edge42, cloud42, 20).
```

◇

Eligible Placement. An eligible `Placement` for `AppName` in its `AppVersion`, costing `TotCost` without exceeding `MaxCost`, can be determined by querying the `placement/5` predicate[3] of Fig. 2 (lines 1–5).

Such predicate first generates an eligible `Placement` for each MEL, by means of `melPlacementOK/6` (line 3, and 6–11). The `melPlacementOK/6` predicate scans the list of MELs to be deployed and exploits `placementOK/5` (line 8, and 12–18) to check software (line 15), IoT (line 16), and cumulative hardware requirements (line 17), when placing a MEL M in its version V onto a node N. It is worth noting that, after placing a new MEL, `melPlacementOK/6` also updates the estimated cost `NewCost` of the current partial placement (line 9), immediately pruning out search paths that exceed the given `MaxCost` (line 10).

After an eligible placement of MELs has been determined, `placement/5` exploits the `flowsOK/2` (line 5, and 19–26) to check that latency constraints for MEL to MEL interactions can also be met. The `flowsOK/2` predicate scans the list of `mel2mel/3` related to the placed MELs (line 4) and checks that either both considered MELs are on the same node (lines 20–22), or there exists link between their deployment nodes that can satisfy the set latency requirement (lines 23–26). It is worth noting that the predicates listed in Fig. 2 can be actually executed to determine all eligible placements of an osmotic application to a target Cloud-IoT infrastructure, that do not exceed a maximum operational cost.

---

[3] Conventionally, a Prolog predicate **pred** with N arguments is indicated as **pred/N**. For the sake of readability, the definition of some predicates is omitted in the listing of Fig. 2. Full code is available at: https://github.com/di-unipi-socc/osmolog.

```
1   placement(AppName, AppVersion, MaxCost, Placement, TotCost) :-
2     application((AppName, AppVersion), MELs),
3     melPlacementOK(MELs, Placement, [], 0, TotCost, MaxCost),
4     findall(mel2mel(M1,M2,Latency), mel2mel_in_placement(M1,M2,Latency,Placement), FlowConstraints),
5     flowsOK(FlowConstraints, Placement).

6   melPlacementOK([], [], _, PlacementCost, PlacementCost, _).
7   melPlacementOK([(M, V)| Ss], [on(M, V, N)|P], AllocatedHW, CostUpToNow, TotalCost, MaxCost) :-
8     placementOK((M, V), N, AllocatedHW, NewAllocatedHW, NodeCost),
9     NewCost is CostUpToNow + NodeCost,
10    NewCost =< MaxCost,
11    melPlacementOK(Ss, P, NewAllocatedHW, NewCost, TotalCost, MaxCost).

12  placementOK((M, V), N, AllocatedHW, NewAllocatedHW, NodeCost) :-
13    mel((M, V), SW_Reqs, HW_Reqs, Thing_Reqs),
14    node(N, SW_Caps, HW_Caps, Thing_Caps),
15    swReqsOK(SW_Reqs, SW_Caps, NodeSwCost),
16    thingReqsOK(Thing_Reqs, Thing_Caps, NodeThingCost),
17    hwReqsOK(HW_Reqs, HW_Caps, N, AllocatedHW, NewAllocatedHW, NodeHwCost),
18    NodeCost is NodeSwCost + NodeThingCost + NodeHwCost.

19  flowsOK([], _).
20  flowsOK([mel2mel(S1,S2,_)|SFs], P) :-
21    member(on(S1, _, N), P), member(on(S2, _, N), P),
22    flowsOK(SFs, P).
23  flowsOK([mel2mel(S1,S2,L)|SFs], P) :-
24    member(on(S1, _, N1), P), member(on(S2, _, N2), P), N1 \== N2,
25    e2eLink(N1,N2,Latency), Latency =< L,
26    flowsOK(SFs, P).
```

Fig. 2. Code to determine eligible application placements.

Example. To determine a placement of the `adaptive` version of `vrApp` over the infrastructure declared in the previous examples, without exceeding an estimated monthly cost of 100 euro, it is possible to run the query:

```
?- placement(arApp, adaptive, 100, Placement, TotCost).
```

As a result, the program of Fig. 2 returns only the following eligible placement, and its associated total cost of 99 euro:

```
Placement = [on(usersData, full, cloud42),
             on(videoStorage, medium, cloud42),
             on(movementProcessing, full, cloud42),
             on(arDriver, light, edge42)],
TotCost = 99
```

Increasing the maximum cost to 110 euro leads to determining other two eligible placements and costs, namely:

```
Placement = [on(usersData, full, cloud42),
             on(videoStorage, full, cloud42),
             on(movementProcessing, full, cloud42),
             on(arDriver, light, edge42)],
TotCost = 107
```

and

```
Placement = [on(usersData, full, cloud42),
             on(videoStorage, medium, cloud42),
             on(movementProcessing, full, cloud42),
             on(arDriver, medium, edge42)],
TotCost = 107
```

◇

3.2 Ranking Placements

To identify the best candidate in a set P_s of determined eligible placements, we employ the following ranking function, where P is a placement in the set P_s and V is the preferred deployment version specified by the user:

$$r(P, V, P_s) = 100 \times (\frac{|P^V|}{|P_s|} + \frac{maxCost(P_s) - cost(P)}{maxCost(P_s) - minCost(P_s)})$$

The formula sums the percentage of MELs of P in version V (P^V) with respect to the total number of placements P_s, with the difference between the max cost of P_s placements and the cost of P, normalised over the difference between the max and the min costs in P_s.[4] The values of $r(P, V, P_s)$ range in $[0, 200]$, with higher values identifying better candidate placements.

3.3 Exhaustive Solution

Figure 3 lists the high-level code to find the best candidate placement among all eligible ones. Predicate goForBest/6 is capable of determining the BestPlacement for an AppName in its AppVersion, according to the PreferredeMelVersion and MaxCost specified by the user[5]. The goForBest/6 predicate determines all eligible placements along with their associated cost by relying (line 2–4) on placement/5 of Fig. 2. Afterwards, it exploits evalPlacement/5 (lines 5) to compute the value of $r(P, V, P_s)$ to be associated with each eligible placement, by computing and summing up version compliance and normalised cost values. Finally, the best/3 predicate determines the BestPlacement, i.e. the one which ranks best among those that were found (line 6).

Example. To determine the best ranked placement of the adaptive version of vrApp (with as many full MELs as possible) over the infrastructure declared in the previous examples, and without exceeding an estimated monthly cost of 110 euro, it is possible to run the query:

```
?- goForBest((0,highest), arApp, adaptive, full, 110, BestP).
```

---

[4] If $maxCost(P_s) = minCost(P_s)$, $r(P, V, P_s) = 100 \times (\frac{|P^V|}{|P_s|} + 1)$.

[5] The SortType argument of goForBest/7 can be also instantiated differently to rank the placements only with respect to the number of MELs in the version preferred by the user or only with respect to their relative costs.

```
1   goForBest(SortType, AppName, AppVersion, PreferredMelVersion, MaxCost, BestPlacement) :-
2     findall( (Placement, PlacementCost),
3               placement(AppName, AppVersion, MaxCost, Placement, PlacementCost),
4               Placements ),
5     evalPlacements(AppName, AppVersion, PreferredMelVersion, Placements, EvaluatedPlacements),
6     best(SortType,EvaluatedPlacements,BestPlacement).
```

Fig. 3. Exhaustive solution.

As a result, the program of Fig. 3 returns only the following eligible placement:

```
[175, 75, 107, [on(usersData, full, cloud42), on(videoStorage, full, cloud42),
                on(movementProcessing, full, cloud42), on(arDriver, light, edge42)]]
```

Such a placement has 75% MELs deployed in their `full` version and costs 107 euro, what makes it achieve a ranking score of 175 out of 200.   ◇

3.4   Heuristic Solution

As the time complexity of the considered placement problem is combinatorially exponential, the exhaustive solution described in Sect. 3.3 is not always adequate to handle large problem instances in a reasonably small amount of time. Furthermore, there might be applications that are only deployed for short time periods, for which a sub-optimal eligible placement can represent a good enough alternative when compared to waiting for the optimal solution. For these reasons, we devised a heuristic version of the previous program. Such a heuristic program combines a preprocessing step to determine the list of compatible nodes for each MEL to be placed with a greedy strategy to explore the search space, based on an estimate of the ranking function of Sect. 3.2.

The preprocessing step exploits the `compatible/3` predicate listed in Fig. 4 to compute the list of all nodes that can support the (hardware, software and IoT) requirements of each MEL M in its version V, with the associated Cost. It is worth noting that – at this stage – hardware constraints are checked by considering only the allocation of the considered MEL (line 6).

```
1   compatible(M,V,((M,V),N,Cost) ) :-
2     mel((M, V), SW_Reqs, HW_Reqs, Thing_Reqs),
3     node(N, SW_Caps, (HW_Caps, C), Thing_Caps),
4     swReqsOK(SW_Reqs, SW_Caps, SWCost),
5     thingReqsOK(Thing_Reqs, Thing_Caps, ThingCost),
6     HW_Reqs =< HW_Caps, HwCost is HW_Reqs * C,
7     Cost is SWCost + ThingCost + HwCost.
```

Fig. 4. Preprocessing code.

After preprocessing, the search proceeds by incrementally (i) estimating the ranking function and (ii) building a placement by adding one MEL at a time. At each step, the heuristic version of osmolog decides to place the MEL with fewest compatible nodes and selects the placement associated to the highest estimate of the ranking function. As cumulative hardware requirements (due to the placement of more than one MEL onto a single node) are checked during this phase, it can happen that the candidate compatible nodes get less than they initially were. Once a placement decision is taken, the number of MELs currently placed in the preferred version and the maximum and minimum cost found up to now are suitably updated, to continue to accurately estimate the ranking function. Prolog backtracking to a previous partial placement when the followed search path does not allow to determine a full placement ensures completeness of the heuristic version of osmolog, i.e. that – in the worst case – the whole search space can still be explored. The process continues until a complete placement is found and returned.

Example. To determine a placement of the `adaptive` version of `vrApp` (with as many `full` MELs as possible) over the infrastructure declared in the previous examples, and without exceeding a monthly cost of 110 euro, we query:

```
?- h_placement(arApp, adaptive, full, 110, Placement, VC, Cost).
```

The result will be the same optimal placement found by the exhaustive search:

```
Placement = [on((arDriver, light), edge42), on((movementProcessing, full), cloud42),
             on((usersData, full), cloud42), on((videoStorage, full), cloud42)],
VC = 75, Cost = 107.
```

◇

4   Experimental Assessment

In this section, we provide an experimental assessment and comparison of the exhaustive and heuristic programs described in Sect. 3. To assess the osmolog prototype, we run both the exhaustive and heuristic versions[6] trying to repeatedly place the `adaptive` version of the application of Fig. 1 over 20 different infrastructures built as per the Barabási-Albert model [1] at varying sizes of 2^i with $i \in [3, 11]$, with a preferential attachment of each node to i other nodes.

In all the experiments, we set the maximum execution time to 100 ms, stopping them after the first size of the considered infrastructures for which the average execution time overtakes this threshold. Figure 5 shows the obtained results in terms of execution times across all experiments. The exp-time behaviour of the exhaustive version of osmolog clearly emerges from the plot, with such version exceeding the set threshold of 100 ms at an infrastructure size of 512 nodes. On the contrary, the heuristic version stays below 100 ms until the infrastructure size reaches 1024 nodes, only exceeding the threshold by 40 ms in the case of 2048 nodes. The second column of Table 1 shows the speed-up achieved by the heuristic in comparison with the exhaustive version. Overall, for the sizes

---

[6] Experiments are run on a machine with Apple Silicon M1 CPU and 16 GB of RAM. Experiments code is available at https://github.com/di-unipi-socc/osmolog.

between 8 and 512, such speed-up is on average around 23×, increasing almost linearly from 2× up to 67× as the infrastructures size grows from 8 to 512 nodes.

Finally, we exploit min-max normalisation (i.e. *feature scaling*[7]) to compare the quality of the heuristic solutions with the quality of the optimal solutions obtained by the exhaustive search, for each of the 20 runs of each considered infrastructure size. This scaled value measures how close a heuristic placement is to the optimal, also with respect to the worst placement possible. The third column of Table 1 shows it for the heuristic solutions at varying infrastructure sizes. The quality of the heuristic solutions is always very close to the optimal one, settling around 0.91 (i.e. only 9% far from the optimal), never exceeding 0.86 and often performing above 0.94 (i.e. only 6% far from the optimal). As the infrastructure size grows, this value slightly degrades since the heuristic is more likely to perform local optimisations while searching for a placement.

Overall, experimental assessment shows that the exhaustive version of osmolog can be used interchangeably with the heuristic one only for very small infrastructures (less than 100 nodes) due to the exponential times associated to an exhaustive exploration of the combinatorial search space. For larger infrastructures, the heuristic version shows considerable speed-ups on the execution times (i.e. ≥ 40×) and still guarantees solutions close enough to the optimal one.

Table 1. Heuristic speed-up and solution quality.

Nodes	Speed-up	Sol. Quality
8	2×	0.98
16	4×	0.94
32	8×	0.90
64	12×	0.89
128	12×	0.86
256	53×	0.96
512	67×	0.88

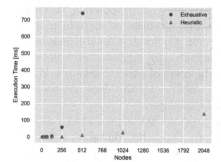

Fig. 5. Execution times.

5   Related Work

Recently, much work has targeted the problem of placing multi-service applications in Cloud-IoT computing scenarios, e.g. as surveyed in [3,16,21]. Osmotic Computing introduces new challenges in this field, as it accounts for the possibility to deploy different versions of a same MEL depending on the contextually

---

[7] The employed *feature scaling* is $r_{scaled} = \frac{r_h - r_{min}}{r_{max} - r_{min}}$ where r_h is the value of the ranking function associated by the exhaustive program to the solution found by the heuristic program, and r_{min} and r_{max} are the minimum and maximum values of the ranking across all eligible placements.

available resources and on QoS targets (e.g. latency, cost, security) [6,23]. Due to space limitations, we limit our discussion only to closely related work relying on declarative solutions, or especially targeting Osmotic Computing.

Declarative approaches were proposed in the past to manage Cloud and network resources (e.g. [14,15,24]). More recently, we have exploited declarative programming to incrementally determine eligible application placements in Fog scenarios [8], to place VNF chains and steer traffic across them [10], and to enable the assessment of the security and trust levels of different placements [9]. Still with a declarative approach, [7] and [18] devised a solution for service coordination based on *aggregate computing*, aiming at managing opportunistic resources via a hybrid centralised/decentralised solution handling node churn and mobility. On a similar line, we proposed a fully decentralised Prolog solution to enforce QoS-aware application management policies [4]. However, none of those declarative approaches considered Osmotic adaptation of services.

By presenting architectures for Osmotic computing platforms, [17,22] highlight the importance of devising multi-criteria optimisation techniques to place and (re-)configure MELs onto target nodes, based on suitable trade-offs between application performance and QoS aspects. Such techniques are to be implemented in the MEL Orchestration Engine so to ensure globally satisfying results. Still targeting Osmotic settings, [19] presented a game-based strategy to place and migrate different types of MELs in mobile augmented reality networks, while optimising resource usage and energy consumption. [11] proposed a load balancing strategy for Cloud infrastructures, based on bio-inspired meta-heuristics. Despite considering MEL migrations, nor [19] nor [11] account for the possibility of a MEL to adapt into different versions. Similarly, [20] proposed an offloading technique to outsource trust management to the users of a social network. While considering trust, latency and resource usage constraints, [20] does not account for different versions of the trust monitor to be deployed.

To the best of our knowledge, none of the previous works presented a declarative solution to place MELs in different versions, depending on target resources and QoS (i.e. latency, cost, version compliance). Hence, osmolog represents a first step towards enabling Osmotic Computing platforms capable of flexibly handling such features of this emerging paradigm, in a declarative manner.

6   Concluding Remarks

In this article, we presented osmolog as a first declarative approach to determine eligible placements of MEL-based applications in Osmotic Computing. We discussed an exhaustive and a heuristic version of the osmolog prototype and we assessed them over a lifelike example considering random infrastructure topologies at varying sizes. In our experiments, the heuristic version showed an average speed-up of 23× compared to the exhaustive version and determined good suboptimal solutions, with an average 9% distance from the optimal one.

Being declarative, osmolog is concise ($\simeq$ 250 lines of code), and easier to understand and extend so to account for new emerging needs if compared to procedural solutions targeting similar placement problems ($\geqslant$ 1000 s lines of code) [8]. Finally, by relying on state-of-the-art resolution engines, osmolog can be extended to get explanations for all its placement decisions.

As future work, we plan to extend osmolog so to consider also security requirements of the MELs to be placed, trust relations among different stakeholders in the Osmotic landscapes, and the possibility to adapt a single MEL into a group of MELs featuring the same functionality. Besides, we aim at studying how to combine osmotic placement of MELs with a fully decentralised architecture, such as the one of [4]. Naturally, we also intend to integrate and experiment our proposal in actual Osmotic platforms, when available.

References

1. Barabási, A.L. (ed.): Network Science. Cambridge University Press, Cambridge (2016)
2. Bellavista, P., Berrocal, J., Corradi, A., Das, S.K., Foschini, L., Zanni, A.: A survey on fog computing for the internet of things. Perv. Mob. Comput. **52**, 71–99 (2019)
3. Brogi, A., Forti, S., Guerrero, C., Lera, I.: How to place your apps in the fog - state of the art and open challenges. Softw. Pract. Exp. **50**(5), 719–740 (2020)
4. Brogi, A., Forti, S., Guerrero, C., Lera, I.: Towards declarative decentralised application management in the fog. In: ISSRE Workshops, pp. 223–230 (2020)
5. Brogi, A., Forti, S., Ibrahim, A.: Optimising QoS-assurance, resource usage and cost of fog application deployments. In: Muñoz, V.M., Ferguson, D., Helfert, M., Pahl, C. (eds.) CLOSER 2018. CCIS, vol. 1073, pp. 168–189. Springer, Cham (2019). https://doi.org/10.1007/978-3-030-29193-8_9
6. Carnevale, L., et al.: From the cloud to edge and IoT: a smart orchestration architecture for enabling osmotic computing. In: AINA, pp. 419–424 (2018)
7. Casadei, R., Viroli, M.: Coordinating computation at the edge: a decentralized, self-organizing, spatial approach. In: FMEC 2019, pp. 60–67 (2019)
8. Forti, S., Brogi, A.: Continuous reasoning for managing next-gen distributed applications. In: ICLP Technical Communications. EPTCS, vol. 325, pp. 164–177 (2020)
9. Forti, S., Ferrari, G.L., Brogi, A.: Secure cloud-edge deployments, with trust. FGCS **102**, 775–788 (2020)
10. Forti, S., Paganelli, F., Brogi, A.: Probabilistic QoS-aware placement of VNF chains at the edge. TPLP (2021, in press)
11. Gamal, M., Rizk, R., Mahdi, H., Elnaghi, B.E.: Osmotic bio-inspired load balancing algorithm in cloud computing. IEEE Access **7**, 42735–42744 (2019)
12. Guerrero, C., Lera, I., Juiz, C.: Evaluation and efficiency comparison of evolutionary algorithms for service placement optimization in fog architectures. FGCS **97**, 131–144 (2019)
13. Hagras, H.: Toward human-understandable, explainable AI. Computer **51**(9), 28–36 (2018)
14. Hinrichs, T.L., Gude, N.S., Casado, M., Mitchell, J.C., Shenker, S.: Practical declarative network management. In: WREN, pp. 1–10 (2009)
15. Kadioglu, S., Colena, M., Sebbah, S.: Heterogeneous resource allocation in cloud management. In: NCA 2016, pp. 35–38 (2016)
16. Mahmud, R., Ramamohanarao, K., Buyya, R.: Application management in fog computing environments: a taxonomy, review and future directions. ACM Comput. Surv. **53**(4), 1–43 (2020)

17. Nardelli, M., Nastic, S., Dustdar, S., Villari, M., Ranjan, R.: Osmotic flow: osmotic computing + IoT workflow. IEEE Cloud Comput. **4**(2), 68–75 (2017)

18. Pianini, D., Casadei, R., Viroli, M., Natali, A.: Partitioned integration and coordination via the self-organising coordination regions pattern. FGCS **114**, 44–68 (2021)

19. Sharma, V., Jayakody, D.N.K., Qaraqe, M.: Osmotic computing-based service migration and resource scheduling in mobile augmented reality networks (MARN). FGCS **102**, 723–737 (2020)

20. Sharma, V., You, I., Kumar, R., Kim, P.: Computational offloading for efficient trust management in pervasive online social networks using osmotic computing. IEEE Access **5**, 5084–5103 (2017)

21. Vaquero, L.M., et al.: Research challenges in nextgen service orchestration. FGCS **90**, 20–38 (2019)

22. Villari, M., Fazio, M., Dustdar, S., Rana, O., Jha, D.N., Ranjan, R.: Osmosis: the osmotic computing platform for microelements in the cloud, edge, and internet of things. IEEE Comput. **52**(8), 14–26 (2019)

23. Villari, M., Fazio, M., Dustdar, S., Rana, O.F., Ranjan, R.: Osmotic computing: a new paradigm for edge/cloud integration. IEEE Cloud Comput. **3**(6), 76–83 (2016)

24. Yin, Q., Schüpbach, A., Cappos, J., Baumann, A., Roscoe, T.: Rhizoma: a runtime for self-deploying, self-managing overlays. In: Bacon, J.M., Cooper, B.F. (eds.) Middleware 2009. LNCS, vol. 5896, pp. 184–204. Springer, Heidelberg (2009). https://doi.org/10.1007/978-3-642-10445-9_10

25. Yousefpour, A., et al.: All one needs to know about fog computing and related edge computing paradigms: a complete survey. J. Syst. Archit. **98**, 289–330 (2019)

Author Index

Printed in the United States
by Baker & Taylor Publisher Services